Winged Words

Winged Words

Flight in Poetry and History

⟡

Piero Boitani

The University of Chicago Press
Chicago and London

Piero Boitani is professor of comparative literature at the University of Rome
(La Sapienza) and winner of the Feltrinelli Prize in 2002.

The University of Chicago Press, Chicago 60637
The University of Chicago Press, Ltd., London
© 2007 by The University of Chicago
All rights reserved. Published 2007
Printed in the United States of America

16 15 14 13 12 11 10 09 08 07 1 2 3 4 5

ISBN-13: 978-0-226-06561-8 (cloth)
ISBN-10: 0-226-06561-8 (cloth)

Originally published as *Parole Alate: Voli nella poesia e nella storia da Omero all'11
settembre.* © 2004 Arnoldo Mondadori Editore SpA, Milano.

Those portions of *Winged Words* not written originally in English were translated from
the Italian by Noeleen Hargan, Anita Weston, and the author.

Library of Congress Cataloging-in-Publication Data

Boitani, Piero.
  [Parole alate. English]
  Winged words : flight in poetry and history / Piero Boitani. — [English-language ed.].
    p. cm.
  Includes bibliographical references and index.
  ISBN-13: 978-0-226-06561-8 (cloth : alk. paper)
  ISBN-10: 0-226-06561-8 (cloth : alk. paper)
  1. Flight in literature.   2. Flight.   I. Title.
  PN56.F54B6513 2007
  809'.93356—dc22   2006036193

♾ The paper used in this publication meets the minimum requirements of the
American National Standard for Information Sciences—Permanence of Paper for
Printed Library Materials, ANSI Z39.48–1992.

For Giuseppe, Jack, and Rachel

Contents

Preface to the English-Language Edition

This is not a book on the history of flying. Several exist, and in the last three years, around or after the centenary of the Wright brothers in 2003, some important ones have come out, which I refer to wherever relevant. Nor is it a book on all kinds of flights, be they mental or real. Every culture has imagined flight—the flight of gods, angels, prophets, and heroes; flight in science fiction; mystical, psychedelic flights; and finally flights in songs (a popular postwar example of this is Domenico Modugno's "Volare"). Actual flight occurs thousands of times every day in every direction. Hundreds of satellites have been orbiting our planet for decades; by flying, human beings have reached the Moon and sent machines to explore the solar system and beyond.

I could not embark on a treatment of air or space crossings of this kind. I would have become decrepit like the protagonist of *2001: A Space Odyssey*, and without even being sure of getting back home before the final flight. I also wanted to avoid too many overlaps with my predecessors in this enterprise, and therefore I do not concern myself with Annunciations, winged penises, ecstasies, sexuality, airy pilgrimages, or levitations of saints.

Instead, I wish to outline a series of personal journeys through the Western imaginary (by which, here as throughout the book, I mean what the French call *imaginaire*, the imaginary, mental world of a civilization), the only one I can discuss with some degree of competence. In these itineraries, the dream or the reality of flight was always present, dominating, at times obsessive. I only wanted to recount them; in 2000 I was offered the opportunity when Harvard University, in the person of Lino Pertile, invited me to give the Lauro de Bosis Lectures the following year. The theme of the lectures was entirely open-ended, but the agreement was that at least one should be devoted to Lauro de Bosis himself, since 2001 would mark the seventieth anniversary of his anti-Fascist flight over Rome, and the centenary of his birth. Lauro de Bosis had attended the same *liceo* where many years later I too had been a student, and I well remembered the solemn occasion when, in the 1960s, an inscription to commemorate him had been dedicated in our school. Furthermore, in the years 2000–2001 I used to drive to work daily through Largo Lauro de Bosis in Rome. This is a curious square, because facing it, just in front of the Olympic Stadium, there still stands a squat white marble obelisk bearing the inscription "MVSSOLINI DVX." Throughout his last years, as well as in the enterprise that led him to death on an airplane called *Pegasus*, Lauro de Bosis had fought against Mussolini, and here they were, tied forever, in perpetual *contrappasso*, by the authorities' ignorance or cunning. There was more: in order to combat Fascism, Lauro de Bosis had founded a political movement called Alleanza Nazionale, the very same name that the Duce's grandchildren had taken on for their party and with which they had been elected to government positions in 2001. Finally, a quarter of a century before all this, a Cambridge friend of mine, the Romance philologist Joseph Cremona, had presented me with a copy of de Bosis's *Icaro* in the now rare edition by Ruth Draper and Gilbert Murray.

How could I, at this point, refuse Harvard's proposal? By accepting it, I would be able to ask myself a few questions about history, about personal and national stories, about the occasions, the right moments—the *kairoi*—in which they occur. And I also planned to pass from Pegasus to Icarus, around whom the imaginary of our past revolves in infinite ascents and descents that take place always at critical points. In 2000, in New York and at Yale University, I had given a lecture on the "mad flight" of Dante's Ulysses in the twentieth century. My friend Angelo Dicuonzo had taken a few pictures for me of a statue of Ulysses (by an Italian artist) in Manhattan that offered an image of the dramatically contrasting options that contemporary global culture was facing. In short, I had compiled almost all my flights for Harvard, the theme for my lectures, and the seed of the future book.

The seed spread out from a four- to a six-branched tree when—after a trip to Brazil—University College, Toronto, in the persons of Paul Perron and Amilcare Iannucci, asked me to give the Alexander Lectures there in 2003. In the meantime, the events of September 11, 2001, had occurred, with their mad flights against the heart of our civilization, and the statue of Ulysses, as readers will see at the end of this book, acquired precise poignancy. An increasingly strong appetite for flight was also growing in me. I had examined the flight of Hermes for Toronto, but I still had an intense desire to explore, after myth, both real and literary flying creatures—birds. Ever since the time of the *liceo*, a fragment by Alcman on halcyons and "Pindaric flights" had fascinated me. Wasn't this the right time finally to study them?

I spent the summer of 2002 in Rome and on the Sabine Hills, thinking about kingfishers (the common English term for halcyons). After Alcman, a look at Ovid—whose Icarus I had already encountered—became inevitable on account of his story of Alcyone. And after him Christoph Ransmayr, whose *Die letzte Welt* I had acquired in Germany as soon as it came out and which I had always loved. It was clear to me that with Hermes and the halcyons I had moved from history to poetry. But Pindar was still hovering above me, a singer both difficult and wonderful. In the fall of 2002 I was at the University of Notre Dame, Indiana, where I taught medieval literature and some of its modern descendants. I embarked on a series of actual flights throughout North America and began to make my acquaintance with eagles. Pindar had opened his first Pythian ode precisely with the eagle sleeping on Zeus' scepter; as I proceeded, an exceptional *kairos* presented itself to me, the opportunity of connecting Pindar's flights to those of Horace, Dante, and the Hebrew and Christian Bible.

Yet this flight, exalting as it was, threatened to drive me down to earth from every pinnacle I thought I had reached. Ted Cachey, trying to keep me on the "middle course" recommended by Daedalus to Icarus, spurred me on while looking after my sanity. And Rachel Jacoff comforted me by correspondence and by sending the beautiful picture of the Eagle Nebula which is so similar to—and so different from—Dante's figure of divine justice in the *Paradiso*. To her I owe more than I can say here.

But I hadn't finished. Ever since the intense month I had spent at Harvard, in F. O. Matthiessen's room at Eliot College—in between chats and furtive cigars (rigorously smoked in the garden) with Lino Pertile, cups of coffee, lunches, and dinners with Rachel, and strolling conversations with Giuseppe Bonfrate—I knew that I had to study at least one fascinating and enigmatic painting, Pieter Bruegel's *Fall of Icarus*, and its literary interpretations in the twentieth century. I was aware, too, that I couldn't avoid poking my nose into the works of Antoine de Saint-Exupéry and Daniele Del Giudice, both true pilots, and authors of books that were very dear to me.

I spent a whole year, all the while encouraged by Pietro Citati, in conceiving, writing, and enjoying these last flights. On December 27, 2003, as I was almost ready to land, I wandered through the center of Rome with my friend Barbara Calvo on a magnificent "halcyon day." In the window of an antiquarian bookshop I used to visit often as a young man I saw the original print of Matisse's *Chute d'Icare*. It was obviously a sign—ambiguous and possibly ominous, given the subject, but in its beauty also clear, as well as dear. Two days later, I raced to buy it with my wife. I had found the illustration for the cover of the Italian edition of this book and a present for what in Rome people call "la Befana," the old hag who flies through the air on a broomstick and who, through a long and devious itinerary across popular culture, represents the Epiphany. Indeed, I completed the book on the evening of January 6, 2004.

As I printed chapter after chapter my son Jack read them and reassured me that even people in their early twenties could be interested in the work. Renata Colorni of Mondadori took it immediately and published it in record time. Rachel Jacoff and Robert Harrison thought it should come out in English and were instrumental in finding a publisher in the United States. I set about preparing the U.S. edition of this book conceived between Europe and North America, and which I believed would need a little adjusting to the needs of a different audience. A word may be appropriate here about the book's language. I had written chapters 1–4 and 8 in Rome, in English, and these needed revisions, which Anita Weston and above all Noeleen Hargan generously provided. For reasons that I do not really know, chapter 5 was written in Italian in the United States, and the remaining two chapters, more normally, in Italian in Italy. These sections had to be translated into English, and again Anita Weston, then with great patience Noeleen Hargan, produced a version that I later revised with the help of my wife, Joan, and my friends Rachel Jacoff and Emma Tristram. My gratitude to these five readers should be recorded here.

I would also like to thank all the people who have given me the opportunity for writing this book and patiently helped me. They will not be charged if my flight is rough or ends in disaster: that responsibility is mine alone. I would also like to thank Daniele Del Giudice, who has supplied me with precious material and read about himself without repugnance, and Alan Thomas and the staff of the University of Chicago Press for seeing the book through production. But finally I ought to remember here the presence of my friend, whom I have often felt smiling ironically over my shoulder, Joan's love, and the wisdom and affection of my three readers *in itinere*, Rachel, Giuseppe, and Jack.

Piero Boitani
Rome, Ferragosto, 2005

Note on Texts and Translations

I indicate in the notes the texts from which I quote. Unless otherwise specified, texts of Greek and Latin classics are from the Loeb series (at times—but this is always pointed out in the notes—they are from the Lorenzo Valla collection of Scrittori Greci e Latini [Milan, 1974–], which publishes critical texts with apparatus and commentary). All English translations and paraphrases are mine unless otherwise specified. In the notes, I also give short bibliographies of critical material that has helped me shape my ideas on a subject.

The English Bible I quote from or refer to is, unless otherwise indicated, the Authorized (King James) Version published by Oxford University Press in 1997. The text of the Vulgate is that of the *Biblia Sacra iuxta Vulgatam Versionem* (Stuttgart, 1994). For Dante's *Comedy* I have used G. Petrocchi's text in *La Commedia secondo l'antica vulgata*, 2nd ed. (Florence, 1994); the English translation is basically that of Allen Mandelbaum (Berkeley, 1980–84), which I have modified in places.

Introduction

There are three intertwining patterns in this book, a historical, a mythical, and a poetic one. To begin with history, let me point out a sequence of significant dates spanning the twentieth century that emerges from what I write. On December 17, 1903, the Wright brothers' first flight in an airplane; June 16, 1904, Leopold Bloom's journey through Dublin in Joyce's *Ulysses*, published in 1922; October 3, 1931, Lauro de Bosis's tragic anti-Fascist flight over Rome; July 31, 1944, Antoine de Saint-Exupéry goes missing in action; February 13, 1945, the bombing of Dresden by Allied forces; June 27, 1980, the Ustica disaster in Italy, when a civilian aircraft with its crew and passengers was destroyed, almost certainly by warplanes on military practice over the Tyrrhenian Sea; *2001: A Space Odyssey* invented by Stanley Kubrick; finally, in 2001, September 11. It will be obvious to the reader that this sequence is made up of both joyous and tragic events. Everyone will also be aware that it is composed of actual historical events and fictional ones. In the mythical pattern, Pegasus is tied to Icarus, and Hermes to Ulysses, Icarus, and Goethe's Euphorion. Within the poetic imagination, Hermes is linked to the angels, while the Greek gods are intimately connected with birds, and in the sky of the halcyons and eagles all flying creatures meet.

I shall try to explain how these patterns relate to each other by outlining what I intend to do in this volume. I start out, in chapter 1, from history and politics, with the episode of Lauro de Bosis impelled to his flight and death by myth and literature, and I ask myself, along with Hamlet, what Pegasus and Icarus might be to him, and he to them; what is a man acting within history to a shadow of the imagination?

1

De Bosis's *Icaro* may not be a great work of art, but it is a drama catalyzing problems of attitude towards myth on the one hand and political action on the other. No explicit mention is made in the play of Ulysses, though Dante's "mad flight" image is deployed, and this leads me to ask why Ulysses is absent, given the Italian imaginary in the early part of the twentieth century.

This is the question dominating chapter 2, on Icarus, which begins and ends with D'Annunzio, exploring myth as the expression of the *culture* of our past: where language and history mingle, at the crucial turning points, in infinite literary rises and falls, from Ovid to Apollodorus, from Bersuire to Leonardo and Bacon, from Bruno to Goethe, Nietzsche, Baudelaire, Mallarmé, and Joyce. Icarus's *cupido caeli* here becomes *psykhagogia*, *furor*, *streben*, an entire civilization's compulsion towards falling.

It should be obvious so far that one cannot keep history, myth, and poetry separate. Each, as I show in the first two chapters, impinges on the other, conditions the other. I turn more decisively toward stories and poetry in chapter 3, on Hermes. With his transformations from Homer to Virgil, and later, in the form of an angel from Dante to Tasso and Milton, flying Hermes marks the entrance of the divine into human experience. It is for this reason that I also compare his flight to those of God in the Old and New Testaments. But Hermes' flight also teaches us something about the type and qualities of the poetry describing it: cosmic and sublime, mimetic and metamorphic, beautiful and pure, exegetic and baroque. Reasoning on myth thus becomes an opportunity to discuss the identification between reader and poet, reading as recognition, the appropriateness and justness of poetic language, the poetry of becoming within the poetry of being, the indeterminacy of certain texts: and also the pity or love of the gods.

Those who have seen Jacques Perrin's excellent documentary, *Le peuple migrateur* (again, 2001, translated as *Winged Migration*), will have been struck by the flights of birds occurring throughout and filling our planet with continuous movement towards life—flight paths toward survival, outbound and inbound journeys from one end of the earth to the other. These are the flights I focus on in chapter 4. Here the poet Alcman reveals the way kingfishers skim the waves, claiming that he sings according to and in tune with birdsong. This is where poetry originates, with its immense desire for mimesis and consolation. The story of Alcyone and Ceyx as narrated by Ovid celebrates the union between male and female, the continuation of the species. It sings of life and human things but through metamorphosis evokes continuity beyond death, and even resurrection. When this story is rewritten in Christoph Ransmayr's postmodern hand, we witness the actual birth of poetry, in weightlessness, from the smallest of things: the minimal and primordial traces of the tiny feathered fledgling. Turning to Montale, we discover in the kingfisher a thread of hope. In T. S. Eliot's *Four Quartets*, we see poetry sing time that destroys and time that preserves, being in becoming.

With the high-flying eagles of chapter 5, the story takes another turn. According to tradition they are gifted with vision so sharp that they can gaze at the sun: swift and precise, these birds of prey nurture their young and, it is said, carry them on their wings. The eagle in flight is one of Pindar's favorite images, and he is himself eaglelike, moving with incredible speed, telescopic vision, and perfect aim; his target is history and politics, but above all the event, *kairos*, the right moment. His point of departure is the enchantment of the golden lyre, which lulls the eagle on Zeus's scepter and which is at times the way we experience poetry. He flies toward the eruption of Etna, the magma of the earth, the Greek battles, the Trojan myth, the God who governs all: toward an ethic of what is beautiful, just, and true. He remains constantly to the *point*, with winged words hitting their target like an arrow.

While Aristophanes makes fun of poets who picture themselves as birds, swans, larks, nightingales, sparrows, and the albatross are to be found everywhere in Western poetry, from the ancients to Shelley, Keats, Leopardi, Baudelaire, Mallarmé, and Yeats: each of them speaks to us of the place and task of poetry. I deal with them briefly, dwelling more on Horace, who develops Pindar's images in his own unique way: he is less fond of eagles, preferring the poetry of small things, and senses the danger that becoming a poet entails. He nonetheless outshines Pindar in Pindaric flight, in the end celebrating the imperial eagle of Rome—war, power, government, laws.

The eagle also dominates the Biblical imagination, where it becomes a sign of God's love, of providence, of the continuing work of Creation, remaining, of course, in its eschatological function, a symbol of the empires of this world. Gradually the eagle comes to incarnate resurrection and ascension, becoming the emblem of the new Christian sublime: John, the fourth evangelist, is seen by the early Church Fathers and by Dante as "Christ's eagle." According to Origen, John characteristically rests upon Jesus' breast in order to listen and then soar: his sublime song flies toward the beginning of things, indicating the purpose of reading: a re-turning to something and an experiencing of it. The Church Fathers who read John are captivated by his boldness: they perceive poetry in his eagle ways, looking upon him as supreme transcendence of contemplation and developing a theology of beauty. I would be happy if readers considered this moment in the book carefully, since it has been around for almost fifteen hundred years, touching on the very spirit of what it means to approach and interpret the Book.

The spaces within it are transcendent and potentially infinite, but they are opened up on the earth, here and now.

When Dante journeys through these spaces, drawing on a whole tradition, a miracle occurs. He sees the eagle as supreme poetry. Homer, of whom he knows very little, is *quel signor de l'altissimo canto / che sovra li altri com'aquila vola* ("the lord of loftiest song / who like an eagle soars above the rest"). But Dante sees the eagle also as poetry *of history*, of the Roman eagle and Christian salvation, and poetry of *divine justice*. The sequence in *Paradiso* from cantos XVIII to XX, where the stars of the just spirits move like flocks of birds to form a golden eagle in the sky, has an extraordinary intensity. It outlines an aesthetic of the primordial elements that continues to astound us, a poetic of the dawn light, in deep, steady, and dramatic meditation of the justness of what is. Dante encounters John the eagle, who questions him on love and charity: here he aims to compose a *theody,* an epinikion to God like David's, and an *alto preconio*, a "sublime announcement," like John's prologue: aiming to become an eagle, like John, and like Paul, Dante becomes the Christian Pindar and Homer.

The modern world may seem to have abandoned such lofty concerns, but that is not true. Pieter Bruegel the Elder's sixteenth-century *Fall of Icarus* provides me with a kind of synecdoche for the entire book. It is a painting of stunning beauty but full of mystery. I attempt to make sense of it in chapter 6: what do the plowman, fisherman, and shepherd represent with their gaze *not* turned toward Icarus as he falls into the sea? The light in the painting may be the sunset or dawn: it is still there, filtering through. Does it mean life or death? The point is that this painting has become an icon, a topos of twentieth-century literature: W. H. Auden, Raïssa Maritain, Allan Curnow, William Carlos Williams, and Polish, German, and Dutch writers interpret it in a hundred different ways: it is the ironic wisdom derived from suffering, the beauty of the world, a boy disappearing at the hands of the Gestapo, an airman dying in the Battle of Britain. It thus acquires an ethical, metaphysical, political, and—once more—historical dimension. Starting from Bruegel, Wolf Biermann—before the fall of the Berlin Wall— put forward two ethical proposals, one for the West and another for the East. More recently, he has linked his vision to Icarus and to Paul Klee's and Walter Benjamin's *Angelus Novus*: the angel of history. Interpretation of the painting tells us that we all have the potential for *poietike*, the ability to recreate a picture, gauging upon it an ethical project directed at reconciling individual good with the good of all.

This same ethical tension within literature is my focus in chapter 7, "Night Flights": with airplanes, flying has become reality, and reality once again turns into literature. Yeats's Irish airman, who foresees his death in war, preaches Hamlet's readiness, the balance between life and death. Antoine de Saint-Exupéry, pilot and writer, draws up an ethic of responsibility deriving from flight, discusses Kant's categorical imperative, aims for creation, maturity, and rebirth from above and from the spirit, wishes to cultivate the tree's desire for being. In him, flight becomes writing and a metaphysical proposal to which we should pay attention. Daniele Del Giudice takes up Saint-Exupéry's ethic of responsibility, focusing on precision in writing and the new "knowledge" of the pilot. He wants to link science, technology, and literature; seeing, creating, and feeling. He perceives flight as history, geography, faith, oblivion, conduct: the extreme "accident" in which the very "substance" of life unfolds. Del Giudice also heads straight for the critical point: the Ustica air disaster, which took place in Italy in 1980, yet another encounter with history, violence, and war.

Most of the flights I discuss in this book converge around the year 2001: the year of A Space Odyssey. In my final chapter I return to Ulysses, to his Dantean "mad flight." Ulysses strikes me as an icon of our times, from June 16, 1904—the day in which Joyce's Leopold Bloom, the modern-day Ulysses, experiences his Dublin odyssey and dreams of a flight through infinite space—to September 11, the day in which two airplanes, in truly mad flight, reduce New York's Twin Towers to ashes. Thus, after making an appearance in the first two chapters, Ulysses reemerges at the end. Joyce writes that Bloom's flight was to take place among people and events, namely, within history. It is this trajectory I intend to follow here, at the same time hoping to show that if poets and novelists use flights as images and patterns for their works, the critic, too, can, and perhaps should, model his or her own itinerary as a flight.

Thus, I outline a swift journey through history and through the thought and literature of the past one hundred years: from Victor Klemperer, German and Jewish philologist, who compares himself to a Ulysses about to be devoured by a Nazi Polyphemus, to Primo Levi, Benjamin Fondane, and Paul Celan, with whom Ulysses ends up at Auschwitz, the Dantean flame changing into the flame of a crematorium. In that death camp, something in European culture and Western history falls. In this connection I question the Ulyssean philosophers: Nietzsche, Bloch, Horkheimer and Adorno, Levinas, Benjamin, De Man, Derrida. I look to a plethora of writers from all over the world, all of them linked by Ulysses: the Jewish Kafka and the Anglo-Indian Anita Desai, the Syrian Adonis, Palestinian and Lebanese poets, the director of Ulysses' Gaze, Theo Angelopoulos, the African writer Soyinka, the Czech Milan Kundera, the Brazilian Haroldo de Campos, the Caribbean

Derek Walcott. History does *not* end at Auschwitz, but continues in the hell that each person inhabits. On the one hand, Ulysses' flight leads to conflict, and on the other to syncretism, to *métissage*: it may lead to the Trojan War but also to the *Odyssey*. I believe that this is the crossroads at which our civilization now finds itself, now more than ever before. Like Icarus before him, Ulysses *hovers* above it: his mad flight lies in juxtaposition to the "just" journey, the love that, as Walcott writes echoing Dante, "moves round the heart." A statue of Ulysses may have threatened the World Trade Center, it alone escaping the planes that crashed into the Twin Towers, but it is up to each of us to choose: either ground zero, Troy, or the sea drizzle tightened into the strings of a harp on which Walcott's Homer, "a man with clouded eyes," plucks the first line of the *Odyssey*. Perhaps, with history and myth in our harps, we need to go back home, back to poetry.

Pegasus 1

"To-morrow at three o'clock, in a meadow on the Côte d'Azur, I have a rendezvous with Pegasus."[1] Thus opens a letter entitled *The Story of My Death* written in French in 1931 by a young Italian named Lauro de Bosis in a Marseilles hotel the evening before boarding a recently purchased aircraft that he had renamed *Pegasus*. De Bosis was about to embark upon what he had come to consider his supreme mission: to fly over Rome and drop upon the city some hundreds of thousands of anti-Fascist leaflets. The manuscript of his *Story* was sent to the editor of the Belgian newspaper *Le Soir* so that it might be published in the event of its author's death. On 3 October 1931, two months before his thirtieth birthday, de Bosis departed from Marignane aboard his aircraft and flew to Rome. Arriving around eight o'clock that same evening, he dropped the leaflets from his plane, undisturbed by antiaircraft artillery and the Italian Air Force for at least half an hour. He then turned westward and disappeared, never to be seen again.

Under the censors' vigilance, the Italian press reported the episode in just a few lines. The foreign press, however, immediately investigated the event, which was shrouded in mystery from the start. Subsequently, *Le Soir* and the *New York Times* published *The Story of My Death* in its entirety. The *London Times* and *München Post* were among the newspapers that devoted considerable attention to de Bosis's *Story*. It was not the first time that someone had undertaken an action of this kind. On 9 August 1918, at the height of the First World War, Gabriele D'Annunzio had flown over Vienna to drop his Italian nationalist pamphlets. On 11 July 1930, one-and-a-half years before de Bosis, Giovanni Bassanesi had flown from Switzerland in order to drop *Giustizia e*

Libertà leaflets over Milan.[2] In the case of de Bosis, however, what caused an uproar was the fact that an aircraft flown by an amateur pilot should actually succeed in reaching Rome, Mussolini's capital, in a country whose air force was considered one of the strongest in the world, thanks also to the transatlantic flights of Fascist hero and minister Italo Balbo.

Moreover, the name of Lauro de Bosis was rather well known, surrounded as it was by a romantic literary aura. Born in Rome of an Italian father, Adolfo de Bosis, and an American mother, Lillian Vernon, the young Lauro had grown up among intellectuals and writers. His father was a poet and translator of Shelley and had founded and edited the literary review *Il Convito*, publishing work by Italian authors Carducci, Pascoli, and D'Annunzio. The young Lauro had attended the Torquato Tasso Liceo of Rome, one of Italy's most prestigious schools for humanistic studies, and had taken a degree in chemistry at the University of Rome. He spoke several languages and was equally at ease in France, England, Switzerland, Germany, and the United States. He had lectured at Harvard, had been secretary of the Italy America Society in New York, and had a wonderfully happy relationship with the well-known American actress Ruth Draper. Among his acquaintances were Thornton Wilder, Prezzolini, Croce, Santillana, and Pound.[3] He had translated classical works by Aeschylus (*Prometheus Bound*) and Sophocles (*Oedipus Rex* and *Antigone*) into Italian, had published in Italy an abridged translation of Frazer's *Golden Bough* and was about to publish the *Golden Book of Italian Poetry* in England.[4] In 1928 he had won Amsterdam's Olympic Award for his 1927 play, *Icaro*. He was thoroughly acquainted with literature, philosophy, and science and had the thirst for learning that one might expect of someone coming from a family so dedicated to the arts and receiving the classical, humanistic education of the time.

Lauro de Bosis was cultivated and intelligent but by no means only an aesthete. Imbued with the values of poetry and idealism, and a follower of D'Annunzio, he had at first enthusiastically welcomed the arrival of Mussolini and Fascism. As he gained experience of life and politics, however, he became aware of the increasingly dictatorial nature of the Fascist regime and gradually began to dissociate himself from it. At the time, the other Western European countries and the United States were governed by liberal democracies. Neither revolutionary nor left-wing but a self-defined "enlightened conservative," De Bosis considered these countries as relevant models for post-Risorgimento Italy. He disagreed with the positions of both *Giustizia e Libertà* and Gaetano Salvemini, with whom he nevertheless maintained a close friendship and lively ongoing debate. De Bosis believed that in order to overthrow Fascism, Italians would have to unite under the flags of the monarchy and the Church, and that the king, Victor Emmanuel III, would have to restore the constitutional guarantees of Italy's Statute. The National Alliance for Liberty, the movement founded by de Bosis in 1930, aimed to promote such developments and, to this end, to sensitize opinion among the highest and most politically aware echelons of the Italian bourgeoisie. Already caught up in a whirlwind of commitments, the young poet spun into action. Upon his return to Rome from New York for the summer of 1930, he devoted himself, together with journalists Mario Vinciguerra and Renzo Rendi, to drawing up, printing, and distributing six hundred copies of eight anti-Fascist "circulars" (the Alliance produced eleven in all). Each letter contained an invitation to the addressee to reprint and distribute at least another six hundred copies, including two Fascists as recipients, in what resembled a chain-mail letter of sorts.

The system worked, but the Italian secret police did not simply stand by and watch. De Bosis returned to the United States in October, both to deliver his resignation as secretary of the Italy America Society, since he wanted to sever his ties with Italy's Fascist regime, and to obtain the post of director of the Rome branch of the Institute of International Education, an agency of the New York—based Carnegie Foundation. To support de Bosis's nomination for this post, the Italian ambassador requested a written declaration of his support for Fascism. The hapless de Bosis complied.

The following month, he departed for Europe. As his ship pulled in to Southampton on 1 December 1930, he received a telegram with the news that Vinciguerra and Rendi had been arrested, along with his mother, sister, and brother. The police had seized the envelopes with the Alliance circulars and had traced those responsible for mailing them. They had found copies of the material at de Bosis's home in Rome and printing apparatus underneath Lillian Vernon's bed.

Mussolini's police-judiciary apparatus had also been busy. De Bosis's friends convinced him not to give himself up, and he fled from England to Switzerland. Meanwhile, the trial of those arrested went rapidly ahead. Lauro's brothers and sisters dissociated themselves from him, and his mother was persuaded by her lawyer to seek pardon directly from the Duce. When the Special Tribunal opened its hearings, in full presence of the foreign press, the prosecution, having obtained evidence and confessions from all the defendants, read out the mother's letter to Mussolini and de Bosis's letter to the Italian ambassador. Just before Christmas, Lillian Vernon was "pardoned" and released, Vinciguerra and Rendi were each given a fifteen-year sentence, and Lauro de Bosis was deliberately ignored in order to avoid any publicity that might work to his advantage.

Meanwhile, de Bosis moved to Paris, where Ruth Draper helped him to recover from the events of the previous weeks. Following her departure, de Bosis started work in February 1931 as a doorman at the Hotel Victor Emmanuel III. He continued to plan his flight to Rome, an idea he had already been mulling over for a couple of years. Moving constantly between France, Germany, and England, de Bosis continued to write and to develop a political strategy. He started work on *The Story of My Death*, took flying lessons, purchased his first aircraft (the first *Pegasus*), and made his first attempt at flying, which ended in near-disaster in Corsica. In Munich in August 1931, he purchased his second *Pegasus*. After various setbacks, on 2 October that year the plane was finally delivered to him. The next day, shortly after midday, the author of *Icaro* departed for Rome aboard his *Pegasus*.

∽○∽

The life and death of Lauro de Bosis are history now, history that is already turning into myth. He shaped his destiny through myth and literature by writing a play about Icarus, by flying an aircraft named *Pegasus*, and by writing *A Story* about his own death. Today, seventy years after his death and a century after his birth, he appears to be the very stuff of myth. Bright and handsome—in a photo taken on the Adriatic shore he resembles Hermes, or Icarus, ready to fly off. In the photos taken of him in Munich in 1931 standing next to his plane, he looks like a Bellerophon controlling his winged horse. He is truly passionate about Pegasus: he produces drawings of it, giving the same name to two aircraft. When he announces at the start of his *Story* that he has a rendezvous with Pegasus in a meadow on the Côte d'Azur, he shows his awareness of the bond between myth and the present, between the winged horse and the flying machine:

> It [my aircraft] has a russet body and white wings; and though it is as strong as eighty horses, it is as slim as a swallow. Drunk with petrol, it leaps through the sky like its brother of old, but in the night it glides at will through the air like a phantom.[5]

Moreover, this bond stems from his own personal experience, from the evolution of his sensibility. Prior to his flight that ended in near-disaster in Corsica, de Bosis recalls in an unposted letter to his mother the days when she used to tell him the story of Bellerophon and his horse Pegasus. Myth and life are one and the same.

To understand this, let us turn our attention first to the myth. The mythical winged horse, offspring of Poseidon, was born close to the ocean sources from the blood of the Gorgon Medusa as she was beheaded by the hero Perseus. This horse, Pegasus, was tamed by either Athena, or Bellerophon, who killed the monstrous Chimera while astride the soaring steed and tried to reach Mount Olympus, only to be sent back to the earth by Zeus. Once Bellerophon was dead, Pegasus returned to the dwelling place of the gods and to the greatest among them. Zeus used Pegasus once more, this time to punish Mount Helicon, which had swollen up excessively out of pride for the Muses, who dwelt there. With a stamp of his hoof, Pegasus convinced the mountain to shrink back to size. But as it struck the ground, Pegasus's hoof caused a fountain named Hippocrene or Castalia to spring forth on Mount Helicon. This fountain became sacred to the Muses and is thought to inspire poetry in all those who drink from it.[6] According to Ovid, Pegasus, who flies amid the clouds and stars with the sky as his earth and with wings for feet, was awarded the supreme metamorphosis: he now dwells rapturous in the skies, which previously he had tried to reach in flight, and shines brightly within a constellation of fifteen glittering stars.[7]

The elements gathered together in the Pegasus myth are profound and powerful constructs of the imaginary of the Western world: the mystery of the sources of the sea; the hypnosis, enchantment, and terror of the petrifying Medusa; blood, the rich nourishment for life and the human body; the constant aspiration to flight, air, and light, to an existence that is not merely material; the purity of inspiration, the water from the spring; the enchanted voice of the Muses; the brightness of the stars. It is impossible to forget the winged horse: it passes from Hesiod to Pindar right up to Ovid, reemerging in the Middle Ages in a trail of light (and in the process acquiring monsterlike features, complete with horns, flaming tongue, and iron hooves, and turning into a winged vehicle);[8] it shines brightly throughout the Renaissance, with poets or Apollo himself astride it, and transformed by Ariosto into the hippogryph; it comes alive in the minds of Voltaire, Schiller, and Blake; it achieves modernity through the eyes of Picasso, De Chirico and Dali.[9]

The winged horse has been perceived as a figure of fame in a tradition lasting for over a thousand years, combining pagan wisdom with Christian morality. As Fulgentius comments,[10] Pegasus was born of the blood of the Gorgon (terror), who was killed by Perseus with Minerva's help—in other words, born of virtue assisted by wisdom. And, by eliminating terror, virtue generates fame, which, like Pegasus, flies. Fear, on the other hand, as maintained in Proverbs, Psalms, and Ecclesiastes, is the beginning of wisdom. Bellerophon, *bona consultatio*, cannot avoid mounting Pegasus: indeed the very name, derived from *pegaseon*, means "eternal source," and wisdom is the eternal source of good counsel. Pegasus has wings: he moves throughout the universe, across all of nature, in a swift procession of thought. He creates the spring of the Muses with a kick of his hoof, on the one hand because the Muses show how to describe the fame of the ancient heroes, and on the other because wisdom alone is the source of poetry.

Glory, thought, wisdom, poetry: this is the Pegasus constellation. In one of the most subtle and solemn moments in *Paradiso*, Dante invokes the heavenly Muse as a *diva Pegasëa*, a "Pegasean goddess," who renders poetic inspiration glorious and lasting.[11] Giordano Bruno, who wrote a "Cabala del cavallo pegaseo," describes its nature thus: "ecco il Furor divino, Entusiasmo, Rapto, Vaticinio e Contrazzione, che versano nel campo de l'Inspirazione" [here are divine Frenzy, Enthusiasm, Rapture, Prophecy and Concentration, which belong to the field of Inspiration].[12] In 1918 Paul Valéry evoked the "ambitious hind leg of the Horse," in which he combined the memory of the imaginary beast, symbolizing the traditional work of poets, with a new ambition to caress lovingly, in rivalry with the Dryads, the smooth body of the sycamore—vegetable, candid, shadowy, airy, yet grounded in the earth's immobility.[13] William Butler Yeats, too, celebrated "our colt," which had "holy blood" and "leaped from cloud to cloud"—Pegasus as inspiration.[14] More typically perhaps, shortly before this Ruben Darío had imagined himself astride Pegasus naked but crowned with the laurel of the sun. Knight of human energy, tamer of the diamond-shod steed, he goes forth "in great flight," never stopping, with the dawn light to guide him like an icon of the unbridled energy that inebriated so much of Western culture at the end of the nineteenth century.[15]

✧

The Story of My Death begins here, on Mount Helicon. But de Bosis is well aware that his flight of October 3, 1931, belongs to reality and to political struggle. As he writes in his opening lines, "And yet we are not going in search of chimeras, but to bear a message of liberty across the sea to a people in chains." "Leaving aside figures of speech," he adds, clearly aware that he is moving away from the realm of poetry, he and Pegasus "are flying to Rome to scatter from the air these words of liberty which, for seven years now, have been forbidden as though they were a criminal act." *The Story of My Death* is a letter that many have read and continue to read as emerging from the threshold between life and death. It is in fact a testament initiated by poetry and bound for history. The heroic political gesture it describes, the deadly engagement with reality, would have been impossible without twenty-five centuries of imagination.

In the unposted letter to his mother written in the summer of 1931, de Bosis seems to anticipate his act, blending life and myth unhesitatingly.[16] He describes, for example, the previous six months of endless activity: having overcome the uncertainty of the first few days, he has spent six months "totally caught up and besieged by the great dream" he has been nursing. Twenty times it looked as if that dream had been shattered forever. Twenty times he put it back on its feet. He crossed the sea three times, took up ten different names, coped with enormous difficulties and solved ten thousand minor problems. Then, suddenly, his mind returns to myth and to childhood memories: "It seems like only yesterday," he now tells his mother, "that you told me the story of Bellerophon and how he tamed Pegasus." He uses his upbringing in a cultivated family as a means of comparing myth with the present: Bellerophon's difficulties were nothing compared to his now. The customers of the Hotel Victor-Emmanuel III ("what a name!" he comments, alluding to the reigning king of Italy who had surrendered the country to Mussolini), seeing the concierge shout on the stairs, "Irma, un double beurre au trente-six," "Hélène, un bain au vingt-huit," were unaware that de Bosis was sitting at his desk typing away on the back of a hotel bill, drafting a proclamation to the king and another to the citizens of Rome.

Pegasus the airplane and Pegasus the myth are both present here. It is impossible to separate them. Nor is it possible to detach them from Icarus. "Today, I don't know whether the thing will succeed," de Bosis continues in his letter to his mother, "or whether I shall meet the same end as Icarus." In either case, he proclaims, the enterprise would indeed be worth dying for. He wouldn't regret it in the slightest, for he has good, serious, and "sober" reasons for undertaking his mission: it is his duty as an Italian, as leader of the National Alliance, and as a fighting companion of two friends now in jail while he goes free. "But having recognized this, I cannot but taste the joy and satisfaction of telling myself I have a fourth reason, and that is as author of *Icaro*. I hope no one will say any longer that it is full of rhetoric."

His 1927 play about Icarus is more than a mere coincidence, and more even than the cultural or ideological background to his 1931 flight over Rome. What Lauro is actually telling his mother is that the flight will *prove* to people that *Icaro* was not mere rhetoric. If this will not stand as a defense of *poietike*, it does stand as existential defense of *praxis* when the action is motivated by, amongst other things, literature. The flight over Rome gives meaning to a whole life. It joins the Pegasus of childhood to the Icarus of a few years earlier and to the Pegasus of the moment. De Bosis writes in his letter to his mother, "Does Mussolini think, then, that he can stop me from returning to Italy? Does he think he has destroyed the Alliance and caused me to give up? Well, his three hundred thousand bayonets and fifty thousand spies are no match against my *Pegasus*. Pegasus is my beautiful winged horse, tamed by me three days ago, which now flies me through the skies with a grace of its own." The aircraft is what Icarus, with his wings made of feathers joined by wax, could not be: the mythical yet real means by which to blow up a dictatorship in which rhetoric played a major role.

Shortly afterwards in this same letter, however, de Bosis harkens back to Icarus. He will fly over his house in Rome, he says, and hopes that some of his leaflets might fall on the terrace. "Will you recognize the style? Not of the leaflets, I mean, but of the enterprise? Will you understand that it cannot be but me?" he asks his family, "Will you be troubled? Will you be proud? Will you think of Italy? . . . Will you take another look at *Icaro*?" This last question tells us that de Bosis wanted his play to be interpreted in the light of his final mission, that he wanted a piece of theater to be read in the light of life, the latter authenticating, as it were, the former, but the former announcing and foreshadowing the latter. Importantly, the play was dedicated to the memory of Lauro's aviator brother Valente, who died during the First World War, and to "those who had the spirit and fate of Icarus." From a general standpoint, therefore, the issue broadens, and could be summed up in the ancient double question as formulated three centuries earlier by Hamlet.[17] Try substituting Hecuba with Icarus: "What's Hecuba—Icarus—to him, or he to Hecuba?"

I shall return to this question shortly. Before I do so, however, let me articulate some of my assumptions. First, de Bosis's flight over Rome belongs to a rhetoric we need to investigate. Second, the rhetoric of Pegasus develops and fulfils that of Icarus. Third, and perhaps most important, the rhetoric of *The Story of My Death* is completely different from either. Although de Bosis now presents himself as a Flying Dutchman, *The Story* is absolutely nonrhetorical in terms of the political rhetoric of the 1930s. Its prose and strategy are terse, ironic, swift, sober—the exact opposite of Mussolini's. In no more than seven printed pages, *The Story* says all there is to say. It destroys Fascism as a regime and as an ideology. It deflates the myth of Mussolini. It describes both the aims of the National Alliance and the preparations for and the schedule and itinerary of the flight to Rome, dealing briefly with the risks involved. It ends by evoking Italo Balbo, Fascist boss, famous aviator, and air force minister under Mussolini: "If my friend Balbo has done his duty, they [Mussolini's planes] will be there waiting for me. So much the better; I shall be worth more dead than alive." Had de Bosis dropped *The Story of My Death* over the streets and squares of Rome together with his leaflets and the copies of Bolton King's *Fascism in Italy*, the whole rhetoric of Fascism would have exploded.

Though no literary masterpiece, *Icaro*[18] is a poetic statement, a mythological rewriting, a historical reconstruction, and a political promise: all somewhat excessive, but not insignificant. As the play opens, we find ourselves on the threshold between the Bronze and Iron Ages. Daedalus, who by de Bosis's explicit directions has "the appearance of Leonardo da Vinci's self-portrait in red chalk," has just drawn from the entrails of the earth a "dark obedient genius to serve man": iron. Minos, tyrant-king of Crete, immediately realizes the potential of the new metal and promises Daedalus he will allow him to go back to Athens in return for iron. Daedalus accepts the pact. Icarus enters the stage on a white horse, carrying two dead eagles and telling his father he has now provided him with the feathers of a hundred birds. Daedalus does not yet wish to reveal his secret, but tells him that if he succeeds in his as-yet-undisclosed project they shall both be "equal to the gods" and that he has given Minos the new iron sword. "What? My iron sword?" exclaims Icarus, "The sword I dreamed of brandishing to liberate the people? Given to the tyrant!" But Daedalus replies that tyrants and liberty pass away and that "thought alone advances . . . and raises a temple, knowledge, compared to which the kingdom of earth is nothing."

As soon as the Prologue is over, the Chorus recites a *parodos* that retraces the history of humankind, from the caves where people once lived in terror of wild beasts, to the discovery of fire and the first splintering of rocks, to human speech, the taming of wild beasts, sailing, right up to the creation of "the first useless thing": the dawn of the "first artist." Daedalus, the Chorus proclaims, is the greatest of all artist-scientists: "He knows the laws of the heavens and has conquered the sail and the horse."

Icarus is presented from the beginning as *aedo*, a singer, a bard, a poet. At the beginning of act 1 he tells the Chorus he wants his dream "in the midst of the fight," "real and armed." The poet's mission, he declares, is to act as messenger between two worlds: this murky world from which he raises hearts to ethereal music; and the world of light, in which he finds the sparks to fertilize the ripe earth. Taking up a lyre, he then sings a hymn to the waves of the sea, guided in their "mad flight" between birth and death by a single harmonious impulse, "brief syllables of an immense chorus."

Minos's queen, Pasiphae, now approaches, inviting him to join her in the tower. Pasiphae, whose affair with the bull is never mentioned in the play, is in love with Icarus. When he rejects both her and her offer of the kingdom, she curses him and invokes the Sun's revenge on him. Icarus, on the other hand, loves Phaedra. After rejecting him in act 1, she declares her love for him in act 3. The love subplots are thinly interwoven with the main plot: Phaedra will love Icarus only when he becomes the perfect hero of flight, and the Sun will take revenge against Icarus presumably by melting the wax that keeps his wings together. While in the first *stasimon* the Chorus celebrates Love as a universal power, inextricably bound to suffering, Icarus in act 1 recounts to Ariadne a "myth" that another singer has heard from Orpheus. This is a cosmogony myth, in which a "god of ineffable name" drew from his own singing spirit, in the dawn of time, a sublime harmony that spread "like a rainbow veil in the midst of the heavens." Then came Kronos, who broke the rhythm that bound the musical notes together, pouring them forth in an immense rain over the sea of being. Each one, according to its nature, became a man, a stag, a tree, a thought. Memories of the happy bond of earlier days, the notes search in vain for each other through black Chaos, while Love and Death aim to restore the ancient harmony.

Midway through act 2, we come to the play's central action. Its development, retracing and rewriting ancient myth, is—in Aristotelian terms—simple, devoid as it is not only of subtlety but also of reversals and recognitions other than the final one, when Icarus falls into the sea, and his body is "recognized" by his *philtatoi*, his relatives and friends. Unlike the Daedalus of classical tradition, de Bosis's Daedalus does not fly with his son but only fits the wings on him, although, very much in line with tradition, he recommends keeping the "middle course." Significantly, Icarus rejoins: "Father, put neither limit nor bounds to my flight. Have faith." Since this is a dramatic piece in the classical style, spectators will not see Icarus's flight and fall on the stage. These are described to us by the other characters, namely, by those who see him ascend (the Cretan court), and by Theseus, who witnesses his death.

Daedalus has invented and created wings: he and his son intend to leave Crete in flight. Accused of sacrilege by a priest who wishes to see him punished by Minos, Daedalus is caught and imprisoned in the royal palace. When Icarus arrives with his sword to free his father, he is taken prisoner by the guards, but Phaedra publicly declares her love for him and asks her father to set him free. After further entreaties from Phaedra, the Chorus, and Icarus himself, Minos allows him to prepare for the first flight to take place on the day Crete celebrates the feast of Prometheus. On that day, Daedalus attaches the wings. After greeting Minos and Phaedra, Icarus ascends the chariot, which takes him to the edge of the rocks overhanging the sea, from which

he leaves for Kithera, promising to return at sunset. The characters see him
fly up into the sky, further and further into the distance until he becomes
a dot and finally disappears. At sunset, Phaedra and Ariadne ask the Herald
to search for Icarus in the skies, but he sees only the sea and a ship sailing
towards Crete with black masts: it is Theseus's ship bearing the annual tribute
of victims for the Minotaur. A funeral procession disembarks from the ship
and heads in the direction of the royal palace. In answer to the questions of
Ariadne and Phaedra, Theseus says that while crossing the Aegean Sea he
saw a man perform an astounding feat: a man who called himself Icarus,
flying like Hermes. Suddenly, however, the young man appeared to be struck
by lightning and, tumbling downwards, "crashed into the purple sea below."
Theseus found his body and is now taking it to Crete. Everyone mourns his
death except for his mother Erigone, who celebrates his glory. One by one,
the others join in with her, and the drama ends with a hymn in honor of
heroes:

> Men, listen to his inspired song;
> wherever in the world a human heart,
> armed against the Fates, burns with eagerness
> and love, there, forever unseen, Icarus watches over him.
> [Uomini, udite il suo canoro afflato;
> dovunque al mondo cuore umano arda
> d'ansia e d'amore, contro i fatti armato,
> sempre, non visto, Icaro lo guarda.][19]

The play's outward structure is most definitely classical, with a prologue
and a *parodos*, four "episodes," each followed by a choral *stasimon*, and a final
exodos, which ends with a *kommos* or dirge. As a translator also of Sophocles
and Aeschylus, de Bosis puts his knowledge of Greek drama to impeccable
use, though with the emphasis of a D'Annunzio. He uses the *parodos* and the
stasimon to have the Chorus pronounce lyrical-philosophical comments on
the action and organizes these thematically either as prelude to or summing
up of the events in each episode. Thus we have the history of mankind in the
parodos and, from the first to the last *stasimon*, Love, Challenge to Heavenly
Laws, Glory, and the "dance of triumph" to celebrate Nike (Victory). The
final *kommos* begins as a lament but ends as a paean in honor of Icarus.

This austere (and slightly maniacal) classical atmosphere envelops the
play's two main Romantic themes, namely, the irresistible urge to fly and
the revolt against tyranny. In a sense, it is as if *Icaro* were constantly braced
between Aeschylus's *Prometheus Bound*, translated by de Bosis himself, and

Shelley's *Prometheus Unbound*, enthusiastically translated by his father. The two impulses at the play's core come to the fore halfway through act 2 when Daedalus tells his son he has solved the enigma of flying by creating wings. Icarus rejoices, proclaiming that he has always felt a "dizzy eagerness for flight," a "yearning for the sky." The "eagerness" and "yearning," *aspra vertigine di volo* and *ansia di cielo*, can be traced, as we shall see, not only to classical sources but also above all to Goethe and D'Annunzio. At the same time, de Bosis's Icarus sees the advent of flight as "the dawn of the times" of his dreams. As he tells his father with characteristic enthusiasm, "Will not the wings perhaps at last sweep away all barriers from the prone earth, will they not bring to men divided and blinded by hate the blue freedom of the birds, and make them all one family under one sky?" Only *égalité* seems missing from this dream of *liberté* and *fraternité* that de Bosis's Icarus shares with the Romantics. When Daedalus replies to his son, urging him to bridle his dreams and accept that "it is not mountains and barriers that divide humankind" and that the only strength that will one day carry people towards love is "the yearning and love of poets," Icarus exclaims, "Both, father! A faith not unarmed, but armed with wings and with sinews, a militant dream!"

Dedalus's point about the yearning and love of poets may sound like strange words from a scientist, but they are the very essence of de Bosis's creed. At the same time, while the plot of *Icaro* leaves no doubt as to how the "militant dream" can be armed with wings, the sinews (*nerbo*) remain rather vague in the play, only fully emerging in de Bosis's mind in the years between 1927 and 1931 and coming to a climax in *The Story of My Death*. Wings alone do not make a dream "militant," and immediately afterward, Icarus can only pray to the Spirit of Life and the Spirit of the Unknown to grant that through him his "desert sky resound with human song."

∽o∾

I will return later to this tension in the play's ideology. For the moment, my focus is on another kind of tension. A cluster of myths is significantly worked into the very texture of *Icaro* and tells us much about the imaginary behind the text. The four most important ones are those of Pegasus, the Argo, Glaucus, and Prometheus. When Icarus reveals the invention of flight to Phaedra, she thinks he might have tamed Pegasus. "Pegasus," he replies, in a line which may astonish readers of *The Story of My Death*, "is only a dream of the poets." Yet further on, in the second *stasimon*'s hymn celebrating those who defy the laws of Heaven, the Chorus praises Perseus, who has killed Medusa, thus causing Pegasus to spring forth from her blood. Above all, it praises Bellerophon, tamer of the winged horse. In *Icaro*, therefore, Pegasus belongs to the past and to poetry, as yet untranslated figuratively into technological reality, into machine or airplane.

Later on, in act 4, Icarus prays to Poseidon, god of the sea, just before launching on his flight. He promises not to touch the waves, to avoid arousing the god's disdain as the "shadow of the Argo" had done in ancient times. This, of course, is a reference to the enterprise of the Argonauts, the first human beings to sail the ocean. The allusion, however, is oblique: not directly to the ancient myth, but mediated by Dante's "shadow of the Argo" (*ombra d'Argo*) in *Paradiso* XXXIII, the final canto of the *Divina Commedia*. And that shadow—not disdained by Neptune but admired—does in fact represent Dante's own enterprise as a man now focusing his enraptured gaze on God and as a poet attempting to recall and describe his vision. For de Bosis too, therefore, the Argo is a poetic fiction, beautiful and remote.

A further reference to Dante appears in the celebration of Icarus as Glaucus, though the character is also present in Ovid's *Metamorphoses*.[20] Later in act 4, when the Cretan court watches Icarus take off and rise ever higher in the sky, the Chorus Leader exclaims: "Seems he not like a god?" Ariadne replies: "He has become one like Glaucus." There is a fairly obvious echo here of Dante's own *trasumanar*, his "passing beyond humanity" in the first canto of *Paradiso*—a metamorphosis similar to that of Ovid's Glaucus, who was "made one among the other gods in the sea." But the echo is fleeting, appearing as it does between references to Apollo and the Chimera and outshone by the eagle that the onlookers see Icarus fight and strangle in his ascent.

The allusions to Prometheus, however, scattered as they are throughout the play, form the true mythical subtext. It is Daedalus himself in act 2 who consecrates Icarus as the second Prometheus. It is on the day when Crete celebrates the memorial feast of Prometheus that Icarus takes off. As Icarus flies out of sight, Minos proclaims that "man has conquered" and that henceforth the two sons of Heaven, Icarus and Prometheus, will be honored together, since (and today's reader will hear the archaizing, decadent echoes) "one with the flower of fire and the other with the conquered azure air, equally they opened the ways of the future." In the concluding *kommos*, it is again Daedalus who extols the "Promethean flame that never languishes," for it now shines through Icarus "in the contested sky."

The mythic figures allied to Icarus link past with future, poetry with knowledge and technique, the human with the divine. Pegasus, the Argo, and Glaucus belong primarily to the realm of poetry and the past. But poetry increasingly seems to fade away: Pegasus is only "a dream of the poets," and the first ship is recalled as a mere shadow. Icarus leaves them behind but never quite becomes a god like Glaucus. The "militant dream" has only one real mythic correlative, namely, Prometheus, who foreshadows the future, Prometheus, whose very name means "forethinker"—the Romantic Titan, the initiator of technology. His presence in the play even seems *institutionalized*. State power, or tyranny, and what we would now call scientific research—Minos and Daedalus, Ludovico il Moro and Leonardo da Vinci— all share Prometheus as a figure of human progress. If we find something disturbing in this consensus, we have only to listen to de Bosis's Icarus himself when, urged by his father, he invokes (again in a somewhat exaggerated manner) Demogorgon, the spirit in Shelley's *Prometheus Unbound*, just before he takes off in flight:

> Soul of the World,
> Force of the Cosmos, Unknown whom I revere!
> These wings and this heart I offer thee. Grant
> that Icarus follow his guardian spirit through the sky,
> and equal in his flight the speed of thought.
> Thou who seeest all things in the immeasurable sea
> of the future, if it is destined that I fall,
> grant that my blood be forever fertile
> and shine again in every age; [. . .]
> . . . .
> Demogorgon, I consecrate to thee in this
> day of glory, in my name, all those
> who, at the price of life, shall carry forward
> toward thy throne the sacred flame of Prometheus
> taken from my hands.
>   [Anima del Mondo,
> nerbo del Cosmo, venerando Ignoto!
> quest'ali t'offro e questo cuore. Lascia
> che il suo vigile demone pel cielo
> Icaro insegua e che il pensiero ei tenti
> con la sua corsa pareggiare. Tu
> che tutto vedi ne l'immenso mare
> de l'avvenire, s'è destin ch'io cada,
> fa che il mio sangue germini nel tempo
> e risfavilli in ciascuna era; . . .
> . . . .

Demogorgone, io ti consacro in questo
giorno di gloria, nel mio nome, quanti
la sacra fiamma di Prometeo, presa
da le mie mani, porteranno innanzi
verso il tuo trono, a prezzo della vita.][21]

In other words, Prometheus constitutes the bridge between the spirit of history as invoked throughout the play and its actualization within history: between Hegel and Croce. Prometheus prefigures Icarus, and Icarus appears as a prefiguration of Charles Lindbergh, whose famous transatlantic flight took place in May 1927. Indeed, *Icaro* contains two prophecies. The first, uttered by the Chorus in the fourth *stasimon*'s hymn to Nike, goddess of victory, clearly alludes to the famous American aviator:

Perhaps some day from where the storms
of the west wind are born, from beyond
the abysses of the immense ocean,
shall come flying people never seen before!

Ah, if it is permitted to look so far beyond,
if this my song resound as prophecy,
Earth, with joy thou shalt look upon thy sons.
Hail to the conquerors of the Atlantic!

Hail to the first, who of the sons of Icarus
Shall bring a message from the Antipodes:
may the great pathway of the Sun open to the youth,
and the heavens bow down to his passage.
[Forse un giorno di là dove si creano
le bufere del vento d'occidente,
d'oltre li abissi de l'immenso oceano
verrà volando non mai vista gente!

Ah, se tant'oltre rimirar si addice,
se profetico splenda questo cantico,
Terra, i tuoi figli guarderai felice:
salute ai vincitori de l'Atlantico!

Salute al primo che d'icaria prole
porterà dagli antipodi il messaggio;
s'apra a l'efebo la gran via del Sole
ed i cieli s'incurvino al passaggio!][22]

In the second prophecy, which occurs in Daedalus's farewell to Icarus's body in the final *kommos*, Prometheus's flame is recalled once more. This time, the stanzas clearly echo Fortune's prophecy concerning the discovery of America by Columbus in canto XV of Tasso's *Jerusalem Delivered* (a passage that de Bosis included in his *Golden Book of Italian Poetry*).[23] Daedalus sees his son Icarus as the forefather and founder of aviation:

> Rest, son. Thou hast not given thy blood
> in vain: the world will follow thy flight.
> The Promethean flame that never languishes
> Shines through thee in the contested sky.
>
> A time shall come when winged ships shall cleave
> The starry vaults amid flashes of lightning,
> and by the hand of man shall be gathered
> the blue harvests of the Elysian fields;
>
> but always, son, thy sacred followers
> will triumph in the glorious name of Icarus;
> before thee shall bow down the bridled
> storms wandering along the paths of the sun.
> [Figlio, riposa. Non invano il sangue
> hai dato: il mondo seguirà il tuo volo.
> La fiamma Prometèa che mai non langue
> per te risplende nel conteso polo.
>
> Tempo verrà che fenderan tra i lampi
> alate navi le sideree volte
> e per mano de l'uom verranno colte
> le azzurre messi degli elisii campi;
>
> ma sempre, figlio, la tua santa prole
> trionferà nel glorioso nome
> d'Icaro; a te s'inchineran le dome
> bufere erranti per le vie del Sole.][24]

Tasso's stanzas had been inspired by *Inferno* XXVI, Dante's canto of Ulysses, and two of Dante's words echo throughout de Bosis's play: *volo* and *polo*, "flight" and "pole." Why, then, isn't Ulysses himself evoked in *Icaro*? Why doesn't he take his place alongside Pegasus, the Argo, Glaucus, and Prometheus as would befit the first great transgressor of the modern era?

There is a curious moment in act 1 when Icarus intones a hymn to the waves of the sea, clearly inspired by Prometheus's invocation in Aeschylus's *Prometheus Bound*. At the end, Icarus explicitly states that the destiny of men on earth—"unconscious syllables of a great melody"—seems to him exactly like the endless movement of the waves—"brief syllables of an immense chorus." "Between birth and death," he says, "one single harmonious impulse guides your mad flight" (*un sol canoro / impeto incurva il vostro folle volo*.)[25] The echo is unmistakable and clearly intentional. No cultivated Italian would have referred to the *folle volo* without intertextual intent, certainly not in the 1920s, and least of all Lauro de Bosis, who included *Inferno* XXVI in his *Golden Book of Italian Poetry* and who found Dante's Ulysses quoted as the epitome of science in James Frazer's *Golden Bough* (to which his play is dedicated).[26] Why, then, doesn't he make more of the association? Why is Ulysses absent from *Icaro*?

∽o∾

Readers will have to wait a while before getting a direct answer to this question. I will begin my devious course toward offering one by returning to Icarus's "militant dream" and focusing on its relationship to Minos. As already seen, Icarus considers his flight as an instrument of progress, freedom, and human fraternity. In the play's imaginary, voiced by the Chorus as well as by Daedalus, flight constitutes a crucial turning point in the evolution of mankind as it develops from prehistory to the present and the future. The problem is that Minos shares this view as much as he shares the Promethean ideology. Minos is no stupid tyrant. He understands perfectly well that iron will be useful—in fact, essential—to his power over the world. He does not hesitate to silence the priest who, after learning of Daedalus's and Icarus's first flight, condemns it as sacrilege. True, when he finally allows Icarus to take off, he orders a slaughter of bulls in sacrifice to the Minotaur, has incense offered on the altars, and commands a hundred white doves to be let loose to the gods. But Minos has no real religious objection to flight. At the same time he never forgets how an authoritarian ruler should behave in order to stay in power. He has Daedalus confined to the palace, and when his great court genius begs to be allowed to fly with Icarus, Minos simply replies, "I have spoken. That is enough." Daedalus will still be useful to him, "more precious," as he says, "than a thousand ships" but precisely because he is not free. Minos is also quick to perceive that, as Phaedra tells him, releasing Icarus will not mean losing him, for he is tied to Crete by his love for Phaedra herself. Neither does he need much persuasion to accept the union between his daughter and a singer, a poet. Phaedra has only to point out that the gods are on the side of Daedalus and Icarus, who have given Crete astronomy, the art of metals, iron. The two have also built the palace and the temple: the future lies with Icarus and Daedalus.

It does not take Minos long to try to *appropriate* Icarus's flight as any astute politician would do. "Conquer, and the King of the Islands will crown thy head with the diadem," he says. Making one important distinction, albeit an abstract one, Icarus accepts. "Master," he replies, "if I conquer, it will be I that will reach forth my hand from on high to crown thee." What other options does Icarus have? He is cornered by his love for Phaedra, by Daedalus's imprisonment, and by his own eagerness to fly. Flying is the only freedom left to him. Flying: risking his life, perhaps dying. "Do you know the terrible risks you're running?" Minos asks him. "All the charm lies in the risk," Icarus replies with Romantic defiance. "What if you fall?" insists Minos, "Don't you fear death?" Icarus ends the exchange by saying, "It does not touch me. As long as there is life, one fights; and then . . . peace! My fate, whate'er it be, I will it." Thus *Icaro* really is the prelude to *The Story of My Death*, showing us what Hecuba is to him, what Icarus is to de Bosis—a poet who flies.

Yet the mythic background of the play is institutionalized, the Promethean flame turned into a state cult. In actual fact, the whole imaginary of the play is itself fairly widespread in the first two decades of the twentieth century. Here is what one Italian journalist wrote on July 22, 1909, in the socialist newspaper *Popolo di Trento*, edited by Cesare Battisti, after the Wright brothers had flown at Kitty Hawk in 1903 and had flown again in France in 1908, in the days when Hubert Latham was attempting, without much success, to fly across the Channel, and just a few days before Blériot managed to do so on July 25, 1909:

> Our age is perhaps more heroic than ancient times. Mercantilism has not strangled the anguished but healthy agony of research. Nowadays, as in the mythological times of the Argonauts, man feels nostalgia for great dangers and great conquests. Today's heroes are called Nansen, Luigi di Savoia, Shackleton, Latham . . . The four primordial elements are now in human hands. The law that forced us to crawl on the ground has been superseded. The dream of Icarus, the dream of all generations, is being translated into reality. Mankind has conquered the air. And just as Mount Pelion from where Jason moved

on fragile ships to mysterious Colchis was transmitted in legend, so the cliff of Sangatte from which Latham launched himself into the "mad flight" will remain in history.

Icarus, the Argonauts, the "mad flight" of Dante's Ulysses—every icon fits, none is out of place. Latham is with Nansen, explorer of the North, Luigi di Savoia, man of the Arctic and the Karakorum Mountains, and Shackleton, unfortunate hero of the Antarctic. The passage might have been written by Lauro de Bosis, had he not been only eight years old when it was published. He, or at least his Ariadne, his Phaedra, his Chorus, might also have penned the paragraph which came next:

> May then the poet come, to celebrate the newest daring of our age, to raise a hymn to modern heroes, to sing the perennial nature of this old human race, which is increasingly distancing itself from that of the animals.

The article was in fact signed by Benito Mussolini, and the only passage in which its rhetoric and ideology would have made Lauro de Bosis uneasy (but only in 1927) is this:

> O Zarathustra, is it perhaps from the steep cliff of Sangatte that the dawn of the super-man has been announced? Has our painful prehistory perhaps come to an end?[27]

Mussolini and the myth of Icarus. Minos, the autocrat in love with technology, the tyrant quick to seize on progress, ready to exploit Daedalus, to appropriate Icarus and Prometheus. Minos—Mussolini. The life, work, and death of de Bosis, as well as his afterlife in history, are locked in a century-long struggle with Mussolini. Thus, the poet flies against Mussolini as soon as he finds *Pegasus*. But this is not sufficient. We also have Mussolini and Dante's Ulysses. The future Duce was passionate about the "mad flight," citing it again in 1925 upon De Pinedo's return from his 55,000 kilometer seaplane test flight, and reading *Inferno* XXVI to his mother before leaving for Lausanne. Is this perhaps the reason why the "mad flight" is absent in *Icaro*, why Dante's Ulysses is absent from the play's mythical texture?

We shall have to read further to find out, for anyone who wrote a play about Icarus in Italy in the 1920s would have had to deal not just with Mussolini but with D'Annunzio as well. And D'Annunzio, a regular guest at the de Bosis home in Rome, simply represented what was then the terminal point of the Icarus myth in literature and history. There, perhaps, we will find an answer to Hamlet's second and apparently absurd question, "What's Hecuba to him, *or he to her?*" What the player who recites the story of Hecuba is to the mythical character of his theatrical fiction; what de Bosis is to Pegasus and to Icarus; what the man acting within history is to a shadow of the imagination—to a myth, a literary figure.

Icarus   2

"It is the Icarus myth," wrote Lauro de Bosis, "which incarnates more than any other the spirit of today."[1] We need to ask ourselves how, as well as why, it did so. Composing a play about Icarus in Italy in the 1920s cannot have been a straightforward matter. From the very beginning of the century, Italian culture had been dominated by the Icarian dreams of Gabriele D'Annunzio. On August 9, 1918, D'Annunzio flew over Vienna to drop mocking leaflets that announced that it was suicidal for Austria to continue to fight in the First World War: "On the wind of victory that is rising from the rivers of liberty," he wrote in his message to the people of Vienna, "we only came for the joy of the exploit and in order to demonstrate what we can dare and do when we want, at the time that we choose."[2] His enterprise, if not his message, doubtless inspired de Bosis as well as the other anti-Fascist flyers of the 1930s.[3]

By 1910, D'Annunzio had already published a novel, *Forse che sì, forse che no,* in which he recounted the complex, morbid relationships in a love triangle formed by Paolo Tarsis, his voluptuous and perverse lover Isabella Inghirami, and her sister Vana. It is through flying that Paolo, the aviator protagonist, finds life and liberation from Isabella. His best friend Giulio, also an aviator, flies to the altitude required to win the prize in a competition, only to meet his death by trying to fly even higher. In a couple of pages in book 1, D'Annunzio even offers a truly hyper-Pindaric history of flying, from Daedalus and Icarus—likened to Prometheus—to Leonardo da Vinci, Otto Lilienthal, and the Wright brothers, the "two silent brothers, sons of placid Ohio" who, "working tirelessly trial after trial, had added the strength of two propellers to the stubbornness of their two hearts in order to move their winged vehicle."[4] The passage opens, however, with a quotation from the *poeta della stirpe*, the poet of the Latin-Italian race, namely, D'Annunzio himself: "Now suddenly, the Latin people remembered the first human wing which had fallen into the Mediterranean, the Icarian wing made up of hazel sticks, dried omentum of ox, and quill feathers from birds of prey." *Un'ala sul Mare è solitaria*, the poet of the race had cried to the lookouts. "A solitary wing is on the Sea . . . Who shall pick it up? Who with stronger bond / will be able to join again the scattered / feathers, to try once more the mad flight?"[5]

D'Annunzio's self-quotation in *Forse che sì* comes from a poem entitled "L'ala sul mare" that he had included in his best collection, *Alcyone*, published in 1903 and constituting the third of the five *Laudi*, praises of the "sky, sea, earth, and heroes," which he named after five of the Pleiades. At the end of the poem, D'Annunzio had exclaimed:

> O high destiny of Daedalus's son!
> The valiant hero kept himself far from the middle way,
> and alone fell into the whirlpool.
> [Oh del figlio di Dedalo alta sorte!
> Lungi dal medio limite si tenne
> il prode, e ruinò nei gorghi solo.][6]

In the composition immediately following "L'ala sul mare," the shadow of Icarus haunts the poet from its very Ovidian title, "Altius egit iter" (He made a higher journey). *L'ombra d'Icaro*, the shadow of Icarus, writes D'Annunzio, still wanders over the warm gulfs of the Mediterranean, following in the wake of the fastest ships, emulating the speed of winds. In the whirlwind, this shadow of Icarus loves the imperious voices of those who command, despising the cries for help of those who suffer shipwreck. As he rowed his boat across the sea, in the sunset the poet saw this shadow standing naked between himself and his *Dèspota*, his inner demon. Icarus's limbs had taken on the color of the sea, but his eyes were sunlike. On his body are the ruby signs of the wings' tying pins, *simili a inermi baltei di porpora*, like unarmed purple shields. And then Icarus cries out:

> O Master . . . this is my ancient
> brother. I love renewing his trials
> in the unknown. Allow, you Unvanquished One, this
> my avidity for heights and abysses!

[O Dèspota, costui è l'antico
fratel mio. Le sue prove amo innovare
io nell'ignoto. Indulgi, o Invitto, a questa
mia d'altezze e d'abissi avidità!]⁷

D'altezze e d'abissi avidità: the expression resembles quite closely the "dizzy eagerness for flight," the "yearning for the sky," which we saw de Bosis's Icarus declare as his prevailing sentiments. With, of course, one basic difference: in typically decadent fashion, and doubtless inspired by Baudelaire, D'Annunzio longs not only for the heights, but also for the abyss. Icarus, however, is not merely the poet's brother, but also his very soul and body, his distress as a man without wings, his anxiety for flight (*ansietà di volo*), his restless desire for *eccesso* and *oltranza*, excess and *outrance.*⁸

On October 13, 1903, two months before the "silent brothers, sons of placid Ohio" first flew an airplane, D'Annunzio composed the *Dithyramb,* which was to become the fourth in *Alcyone* and that, coming directly after "Altius aegit iter," once more recounts the story of Icarus. This time the story is told by the protagonist himself, with each of the poem's eight sections introduced by *Icaro disse,* Icarus said. The first part of the narrative, however, rewrites Ovid in typical D'Annunzio fashion. Icarus is sensually attracted by Pasiphae (this motif is reversed in de Bosis's *Icaro*) and one day witnesses the union between her and Minos's white bull as she lies hidden in the artificial cow created by Daedalus. He hunts an eagle, killing it after a tremendous struggle on a solitary rock and sacrificing it to the sun as if to purify Pasiphae's unnatural passion. He then gives Daedalus the bird's feathers, and his father uses them to build wings for himself and his son. The sight of Pasiphae's degradation, with the monstrous fetus of the Minotaur moving in her womb, produces in Icarus a strong desire for purity and altitude. Father and son prepare for the flight, time now being marked by the continuous repetition of *È l'ora,* it is time. Although Daedalus urges him to keep the middle way, Icarus aims at the sun itself. As his father calls him, his voice fading into the distance, Icarus rises, ecstatic in his new airy liberty, alone and winged in the immensity, his heart beating as fast as his wings. He sees eleven ships sailing the sea towards a "remote enterprise" and imagines the Argonauts talking to each other about him, Nike's son. Suddenly, shadows cluster around him: the feathers of his wings are falling off. With one last effort, he rises towards the Titan, the sun, contemplating his ineffable face and offering him his unknown human wings. His voice, *che non chiedea mercé / al dio ma lode eterna* (which begged no mercy / of the god but eternal praise), drowns in the roar of the solar chariot's wheels. Then, circling around in the eternal

light, Icarus plunges into the depths of the sea that will bear his name.
D'Annunzio ends the poem by invoking his hero:

> Icarus, Icarus, may I, too, sink
> into the deep sea, may I, too, plunge
> my valor into it, but forever
> may my name be left to the deep sea!
> [Icaro, Icaro, anch'io nel profondo
> Mare precipiti, anch'io v'inabissi
> la mia virtù, ma in eterno in eterno
> il nome mio resti al Mare profondo!][9]

Some years later, D'Annunzio was to recall the feelings and the circumstances
that inspired the *Dithyramb*. While riding his horse in the Apennines, he saw
an eagle take off from the cliffs of Pennabilli and fell into a poetic trance,
possessed by the great shadow. *Se tutto a me diventa poesia, il mondo non è
dunque la mia sostanza?* (If everything becomes poetry to me / is not the
world my substance?), he wondered, at the same time knowing that his
words were now those of the mystic:

> I had never felt in my breast a spirit so tyrannical, so rapacious, so voracious . . .
> I shut myself in, I burnt and smothered. I fumed like a fiery eagle in a blind
> cage, as Icarus must have fumed in the cave where his father too slowly shaped
> his wings. Poetry made a lump in my throat, like weeping, like blood. My will
> to speak broke the measure, overwhelmed the numbers. Every great stanza of
> the *Dithyramb* began for me "Icarus said," began again "Icarus said," repeated
> itself "Icarus said." It was like an implacable agony; it was like a longing to
> drink the breath of the titanic height; it was like an ardor to equal in my breath
> the breathing of Pan.[10]

This Icarian obsession is something more than Plato's poetic *mania:* that *furor*
here becomes an intense struggle, anguish without respite, implacable agony
and existential longing for titanic breath, as for a Nietzschean superman.
This is what D'Annunzio wants to incarnate in both his life and his writings.
The power of the myth appears irresistible, yet what is notable in the passage
is that the myth works only as a persona, a shadow of D'Annunzio's own "I."
The prose tells us not so much what Hecuba—Icarus—is to him, but what he,
D'Annunzio, is to Icarus. There was no Icarus that breathed and cried in him,
for it was the other way round: *he* that cried in Icarus *con tutte le midolle del
mio cuore,* "with every nerve in my heart."[11] In short, D'Annunzio describes

the inner struggle required in order to live according to the myth. Yet this turns mostly into a picture of the birth pangs of composing poetry, namely, of the pain, the "lump in the throat," the "weeping" and "blood," inherent in writing poetry, in rewriting the myth. Whether these are absolutely necessary for the inspiration of every poem we shall see in the chapters that follow, in which we examine images of halcyons and eagles. Perhaps, however, we have already glimpsed a not entirely irrelevant point: *this* Icarus is a figure of a *Wille zur Macht, zum Tod, zur Dichtung*—of a will for power, for death, and for poetry closely connected with eros. He is an icon of nationalism (the Latin-Italian race) and authoritarianism (since his shadow loves the imperious voice of those who command).

I shall return to this theme shortly. Meanwhile, it is worth noting that in D'Annunzio's imagination, Icarus is Ulysses' twin brother. The *Laudi* are presided over by the Dantean shadow of the Greek hero, the role model for the man D'Annunzio wants to be. In the invocation to the Pleiades and the Fates at the beginning of the book, D'Annunzio announces his desire to burn the rudder and figurehead from the ship wrecked in the last storm. To those who ask which god is concealed in the fire, he replies that it is not a god, but Laertes' son, who, seen in Dante's fire, is worth more than the "Galilean" Christ:

> He sails to unknown lands,
> a sleepless spirit. His sole anchor, his virtue,
> subdues the whirlpools of his heart.
> [Ei naviga alle terre sconosciute,
> spirito insonne. Morde, àncora sola,
> I gorghi del suo cor la sua virtute.]

Words worthy of Ulysses arise from the Latin blood, since *il sacro Dante / le diede più grande ala, onde più vola*, the sacred Dante gave / them a greater wing so that they might fly higher. *Re del Mediterraneo*, prays D'Annunzio:

> Mediterranean king, speaking
> in the greater horn of the ancient flame,
> speak to me in this flame-tossed pyre!
> . . . .
> O you who with your heart was wont
> to turn your keel against all dangers,
> following your Siren spirit,
> until the Sea was closed over you!

[parlante
nel maggior corno della fiamma antica,
parlami in questo rogo fiammeggiante!
. . . .
o tu che col tuo cor la tua carena
contro i perigli spingere fosti uso
dietro l'anima tua fatta Sirena,
infin che il Mar fu sopra te richiuso!]¹²

And Ulysses, a recurring figure throughout D'Annunzio's work, is indeed the
first and greatest shadow the poet meets in the sea journey towards Greece
recounted in the first book of *Laudi* entitled *Maia*. D'Annunzio rewrote
Icarus precisely as such a Ulysses-like hero. At least two quotations from the
Odyssey are planted in the post-Ovidian text of *Alcyone*'s Dithyramb IV, but
the Dantean source of D'Annunzio's Icarus is unmistakable. *Un'ala sul mare è
solitaria*, the poet of the Italian race had cried, "A solitary wing is on the sea,"

Who shall pick it up? Who with stronger
bond will be able to join again the scattered
feathers, to try once more the mad flight?
[Chi la raccoglierà? Chi con più forte
lega saprà rigiugnere le penne
sparse per ritentare il folle volo?]

This was the question in "L'ala sul mare," reiterated in *Forse che sì, forse che
no*. Dante's mad flight is appropriated again. And at this point perhaps we
understand why Lauro de Bosis felt compelled to use Ulysses so obliquely in
his own *Icaro*. Fascinated and dominated as he was by D'Annunzio's image
of Icarus, he could not risk an identification that would bring his character
wholly within the sphere of Nietzsche, D'Annunzio, and Mussolini. If we
reconsider De Bosis's *Storia della mia morte* and *Icaro* in this light, we can see
the man acting within history by reacting to a shadow of the imagination.

∽o∾

Although the first three decades of the twentieth century have been called
the "age of Icarus,"¹³ the icon upon which this idea hinges clearly derives
from a much earlier period. We must therefore take off on a rapid flight
through literature to discover its history.¹⁴ What interests me here is the
cultural significance of poetry that uses Icarus as a figure, rather than its

actual poetic value. In other words, we are looking at the intersection of literature and history.

One would normally associate the Icarus of classical tradition with the pathetic and tragic and not with the superhuman. In *Aeneid* VI, Virgil refrains from telling the story, or rather, he refrains from having Daedalus sculpt it in gold in the temple of Apollo, precisely because this would entail too much "pain" (*dolor*).[15] Ovid, of course, recounts it several times in his works, and always with extreme pathos. He associates it with love in the *Ars amandi* and with poetry in the *Tristia*.[16] The former contains a line that may be of interest to us: when Daedalus decides to make wings in order to flee from Crete, he tells himself, *sunt mihi naturae iura novanda meae* (I must subvert the laws of my nature).[17] Thus, right from the start, flight implies overcoming the laws of nature through the discoveries of which the human mind is capable. Yet Icarus's flight itself is seen in the *Ars amandi* simply as a "daring art," a new, exciting technique akin to that of Ovid's love poetry.

In the famous account in Ovid's own *Metamorphoses*, these features are repeated, and two more added.[18] Tired of being confined to Crete, where he has nonetheless built the cow for the "unearthly adultery" of Pasiphae and the Labyrinth, Daedalus thinks of escaping by air. He sets his mind to work on an unknown art and changes the laws of nature (*ignotas animum dimittit in artes / naturamque novat*). He lines up some feathers according to size, starting with the smallest then adding longer ones, and so his creation grows, just as the shepherd's pipe is made up of reeds of different lengths. He then ties the feathers together with string, binding them with wax at the bottom, and curving them slightly so that they resemble real birds' wings. The astonishing invention thus comes about through mimesis. Later, after tying the wings to Icarus, Daedalus advises him to fly at midheight: the damp air will weigh down his feathers if he goes too low, and the heat of the sun will burn them if he should go too high. Fly behind me, he urges, I will be your guide: *me duce carpe viam*. The two of them take off and fly over the sea. The father flies in front of the son, "just like a bird who has brought her tender fledglings out of their nest in the treetops, and launched them into the air," urging him not to lag behind, instructing him in that dangerous art, beating his own wings and turning round to look at those of the boy. A fisherman with his rod, a shepherd leaning on his stick, and a farmer bent over his plow handle all watch them in astonishment, thinking that those creatures capable of moving through the skies are gods. Father and son fly on, leaving the islands of Samos and Delos behind. But soon Icarus begins to rejoice (*gaudere*) in his bold flight and, led by a desire for the open sky, flies higher (*caelique cupidine tractus / altius egit iter*). The sun softens and melts the wax that held the feathers together—incongruously, as Leopardi noted, *poiché nell'alta region del cielo / non suole il caldo soverchiar ma il gelo,*[19] since in the lofty reaches of the sky, it is the chill that overpowers and not the heat—and Icarus beats his now-bare arms in vain. Calling out for his father, he plunges headlong downwards, but his shouts drown in the blue waters that are to bear his name.

There is not only innovation in science and art, or technique, but also a rejoicing in the flight, and above all a *cupido caeli*, a desire for the sky, an element upon which all subsequent accounts of the myth were to build. Indeed, D'Annunzio uses the second line of this quote as the title of his second Icarian poem: "Altius egit iter." In Ovid's *Metamorphoses*, however, as in all the classical treatments of the theme, this *cupido* seems unconscious: Icarus does not look for it, nor does he deliberately foster it; he is simply subjected to it, *tractus*, driven by it. Offering a short summary of the story in his *Epitome*, Apollodorus uses the word *psykhagogoùmenos*, infatuated, exalted.[20] *Psykhagogia* originally indicated Hermes' action of leading the souls of the departed to the netherworld, later coming to mean the evocation of the dead and, metaphorically, attracting the souls of the living, persuading, winning over, alluring; in a derogatory sense, deluding. Icarus is, as it were, led to Hades, as though already a shadow in classical times, well before D'Annunzio. His great *cupido caeli* is suspended between life and death, between allurement and delusion. Love and poetry, therefore, are the only fields to which his flight and fall can apply. In *Ars amandi*, Ovid sees to the former, and at the end of *Carmina* II Horace proclaims—as I will show in greater detail further on—that he, the son of poor parents, will be brought by unwonted wings through the flowing air. He shall not die but, changed into a bird, will fly over the entire earth "more famous than Icarus."[21]

An *Icarus* also appears among the theatrical productions of the emperor Nero. The Pyrrhic dances he directed featured not only the bull that mounted Pasiphae as she hid within the wooden cow, but also an Icarus who, while attempting his first flight, fell beside the emperor's couch and spattered him with blood: a truly realistic scene, if of dubious taste.[22] Nonetheless, despite continued attempts and numerous rumors, it seems that the ancients knew of only one successful attempt to fly: around 400 B.C., the Pythagorean Archytas of Tarentum, the philosopher and mathematician who founded scientific mechanics, had apparently built a wooden dove capable of flight.[23] Greek and Roman authors were therefore quick to rationalize the Icarus myth. One "intellectual" interpretation, recorded by Lucian, the extraordinary inventor of the *Icaromenippus*, has Daedalus (representing science) teach astronomy to Icarus who, launching into overelevated speculations, falls into madness.[24]

But for most classical writers, as well as for medieval successors such as Dante's friend Giovanni del Virgilio, "flying" stood for "sailing." Diodorus, for instance, maintained that Daedalus and Icarus fled from Crete in a ship provided by Pasiphae and that Icarus fell into the sea while landing on an island, and was drowned.[25] According to Pausanias, father and son sailed on separate ships, both of which had been rigged with sails invented by Daedalus for the occasion. Although the father's ship managed to ride the waves, Icarus's ship overturned.[26] In his short history of navigation, Pliny the Elder tells us that Icarus invented sails, Daedalus the mast and yard.[27] Moreover, from very early on Daedalus's activity is associated with that of Ulysses: he possesses similar *metis* and *tekhne,* a multifarious mind and the artistic-technical ability of building.[28] In describing how his hero built and decorated his nuptial bed using the olive tree, Homer uses the verb *daidallein.*[29]

⧔

It is easy to see how Ovid's account could lead to a moralizing interpretation: all one had to do, particularly in a Christian milieu, was to read hubris and disobedience into Icarus's *cupido caeli.* In the fourteenth century, for instance, Pierre Bersuire believed that he who "elevates himself through presumptuousness and pride and thinks himself better than others or seeks a higher status beyond personal sufficiency, his inner feathers, that is, his virtues, get burnt, and his outer feathers, that is, his nobility and worldly power, get dissolved and destroyed." According to Bersuire, Ovid's account should be applied in "exemplary" fashion to the "disobedient and presumptuous children who do not want to follow their fathers, nor prelates or wise men." They cannot persevere in their high flights and must perforce fall. They behave, Bersuire continues, like Jeroboam, who "preferred" himself to his wise father Solomon and said, "My little finger shall be thicker than my father's loins."[30] Those who wish to fly either spiritually, through virtuous works, or temporally, by means of secular power, must keep the middle way, follow their elders and avoid drifting from their example—*id est maiores sequi nec ab eorum exemplis et regulis declinare.* Ovid had already highlighted the father-son conflict. In his magnificent blend of biblical and pagan wisdom, Bersuire develops this into a struggle between tradition and innovation, proclaiming, in typical medieval fashion, the absolute value of the former.

In the early fifteenth-century *Ovide moralisé en prose,* which took its inspiration from a century-old poetry version of the story,[31] the treatment becomes more broadly allegorical, spanning from anagogy to moralizing. Here,

Daedalus's flight prefigures Christ's Ascension, and Icarus's fall the image of
the dangers inherent in a misguided *imitatio Christi*. By means of his word
and infinite divine power, the Son of God, the "sovereign carpenter," created
the firmament, the earth, and the elements. He was so valiant that when
he became flesh, the devil, who had already levied his tribute of death on
the human race, was beaten. But when Jesus had done all he had descended
on earth to do, he wished to rise and fly back to his home in Heaven and,
in so doing, taught his human creatures how to fly after him: neither too
high nor too low. In order to fly, they must have two wings, the right one
being love for God, the left one being love for their fellow men. Those who
fly too low because they love the world too much, plunge and drown in it.
Those who fly too high pride themselves on the gifts received from God:
they stumble and fall after their lord and master, Lucifer, and follow him all
the way to Hell. Thus, the Middle Ages can read the whole Cretan myth and
the Daedalus-Icarus story as the great history of the whole universe from
Creation onward, and particularly as *Heilsgeschichte*, the supreme history of
salvation.

Nonetheless, the Middle Ages, the civilization that clings to tradition,
celebrates the flights desired by God: fluttering angels, levitating saints;[32]
Paul's *raptus* to the third heaven;[33] Elijah ascending into the whirlwind in
a chariot of fire;[34] Mohammed astride Burak, a winged white steed halfway
between a horse and a mule, flying by night from the Sacred Temple (of
Mecca) to the Farther Temple (of Jerusalem), ascending to the sky and
visiting hell.[35] Countless mystics follow, both men and women, from both
Christianity and Islam. And in poetry we have Dante's spectacular flights
through paradise, and Chaucer's flight to the House of Fame. I shall return
to these later.

This desire for flight, which burned from prehistory to classical times,
was not abandoned in the Middle Ages.[36] Alexander the Great has a metal
cage built with griffins tied at the front of it, placing before them sharpened
sticks onto which pieces of meat have been pinned. To reach the food, the
griffins are deceived into taking flight. Pulling the cage behind them, with
Alexander inside, they reach an altitude from which the land looks like a
flowerbed and the sea a dragon wallowing in the mud. Then God's power
casts a shadow over the griffins' eyes, throwing the animals to the fields:
thanks to the metal cage, however, Alexander suffers not even the slightest
scratch.[37]

An architect (a Daedalus, therefore) builds a tower at Hamadhan for the
king of Persia, who then locks him in it. But the architect asks for some wood
to build himself a hut in order to protect his body from the vultures; with this

wood he makes wings for himself, and rises with the help of the wind, landing unhurt far from the tower. Around A.D. 875, the Andalusian physician Abul Qasim ibn Firnas, said to be the first to make glass with clay, covers himself with feathers, pinning two wings to his body. Taking off from a high spot, he flies "for a considerable distance, as though he were a bird": upon landing at the place from which he took off, however, he seriously injures his back because he did not know that birds use their tails while landing, and he had not made one for himself. The great lexicographer, philosopher, and theologian Abu Nasr Ism'il ibn Hammad, known as al-Jawhari, dies while trying to fly with the help of two wooden wings: throwing himself into the air from the roof of the Nisābūr Mosque, he immediately falls to the ground. I like to think, and not without some historical foundation, that this took place in December 1003, nine hundred years before the short airplane flight made by the Wright brothers.[38]

There is also the magnificent comic scene narrated by the historian Nicetas Acominatus: in 1161, after conquering the sultan of Rum, the emperor Manuel Comnenos invites him to Constantinople. The sultan arrives the following year and is welcomed with much celebration. A Turk in his retinue climbs up the tower overlooking the celebrations and begins to announce his intention to fly over the stadium. He is standing on the tower "as though at a starting line, wearing a wide robe that reaches his feet." The robe is white, and reeds set out in a circle swell its billowing folds: his plan is that he will be lifted into the air by the robe "as by a sail." The onlookers urge him to take off, the emperor tries to stop him, and the sultan sweats and his teeth tremble in concern for the uncertain outcome of the enterprise, "both proud of his fellow countryman and full of fear for him." The Turk takes several gulps of air, tests the wind, lifts his hands several times into the position of wings, then steps back, praying to the wind; finally "he shakes himself like a bird, believing that he can walk in the air." He throws himself into the air: "but he was a more wretched sky-walker than Icarus: he dropped to the ground like a body drawn by gravity, and did not fly like a light creature; in the end he fell down, shattering his soul, bursting his calf muscles, hands and every bone in his body." For days afterwards, the inhabitants of Constantinople talked only of this flight to deride and jeer at the Turks in the sultan's retinue.[39]

The Daedalus-Icarus figure is thus not restricted to the Western imagination but also pervades the Islamic East, at that time more open to innovation and progress. And Western Christianity, all the while advocating the middle way and tradition, is on a par with Islam. William of Malmesbury tells the story of an Anglo-Saxon monk named Eilmer from his abbey who also attempted to fly, a few decades before Halley's comet, some time before the

Norman invasion of England in 1066. Eilmer tied wings to his hands and feet, "thus mistaking fable for truth, so as to be able to fly like Daedalus." Aided by the wind at the top of a tower, he takes off and flies for a distance of one stadium. Tossed violently by the wind, however, and by the whirling of the air and his own fear, he falls and breaks his legs, and is left permanently lame. He too believed that the reason for his failure was that he forgot to attach a tail behind him.[40]

Eilmer's descent was later held to be Europe's first flight. It could, with some semblance of truth, be collocated in 1003, the same symbolic year in which al-Jawhari's ill-fated flight took place. Medieval England must have had a passion for flight similar to that witnessed in Italy,[41] however, for in the mid-thirteenth century, the philosopher Roger Bacon announced in his *De mirabili potestate artis et naturae*, "It's possible to make Engines for flying, a man sitting in the midst whereof, by turning onely about an Instrument, which moves artificiall Wings made to beat the Aire, much after the fashion of a Birds flight." Bacon cunningly adds that he has never seen such an engine nor known anyone who has, but that he is well "acquainted with a very prudent man, who hath invented the whole Artifice."[42] Thus, since no one has ever discovered who he was talking about, the sole airplane of the Middle Ages remains suitably enshrouded in mystery.

∞

From a historical and imaginative perspective, it is enlightening to compare Bacon's claim with that made by Leonardo da Vinci more than two centuries later: "The great bird shall take its first flight above the hill of its great Cecero, filling the universe with stupor, filling all writings with its fame, and giving eternal glory to the nest where it was born."[43] What differs here is the tone, the visionary certainty with which Leonardo anticipates the first flight of the "great bird" that he himself is designing, after studying at length the flight of real birds: he was to build and launch it from the nearby Mount Cecero for the greater glory of Florence. As we know, nothing actually came of it, but the cry of exultation rises nonetheless, irrepressibly, from the lips of the artist, scientist, and inventor and turns four of the five lines into eleven-syllable verses. As he seems to intimate in other fragments, Leonardo *knows* human beings will fly. Leaving aside the complexes rooted in his sexuality, as discussed by Freud in his famous article, and their significant connections with birds and flying,[44] we can see that Leonardo possesses both the *metis* and the *tekhne* of Daedalus. It would be impossible, therefore, *not* to associate him with Daedalus, as indeed it was impossible for D'Annunzio and de Bosis.

There is of course no better passage than this for those who wish to exalt the "new" Renaissance spirit. Toward this myth, however, the Renaissance has a much more complex and ambivalent attitude. Rather than venture into details discussed by others,[45] I would like to fly once more across the magnificent landscape, delineating, as it were, its salient features. There is, for example, the marvelous hippogriff that Ariosto invents to speed the journeys of some of his characters, thus combining Pegasus with the griffin, Boiardo's *Orlando innamorato* with Pulci's *Morgante*, Virgil's *Eclogues* with Ovid's *Metamorphoses*: a steed that is *non finto, ma naturale*, not artificial, but natural, generated by the coupling of a mare and a griffin. It has the feathers and wings, forefeet and head of its father, and the rest is like its mother. They come, says Ariosto, "but rarely," to the Ryphaean Mountains far beyond the frozen seas, *molto aldilà dagli aghiacciati mari*.[46] Astride this exotic steed, the rather mad Briton Astolfo flies faster than an eagle or falcon above Western Europe, the Mediterranean, from Morocco to Egypt and to Ethiopia, where the emperor takes him to be an angel of God or the new Messiah.[47] And shortly afterward, it is again the hippogriff that enables Astolfo to ascend to the Earthly Paradise and meet John the evangelist.[48] Nonetheless, when John wants to lead the horseman to the moon, where he is to restore Orlando's lost senses, they use a chariot similar to Elijah's to which John yokes four horses redder than flame. Riding one of these chariots, Astolfo and John cross into the sphere of fire and reach the kingdom of the moon, which looks like polished steel without a stain but is as large as the earth with rivers, lakes, fields, and towns. Between two mountains is a deep valley containing everything we lose: fame, prayer and vows, and

> The lover's tears and sighs,
> the pointless time spent in play,
> the lengthy idleness of ignorant men,
> vain designs that never take place.
> [le lacrime e i sospiri degli amanti,
> l'inutil tempo che si perde a giuoco,
> e l'ozio lungo d'uomini ignoranti,
> vani disegni che non han mai loco.][49]

The lively imagination of the Renaissance poet is well suited to the celestial spheres of the medieval cosmos and its theology: the "natural" hippogriff works as far as the earthly paradise; higher up, it becomes necessary to change vehicles and entrust oneself to the biblical chariot of Elijah.

The Renaissance treats the myth of Icarus similarly. There is, on the one hand, an overwhelming lyrical tradition right up to the Baroque period that deploys the Icarus story in *love* poetry. This tradition includes compositions by Ariosto, Tansillo, Ronsard, Garcilaso de la Vega, Herrera, Tasso, Guarini, and many others.[50] In a 1532 sonnet, for example, Luigi Tansillo sings:

> Love spreads my wings, and so high
> does my bold thought raise them
> that, rising ever higher, I hope
> to break open the gates of heaven once more.
> [Amor m'impenna l'ale, e tanto in alto
> le spiega l'animoso mio pensiero,
> che, ad ora ad ora sormontando, spero
> a le porte del ciel far novo assalto.][51]

Alongside and interwoven with this tradition, a thread develops that focuses on *glory*, in particular the glory that derives from boldness of mind, as the most important meaning of Icarus's flight and fall. Many compositions fall into this category: Sannazaro's sonnet "Icaro cadde qui" (which de Bosis includes in his *Golden Book*), its translation into French by Philippe Desportes (the very text that provided de Bosis with the opportunity to write his *Icaro*), William Drummond's "Whilst with audacious wings," Tansillo's "Poi che spiegate ho l'ale" (also published in the *Golden Book*), Ernst Christoph Homburg's "Vergleichung eines Liebhabenden mit dem Ikarus," and dozens of other poems in all of Europe's languages, including the Latin of Alciatus, Shakespeare's English, Calderón's Spanish, and Marino's Italian.[52] This exquisite lyrical poem by Góngora—who also weaves Icarus, Ulysses, and Columbus into the refined plot of the *Soledades*[53]—is exemplary:

> Let not the foolish end of the unfortunate
> bold youth stop your strong, intent thought;
> the humid element was the tomb
> to his daring flight.
> Distend your sweet wings to the soft wind
> and, without the flat sea of your frozen fear
> wetting your feathers, touch, brought on high,
> the flaming region of daring.

Crown the top of the golden sphere
where the imperial bird sharpens its sight
and the wax of noble desire melts.
This shall be great honor to the sea,
and to its shores to which your burial is destined,
that your name shall rob it of its ruin.
[No enfrene tu gallardo pensamiento
del animoso joven mal logrado
el loco fin, de cuyo vuelo osado
fue ilustra tumba el húmido elemento.
Las dulces alas tiende al blando viento,
y sin que el torpe mar del miedo helado
tus plumas moje, toca levantado
la encendida región del ardimiento.
Corona en puntas la dorada esfera
do el pájaro real su vista afina,
y al noble ardor desátese la cera;
que al mar, do tu sepulcro se destina,
gran honra le será, y a su ribera,
que le hurte su nombre tu ruina.][54]

Between the sixteenth and the seventeenth centuries, however, there seem to emerge around Icarus three distinct polarities linked to both past and future. One is represented by Francis Bacon, who calls the Icarus story a "parable" of "mediocritas," the middle way that should be kept in "moral actions." He couples it with the fable of Scylla and Charybdis, also a parable of moderation, this time in doctrine and in science, a moderation it is advisable to maintain *inter distinctionum scopulos, et universalium voragines,* "between the rocks of distinctions and the chasms of universals."[55] Thus, the ancient wisdom of Ovid (but also of Aristotle and Horace, who saw virtue as a *medium* or *meson* among extremes) is reaffirmed well beyond the Middle Ages.

The second polarity is almost the exact opposite. In his *De gli eroici furori,* Giordano Bruno quotes Tansillo's sonnet "Poi che spiegate ho l'ale" to explain how all human beings should "run," doing their best, "because the heroic mind is happier with falling or failing worthily in high enterprises . . . rather than succeeding perfectly in less noble, lower ones."[56] This is quite a turn-about. For Bruno, the fate of Icarus becomes the paradigm of his own life and philosophy. The *furor* of which he speaks is what men need to begin to fly again, leaving the earth and rising again towards the sky, ascending to the infinite, changing from "moles" to "great birds." The metaphor of flight recurs obsessively in Bruno's writings, often coupled with the concept of "folly," and it is not difficult to suspect that its roots lie in the Dantean image of Ulysses' *folle volo*. In order to escape the prison of the movement and change that constitutes the "vicissitude" of all earthly things, the true philosopher must run the risk of *furor* and *follia*, must fly and accept the possibility of catastrophe, of death. As de Bosis says in his note to Tansillo's sonnet in the *Golden Book of Italian Poetry*, Bruno turns "boldness in love" into "boldness of thought in philosophy." Here is the sonnet by Tansillo that Bruno quotes:

> Since I have spread my wings to my beautiful wish,
> the more air I see under my feet,
> the more I offer the wind my swift feathers.
> And I despise the world, and spur myself towards the sky.
> The wretched end of Daedalus's son does not
> Make me bend down—nay, I rise again.
> I am well aware I shall fall down to earth, dead;
> but what life equals my dying?
> I hear my heart's voice resound through the air:
> "Where, foolhardy man, do you bring me? Climb down,
> for too much daring is rarely without woe."
> "Fear not (I reply), a high fall.
> Cleave the clouds safely, and die happy
> if Heaven gives you such glorious death as your fate."
> [Poi che spiegat'ho l'ali al bel desio,
> quanto più sott'il piè l'aria mi scorgo,
> più le veloci penne al vento porgo:
> e spreggio il mondo, e vers'il ciel m'invio.
> Né del figliuol di Dedalo il fin rio
> fa che giù pieghi, anzi via più risorgo;
> ch'i' cadrò morto a terra ben m'accorgo:
> ma qual vita pareggia al morir mio?
> La voce del mio cor per l'aria sento:
> 'Ove mi porti, temerario? China,
> ché raro è senza duol tropp'ardimento';
> 'Non temer (respond'io) l'alta ruina.
> Fendi sicur le nubi, e muor contento:
> s'il ciel sì illustre morte ne destina.']⁵⁷

Bruno himself had announced this message in *De l'infinito, universo e mondi* with a vigor that goes well beyond Tansillo's post-Petrarchan sweetness, coming close to Dante's intensity and harshness:

> Who gives me feathers, and who warms my heart?
> Who lets me not fear fortune or death?
> Who broke those chains and those gates
> from which only few are freed and escape?
> The ages, the years, the months and days and hours,
> Time's daughters and weapons, and that court
> against which neither iron nor diamonds are strong enough,
> have ensured me against its fury.
> Hence, secure, I extend my wings in the air,
> fearing no obstacle—be it of crystal or of glass—
> but cleaving the skies and climbing to the infinite.
> And while I rise from my globe to the other globes
> And penetrate further into the ethereal field,
> I leave behind that which others see from far away.
> [E chi mi impenna, e chi mi scald'il core?
> Chi non mi fa temer fortuna o morte?
> Chi le catene ruppe e quelle porte,
> onde rari son sciolti et escon fore?
> L'etadi, gli anni, i mesi, i giorni e l'ore
> figlie et armi del tempo, e quella corte
> a cui né ferro né diamante è forte,
> assicurato m'han dal suo furore.
> Quindi l'ali sicure a l'aria porgo,
> né temo intoppo di cristall'o vetro;
> ma fendo i cieli, e a l'infinito m'ergo.
> E mentre dal mio globo a gli altri sorgo,
> e per l'eterio campo oltre penetro:
> quel ch'altri lungi vede, lascio al tergo.][58]

Here, then, is the new Icarus, a Prometheus who has broken all chains, who fears neither fate nor death, who cleaves the sky and rises toward the infinite, penetrating the "ethereal field" and leaving behind what other human beings can only glimpse from afar—for Marlowe, both Faustus and Lucifer.[59] And just to give an idea of Bruno's revolution: Sor Juana Inés de la Cruz, the Mexican scholar, poet, and nun, maintained that just as eyes cannot bear the rays of the sun, so the human intellect, like an Icarus drowning in his own cries, fails to comprehend the universe.[60] As we shall see, there are only two further steps from Bruno to D'Annunzio.

Giordano Bruno tried to preach his philosophy at Oxford. It took all of the traditional and traditionalist Oxbridge irony to belittle him, the man who wished to present himself as a great bird, turning him into an "Italian Didapper," an insignificant nobody, literally "a small diving water-fowl."[61] Thirty years earlier, in 1555, it had taken a stroke of genius—and three strokes of the paintbrush—to reduce the great Renaissance image of Icarus to absolute nonrelevance (hence my third polarity). In *The Fall of Icarus,* Pieter Bruegel the Elder had followed Ovid to the letter when he singled out a shepherd, a plowman, and a fisherman as spectators of Icarus's fall. Except that in his painting, as Icarus plunges to the sea, a leg and scattered plumes barely visible on the surface of the water, none actually turns his eyes up, or down, to watch the momentous event: each carries on calmly with his work (see chapter 6). This surprising and healthy reformulation of the myth went more or less unnoticed by literature until 1938—the year of D'Annunzio's death—when Auden wrote his "Musée des Beaux Arts," inaugurating what was to become a topos of modern poetry throughout the world.

The story of Icarus in European culture had not yet come to an end, however. After Leonardo and Galileo, Newton speculated at length about flying, but it was only in 1783 that the Montgolfier brothers succeeded in sending human travelers into the air in a hot air balloon—an event celebrated in the work of many poets, including the famous ode by the Italian Vincenzo Monti, appropriately reprinted by de Bosis in the *Golden Book of Italian Poetry.* And it is here that we begin to notice in the European imagination a distinction between scientific and technological reality on the one hand and the mythical imaginary on the other. Before the French Revolution, Europeans knew they could fly in spite of having no wings and having to help themselves with a device lighter than air.

Yet the dream of Icarus persisted, reaching a momentous peak and historic turning point a few years later. In the third act of part 2 of *Faust,* via Mephistopheles-cum-Phorcyas, Goethe recounts in three hundred lines the life and death of Euphorion, son of Helen and Faust (and according to classical legend, of Achilles and Helen). "Winged spirit" and "demon," Euphorion appears as a "young Apollo," carrying the golden lyre and bearing on his head something shining, a golden crown or the flame of "superhuman intellect." In reality, as Phorcyas reveals, his origins are those of Hermes, the god who flies, plays the lyre, and makes poetry, whom we will meet in the next chapter. But he is a Hermes whose mother warns him not to attempt flight, for it is not his gift to fly freely, and whose father advises him to stay close to earth like Antaeus, for the earth, with its "elastic" virtue, will enable him to "leap," launching him into the skies. Euphorion is only a ghost of the ancient god, a modern Hermes, for the Greek gods have disappeared together with their tales. Today's poetry must come from the "heart," from its depths, not from the dawn in which the Greek gods moved, and which they spread around themselves.

Helen, Faust, and Euphorion start out as a happy trinity, but soon the restless son expresses his desire to soar into the winds. His parents succeed in restraining him for a short time, during which Euphorion chases girls in the forest. Once more he declares that he wants to rise higher and higher: *Krieg* and *Sieg*, war and victory, are the only two goals worth striving for. When Euphorion becomes a young warrior engaged in the struggle for the liberation of Greece, he proclaims the new law:

> No walls, no bastions,
> Every man must be conscious of himself.
> The bronze breast of man is
> A mighty rock, strong to resist.
> [Keine Wälle, keine Mauern,
> Jeder nur sich selbst bewusst!
> Feste Burg, um auszudauern,
> Ist des Mannes ehrne Brust.]

By applying to man what had until now been preached of God (Luther's German translation of Psalm 46 is entitled "Ein feste Burg ist unser Gott"), Euphorion signals a radical change of spirit and worldview, according to which human self-awareness now proceeds in step with the collapse of all walls, with the fall of all the gods. The Chorus responds with a hymn to *Heilige Poesie*, holy poetry, which ascends to Heaven and becomes a shining star, and yet always reaches humankind. Euphorion tells his parents he hears thunder boom from valley to valley, "army against army in the dust and in the waves" and "fury against fury, towards woe and torment": *Und der Tod / Ist Gebot: / Das versteht sich nun einmal*, "and *death is a command*, everyone understands this now." At this point Euphorion sees a pair of wings opening up before him. Crying out, *Ich muss! Ich muss! / Gönnt mir den Flug* ("I must,

I must, / Let me fly"), he leaps up to the sky, his head shining, followed by a trail of light. But as soon as the Chorus exclaims *Ikarus! Ikarus! / Jammer genug* ("Icarus, Icarus, / terrible pain"), a beautiful youth falls to his parents' feet, his body disappearing while his halo rises up to the sky "like a comet." The dead man strikes everyone as being familiar. While Euphorion's voice begs his mother not to abandon him, the Chorus celebrates him as the man who has opposed tradition and the law, who has desired something sublime, and who will be followed by other human beings. Then, in total silence, Helen disappears.[62]

What an astonishing and metamorphic pantomime! In a conversation with Eckermann on December 29, 1829, Goethe said that he intended Euphorion (whose name means "the powerful one") in part 2 of *Faust* as an equivalent of the *Knabe Lenker*, the boy charioteer of part 1 representing Poetry. Euphorion does in effect appear to embody a Dionysiac sort of vitality, Plato's *mania* as well as creative genius. This is the *new* poetry, hermetic yet different from the old. It contains a sense of the sublime, while seeming exaggerated at the same time, and yet it both enchants and moves: between preservation and revolution, between the classical and the Romantic.[63] The *bekannte Gestalt* that Euphorion's dead body resembles is Byron.

But this is not simply about poetry. *Heilige Poesie*, yes, linking antiquity, Renaissance and Romanticism, the poetry of Hermes and Icarus. As we shall see in the chapters that follow, poetry can throw each of us toward the skies, like the halo that rises in the guise of a comet as Euphorion's body disappears. In Goethe's work, however, a thread of culture and spirit emerges whose ideal we have been tracing: this thread links Ovid's *caeli cupido*, Bruno's heroic fury, and the *streben* of Goethe's Euphorion. In classical times Icarus met his death because of *psykhagogia;* with Bruno he accepted it; now he actively *seeks* it. He cannot look at history and reality "from faraway" but wants his share of *Sorg und Not*, of anguish and danger. Faust and Helen consider this kind of life an *Übermut*, a boldness equal to hubris that forebodes *Tödliches Los*, a destiny of death. This, however, is precisely what Euphorion sees as his own imperious "command."

One might of course point out, somewhat simplistically perhaps, that this is indeed what Europe practiced between 1789 and 1945. The cry of *Krieg und Sieg* has been heard on many an occasion during the past two hundred years. It certainly shows little trace of the traditional wisdom of Bersuire, Montaigne, or Bacon, never mind Bruegel's subversive skepticism. Goethe manages to complicate the image of Euphorion, and of poetry, both subtly and evocatively. Yet this is the wisdom consecrated by the new age. One need only read Nietzsche to realize this. After revisiting the myth of Ulysses in the fifth section of the "Seven Seals" chapter of *Zarathustra*, Nietzsche rewrites Icarus thus in the seventh section:

> If ever I spread out a still sky above myself and flew with my own wings into my own sky:
> if, playing, I have swum into deep light-distances and bird-wisdom came to my freedom:
> but thus speaks bird-wisdom: "Behold, there is no above, no below! Fling yourself about, out, back, weightless bird! Sing! speak no more!
> are not all words made for the heavy? Do not all words lie to the light? Sing! speak no more!"
> [Wenn ich je stille Himmel über mir ausspannte und mit eignen Flügeln in eigne Himmel flog:
> wenn ich spielend in tiefen Lichtfernen schwamm und meiner Freiheit Vogel-Weisheit kam: —
> —so aber spricht Vogel-Weisheit: "Siehe, es gibt kein Oben, kein Unten! Wirf dich umher, hinaus, zurück, du Leichter, Singe! Sprich nicht mehr!
> —sind alle Worte nicht für die Schweren gemacht? Lügen dem Leichten nicht alle Worte? Singe! sprich nicht mehr!"][64]

D'Annunzio or Mussolini might have understood this "bird-wisdom" as announcing the death of traditional morality: there is no longer any above or any below, no good or ill; the wings now belong to us. Unlimited freedom has joined the new wisdom: there is no more need for discourse, for rational *logos*. "Sing!" Poetry will take the place of philosophy (D'Annunzio); words, the normal dialectic of politics, are lies made for the heavy. Fantastic, poetrylike propaganda will replace them (Mussolini). *Speak no more:* we shall impose censure!

I am well aware that this is a simplistic version of a popularized and derivative Nietzschean view. Considering the two men invoked, however, it does not stray too far. Of course, there may also have been those who read the new bird-wisdom according to an aesthetic-scientific-technological ideal, as a new, clean, and powerful sublime, with the machine, the airplane, detached from daily reality, from the dirt and chaos of the industrial world. The Futurists serve to testify to such an interpretation.[65]

Some, however, will have understood the emptiness of such dreams even before they became public. In Baudelaire's "Les Plaintes d'un Icare," at the end of the *Nouvelles Fleurs du Mal*, Icarus laments finding his arms broken for having only embraced clouds, and seeing, thanks to the stars shining in the depths of the sky, only "memories of suns." Icarus has tried to experience everything, but his wings fall "under an eye of fire"; he burned for love of the beautiful but now realizes that he will not even have "the sublime honor" of giving his name to the abyss that is to be his grave. The end of the new wisdom is, simply, nihilism:

> In vain I searched for the boundaries
> and center of space;
> under an unknown eye of fire
> I feel my wing breaking;
> and burned by my love of the beautiful,
> I will not have the sublime honor of giving my name
> to the abyss that will serve as my tomb.
> [En vain j'ai voulu de l'espace
> Trouver la fin et le milieu;
> Sous je ne sais quel oeil de feu
> Je sens mon aile qui se casse;
> Et brûlé par l'amour du beau,
> Je n'aurai pas l'honneur sublime
> De donner mon nom à l'abîme
> Qui me servira de tombeau.][66]

The irony with which this poem scorches all modern, Faust-like scientists, would-be Supermen, and all those who increasingly believe in art for art's sake, the traditional Icarus icon as well as Baudelaire's longing for death and the abyss, was certainly not lost on Nietzsche's own countrymen. Between 1902 and 1921, Stefan Zweig and Rainer Maria Rilke both translated "Les Plaintes d'un Icare" into German, and even before that, between 1886 and 1891, both Stefan George and Theodor Fontane dedicated some rather cutting lyrical poems to Icarus.[67] Nor was the irony lost on Mallarmé, who compares himself in "Les Fenêtres" to a dying man in a hospital ward who leaves his bed to go to the window and, forgetting all medicines, herbal drinks, clock, and cough, gazes up at the sky and imagines beautiful golden galleys resembling swans asleep on a purple and perfumed river. Seized by disgust for humanity and his hard soul, the poet flees, clinging "to all the closed windows from which backs are turned on life," and there, "in their glass washed with eternal dew, gilded by Infinity's chaste morning," he looks at himself and—"whether the glass be art or mysticism"—sees himself as an angel who has died and been reborn wearing Beauty like a diadem. But, alas! *ici-bas est maître*, the world below is master, its nausea reaches the poet's nose even in his safe asylum and the "vomit of Stupidity" forces him to "hold

his nose before the blue." Suddenly he feels like an Icarus falling throughout
eternity:

> Is there a way, O Self familiar with bitterness,
> to break the crystal insulted by the monster
> and to escape, with my two featherless wings
> —at the risk of falling throughout eternity?
> [Est-il moyen, ô Moi qui connais l'amertume,
> D'enfoncer le cristal par le monstre insulté
> Et de m'enfuir, avec mes deux ailes sans plume
> —Au risque de tomber pendant l'éternité?][68]

And so in the end the fall of Icarus becomes the image of a decadence that is
not merely one person's feeling of bitterness, but a general existential state
as well, a *tomber pendant l'éternité* that rewrites the Fall of Adam and Eve in
metaphysical terms as man's ultimate destiny.

∽๐๛

Flying rather like Icarus, we return once more to the time of Mussolini,
D'Annunzio, and de Bosis. We are also in the age of the Wright brothers,
Latham, Blériot, Farnam, the flying aces of the First World War. Suddenly,
after December 17, 1903, flight is no longer "mad," but real. People are using
planes more and more, in peace and war. Traveling by plane, people cross
countries, channels, mountains, seas, oceans and the earth's poles, which
they have only recently reached on foot and by sledge. In the process, some
crash to the ground or sink, such as Latham who attempted to fly across the
Channel, or Jorge Chávez, the Peruvian who first flew over the Alps. Some are
brought down by enemy fire, as happened in the end to the famous German
Red Baron. Many die, and many survive. Yet the Western imagination still
clings to the Icarus icon. We find it in Georg Heym, Gottfried Benn, Pascoli
(who celebrates Chávez in one of his *Odi*), Yeats (whose "Irish Airman" can
foresee only his death), and dozens of other writers. As Robert Wohl puts
it, "The West was much too intoxicated by speed and the exhilaration of
flight to refuse the sacrifice of human lives that the conquest of the air would
demand."[69]

And there is more. A *compulsion to fall* seems to dominate all twentieth-
century imaginative recreations of flight, in fiction and film as well as in
poetry. In *Vol de nuit*, the novel that, as we shall see further on, consecrates
the theme of flight in fiction, film, and opera, Antoine de Saint-Exupéry

describes the climax of his character Fabien's experience, his final, Icarus-like rising to the stars and simultaneous falling down, in the following manner:

> He might keep up the struggle, chance his luck; no destiny attacks us from the outside. But within him, man bears his fate and there comes a moment when he knows himself vulnerable; and then, as in vertigo, blunder upon blunder lures him.
>
> [Il aurait pu lutter encore, tenter sa chance: il n'y a pas de fatalité extérieure. Mais il y a une fatalité intérieure: vient une minute où l'on se découvre vulnérable; alors les fautes vous attirent comme un vertige.][70]

It is this "inner fatality," this sudden discovery of vulnerability, this final *psykhagogia* that, paradoxically, is brought to light by the modern, exhilarating conquest of the air. The tragic power of the myth seems stronger than the new technological reality. It is not the sun—not any *fatalité extérieure*—that melts the wax of Icarus's wings. What seizes those who destroy the ancient taboo is a vertiginous attraction towards fallibility.

I suspect that this attraction is what the new "poets of the air" shared before Auden and others rediscovered Bruegel's painting. Yet there are differences. Kafka and D'Annunzio both attended the Brescia Air Show in 1909, the former as a spectator, the latter as a much-celebrated VIP continually asking the pilots to allow him on board for short flights (and succeeding with Blériot). The outcome of Kafka's presence there, beyond the short sketch "The Aeroplanes at Brescia," was fiction where not a single flight is to be found—apart from the imaginary and oblique one of "The Bucket Rider"—and where human beings, even when metamorphosed into beetles, are chained to the ground.[71] In his *Second Notebook,* Kafka notes the events surrounding the siege of a city. In the end the troops manage to storm the city through the south entrance, passing over the corpses of their enemies and forcing their way through the yellow smoke. They arrive at the first house, knocking down the door with pick axes. An old man approaches them. "Strange old man: he had wings. Large open wings whose outside edge stretched beyond his height":

> "He has wings," I cried to my comrades, and we who were at the head drew back a little, as much as those who pressed on our shoulders allowed it. "You wonder," the old man said, "that we all have wings, but they have been no use to us and, if we could tear them off, we would do it." "Why didn't you fly away?" I asked. "Fly away from our city? Leave our fatherland? The dead and the gods?"[72]

In contrast with this striking parable of uselessness and immobility, of attachment to tradition and home, of surrender and desperation, is the product of D'Annunzio's mind, *Forse che sì, forse che no*, a novel that, as we have seen, exploits and sums up both the Icarus and the Ulysses traditions.

Let us turn for a moment to these traditions. Together, these two characters and their stories constitute an explosive mixture in the sphere of existence, history, and literature; life and death, *cupido caeli* and *libido sciendi*, rhetoric, narration, poetry, and music; navigation and aviation. In Italian culture, they are all entangled to the point of producing a constantly recurring *folle volo*. Having composed a *Volo di notte* based on Saint-Exupéry's novel in 1940, the musician Luigi Dallapiccola wrote an *Ulisse* in 1968. Columbus is seen by his contemporaries, and Vespucci sees himself, as the fulfillment in history of Dante's Ulysses.[73] Leonardo is considered a new Daedalus, and Bruno, D'Annunzio, and de Bosis see themselves as new Icaruses. In Italian culture, Ulysses and Icarus together form such a powerful combination that they produce both Fascism and anti-Fascism.

One wonders if these two mythical icons will ever find a way of coexisting without causing extreme disasters. The answer is yes, in fact they already have. James Joyce's epigraph for *A Portrait of the Artist as a Young Man* comes from Ovid's account of Daedalus and Icarus in the *Metamorphoses: ignotas animum dimittit in artes*. Joyce's protagonist in this novel, replete with its images of flight, is called Stephen Dedalus, though in fact he often behaves like an Icarus. In the very last lines of the book, as he prepares to leave Dublin for Paris, he promises himself he will go "to encounter for the millionth time the reality of experience and to forge in the smithy of [his] soul the uncreated conscience of [his] race." The next day, he reports in his diary the following invocation to his mythical father, the Greek Daedalus: "Old father, old artificer, stand me now and forever in good stead." As has been noted, "he is both an Icarus asking for support . . . and an Icarus asking that Daedalus stand in his place—i.e., that the son will become like the father and survive to create his own labyrinth (*Ulysses*; *Finnegans Wake*)."[74] We shall never know exactly what Stephen Dedalus experiences in France, but we do know that when he returns to Dublin, still harping on about Daedalus and Icarus, he meets, in the person of Leopold Bloom, another father: his Ulysses.

After crossing history and culture, we realize the extent to which they constitute a novel, a logical yet surprising plot, possessed by a poetry of its own. We see how necessary it is, at this point, to move on to the literature I have repeatedly mentioned. For it not only illustrates periods and changes but also has its own way of designing flights and shadows, of which history can only dream.

Hermes   3

We shall now leave history for a moment and enter the realm of story and myth, where flying belongs to the birds, and above all to the gods. Unlike their Hebrew counterpart, Greek gods are not endowed with ubiquity. They have to actually move from Olympus to reach their desired destinations, and to do so they must fly, either as birds or assisted by flying horses and chariots. Gods frequently appear as flying creatures, possibly following religious cults dating back to the second millennium B.C. At times they seem to turn into *actual* birds.[1] In the *Iliad*, for example, prior to the duel between Hector and Ajax, Athena and Apollo go to Zeus's sacred oak like vultures; Hypnos, god of Sleep, climbs up a tall pine tree to hide among its branches "for all the world like the bird with a shrill cry, / the mountain bird the immortals call Bronze Throat / and mortals call the Nighthawk." During the ship battle, Apollo swoops down toward Hector like a sparrow-hawk, "the killer of doves, the fastest thing on wings." Then there is Athena, spurred on by Zeus, who leaps from the skies to reach Achilles "like a shrieking, sharp-winged hawk."[2] In the *Odyssey*, the disappearances of Athena, who protects Odysseus and his family, also appear birdlike: one episode has her disguised as Mentes and disappearing as fast as, or in the guise of, a bird, after advising Telemachus to seek out Nestor and Menelaus for news of his father. She takes off at great speed once again, in the form of a vulture, while Telemachus and Nestor are speaking, and is thereby recognized by the latter. In the throes of the massacre of the Suitors, after appearing as Mentor to spur Odysseus on to battle, Athena in a single leap settles upon the main beam of the smoke-filled room, resembling or in the form of a swallow. Even in the midst of the raging storm that batters Odysseus's raft as he sails from Ogygia, Calypso's island, to the land of the Phaeacians, Ino the sacred nymph rises like a petrel from the water to talk to him and offer the boat that will save him from the waves, then dives back into the water like a petrel.[3] There is clearly something in the ancient Greek imagination that links the gods to birds, those creatures of lighting speed in the air, enigmatic shadows with the power of birds of prey, with all-observing eyes like the swallow and with their sudden swooping into and out of the sea.

Hera and Athena reach the plains of Troy, where the Simois and Scamander rivers merge, and set off toward the Greeks, to spur them on to battle and above all to incite Diomedes to fight Ares, the god of war. They are now seen as "wild doves," keen to bring help to the Argos warriors: they quiver in fury and impatience before launching into battle.[4] But Hera and Athena did not fly like birds to reach the earth. Incensed by the number of Greek warriors the Trojans are killing under the spur of Ares, the two goddesses prepare a formidable chariot and yoke horses to it. The gates of heaven open, presided over by the Seasons, and with Zeus's permission Hera whips the horses to a gallop. They fly swiftly, "careering between the earth and starry skies." Neighing loudly, in a single leap they fly as far as a man's look as he scans the dark reflections of the sea from some high place.[5]

Something sensational is happening here: leaving aside the bird iconography, Homer concentrates on the horses' flight, setting it between the two extremes of the world: earth and sky. He then compares the length of a single stride with the space which a man's gaze takes in while looking out across the sea from a high point into the distant horizon. In his commentary on this passage, Longinus says that Homer "measures the mighty leap" of the horses "in terms of cosmic distances," and magnifies (*megethynei*) the gods. To do so, a "great mind" is required, because the sublime is always the echo of a great spirit. The cosmos and divinity are within the poet, their magnitude equal to his innate magnanimity: it is these that are then cultivated, as it were, in the generous transports of the soul. Thus, verging on mania, Homer's breath blows passionately "as a devouring fire rages on the mountains." Longinus particularly appreciates those passages where Homer himself "proposes the divinity as it really is: a pure entity, great and uncontaminated." He gives as an example another passage from the *Iliad*, another godly flight, this time concerning Poseidon.[6] During the ship battle in this episode, the god of the sea, angry with Zeus, contemplates from the topmost crests of Samothrace the defeat by the Trojans that his protected Greeks are suffering. Suddenly, Poseidon strides down the steep mountainside, and as he does so the tall mountain and the forests tremble under his immortal step. He takes three long strides and at the fourth reaches his destination at Aegae, where his magnificent palace lies deep in the sea, shimmering with gold, eternal. Upon his arrival, he yokes to the chariot two golden-maned horses with bronze hooves as fast as the wind. Dressed in gold and carrying a magnificent golden whip, he mounts his chariot and leaps into the waves. The sea monsters dart about joyfully as he passes, rushing from their hiding places to greet their sovereign. The ocean opens up in celebration, even as the chariot's axle remains dry. The horses fly like the wind, carrying the god to the Greek ships in rapid leaps.[7]

Absolute domination over nature and tremendous strength; the huge and solemn leaps; the clothing, mane, and whip of gold, the purest of the elements after water; the joy of the sea parting before him, god of water: this is the pure, great, and uncontaminated divinity of Poseidon. In the end, it is summed up in its *not touching* the waves, in its skimming past, horses flying like the wind and leaping across enormous distances. It is not by chance that Longinus recalls here the similarly sublime nature of Genesis: "Similarly, the law giver of the Jews [was] no ordinary person, for, having formed a high conception of the power of the Divine Being, he gave expression to it. At the beginning of the Bible, immediately after writing, 'And God said,' what does he add? 'Let there be light: and there was light; let there be earth: and there was earth.'"

∽◦∾

I will return to this point shortly. For the moment, I will simply highlight the fact that no Greek god flies faster or more memorably—and without horses—than Hermes, the friend (and deceiver) of humankind, messenger of Zeus.[8] His are nearly always rescue missions, performed upon Zeus's order at crucial moments. We have three such missions in the Homeric poems, one each in the *Iliad*, the *Odyssey*, and the "Hymn to Demeter." Indeed, Hermes' flight is a stock model, first employed in the *Iliad*, and taken up and repeated with variations in the other two poems. In the *Iliad*, Hermes' mission is to help Priam and his herald reach the Greek camp at night. Twelve days earlier, Achilles had killed Hector in combat, and ever since has dragged his corpse along the ground behind his horse, circling around Patroclus's tomb. Priam has decided to go and ask his supreme enemy for Hector's body, ransoming it with innumerable precious gifts. This is of course a mad enterprise, and the Trojans are all against it. But Priam remains stubborn: beseeching Zeus to grant him a safe journey, he mounts his chariot and heads off into the darkness. Zeus pities the old man and orders Hermes, whose "greatest joy" is "escorting men" and hearing out those he favors, to descend to the Trojan plain and take Priam to the Greek camp "so none will see him."

This is clearly a crucial moment. If Hermes fails to protect Priam from the Greek scouts, then the last great scene of the poem, Priam's encounter with Achilles, cannot take place, and the *Iliad* would end without the scene's unexpected and intense celebration of human piety, and without Hector's funeral, which concludes the episode. Homer, however, seems in no hurry to get there, and indeed delays this moment for a further two hundred lines while focusing on Hermes' flight and his conversation with Priam. Of course, Hermes obeys Zeus's order. He immediately fastens to his feet "the supple sandals, / never-dying gold, that wing him over the waves / and boundless earth with the rush of gusting winds." He seizes the wand "that enchants the eyes of men . . . or wakes them up from sleep," and flies, "touching down on Troy and the Hellespont in no time." Then, he proceeds on foot, in the guise of a young prince, until he meets Priam and his herald.[9]

Rather than describing *this* particular flight (if it were not for "Troy" and the "Hellespont," Hermes might well be flying across the Atlantic), this passage gives us an idea of what a flight by Hermes can be: a sudden, rapid wake of gold flashing across sky, sea, and earth, accompanied, indeed winged on, by the breath of the wind. Homer seems more intent on conveying the immensity of the distance covered in a flash and the fact that it comprises waves, earth, and air rather than on showing *how* Hermes actually flies. As we have already seen with the chariot flight of Hera and Athena or that of Poseidon, Homer sets out before us all the natural elements and has the gods' flight cover the entire universe. This is the kind of cosmic poetry that is my focal point.

None of this is present in the third instance mentioned above. In the "Hymn to Demeter,"[10] Hermes has to fly to the underworld to persuade Hades to release Persephone. This is another crucial moment, since without Persephone's return the earth would be kept wholly barren by her mother Demeter; spring would come no more, and the all-important Eleusinian Mysteries, at the center of Greek religion, would never occur. Yet here, and quite rightly, the author is far more interested in Demeter's own theophany—sudden beauty, perfume, and light pervading Celeus's house "as if by lightning"— than in Hermes' flight. Functional as this is to the plot of the hymn, it is dealt with in just two lines: "Hermes obeyed, and forthwith towards the depths of the earth / he launched, leaving the Olympian mansions."

In my second instance, however, from the *Odyssey*, we are back to poetry of the cosmos, and perhaps much more. Here, Hermes' mission is as delicate as ever. Taking advantage of Poseidon's absence, Athena has persuaded Zeus to decide that Odysseus—the poem's protagonist, although readers, now in book V, have not yet encountered him—should at last be granted permission to return home to Ithaca and to his wife Penelope after the ten years of the Trojan War and another ten years of wandering on the sea. He has now spent seven of these years on the distant island of Ogygia, as guest and lover of the nymph Calypso, who even offers him immortality in exchange for staying there with her forever. Odysseus, however, prefers his own mortal and transient life and his ageing wife. Indeed, when Hermes lands on Ogygia, readers find Odysseus sitting "on a headland, weeping there as always, / wrenching his heart with sobs and groans and anguish, / gazing out over the barren sea through blinding tears."

But this is to anticipate. Hermes' mission is to tell Calypso of Zeus's decision: she must release Odysseus. Calypso is a nymph who can bestow immortality, although she is not the powerful Hades—god of the underworld and brother to Zeus himself—of the "Hymn to Demeter." The Ogygia mission does not entail escorting an old king through enemy territory, as was Hermes' task with Priam in the *Iliad*. Yet Homer does his utmost to make it one of the most resonant scenes in the *Odyssey*: because—we must be sure to understand this—Calypso deeply *loves* the man she rescued from the stormy waves and made her companion, and against the power of a goddess's love only the almighty decrees of Zeus can prevail. Hermes' duty is not easy this time either, therefore, and Homer may be indicating this from the very beginning by staging a flight that, while following the stock model, also adds some spectacular and significant details. I quote it in full:[11]

So Zeus decreed and the giant-killing guide obeyed at once.
Quickly under his feet he fastened the supple sandals,
ever-glowing gold, that wing him over the waves
and boundless earth with the rush of gusting winds.
He seized the wand that enchants the eyes of men
whenever Hermes wants, or wakes us up from sleep.
That wand in his grip, the powerful giant-killer,
swooping down from Pieria, down the high clear air,
plunged to the sea and skimmed the waves like a tern
that down the deadly gulfs of the barren salt swells
glides and dives for fish,
dipping its beating wings in bursts of spray—
so Hermes skimmed the crests on endless crests.
But once he gained that island worlds apart,
up from the deep-blue sea he climbed to dry land

and strode on till he reached the spacious cave
where the nymph with lovely braids had made her home,
and he found her there inside . . .

This is again what I have called "cosmic" poetry: the introductory formula once more includes the waves, the "boundless earth," and the "rush of gusting winds" as in *Iliad* book XXIV. The poet then adds width and depth to the view: the "ether," the "high clear air" is now included, and the vista extends to the island "worlds apart." The original, *teloth'eousan,* implies extreme remoteness, suggesting that Ogygia lies at the end of the world because it is at the center of the sea.[12] The width is emphasized by the "many crests" Hermes skims when he reaches the sea. Finally, the points of view change. At first, we have a view from above: Hermes "swoops down" (*epibas*) to Pieria as if beheld by the gods high up on Mount Olympus. Then he suddenly plunges down from the sky to the sea: an observer seems to be following his flight from below, from the water's surface. Immediately afterward, as Hermes skims the waves, the viewpoint becomes horizontal, as if the observer were now seeing him from the land, perhaps from Ogygia itself. In short, space has acquired a third dimension and has opened up to the infinite. The effect is not unlike that evoked by Longinus to define the sublime: Homer, he says, magnifies (*megethynei*) the gods, he "measures the mighty leap" of their horses "in terms of cosmic distances."

The readers' amazement as they follow Hermes' flight is produced by this sublimity. According to Longinus, it "uplifts our souls" so that "we are filled with a proud exaltation and a sense of vaunting joy, just as though we had ourselves produced" what we have read, as though each reader had generated these lines: each, so to speak, a Homer. The greatness of the poetry fills the mind, enriching it; it is "impossible to resist its appeal," and "it remains firmly and ineffaceably in the memory."[13] For readers, it is an unforgettable icon of the divine stretching across the whole universe and moving through it at the speed of light.

Yet one feels that this is not quite the whole story, that some qualification is still needed. The passages examined so far—*Iliad* V, *Iliad* XXIV, *Odyssey* V—are similar in their deployment and breadth, at times even in particular expressions, but they also differ. As indicated above, the first two, Hera and Athena's chariot flight and Hermes' flight to Troy, seem to be concerned with the cosmic distances involved, and not with how the gods fly. In *Odyssey* V, by contrast, we are given a simile that describes precisely this. And what a simile! After "swooping down" and "plunging" to the sea, Hermes skims the waves "like a tern (or a gull) / that down the deadly gulfs of the barren salt swells / glides and dives for fish, / dipping its beating (literally, "solid") wings in bursts of spray." "Like," the text reads: *eoikos*. Scholars claim that it is impossible to decide whether this means "in the manner" or "under the form" of a tern. Homer cannot be pinned down by "scientific" accuracy, and his sublimity entails uncertainty and ambiguity, what Leopardi calls *vaghezza*, indeterminacy: the ability to imagine the nonvisible. And yet at the same time it entails remarkable precision: this is a specific bird, a gull, who glides down to the waves, dives for fish, and dips its wings into the sea. Like the ancient Greeks, we have all seen it, the marvellous scene of a pair of wings poised, tensed, in midair, then gliding, skimming and brushing against the water and the spray, the beak suddenly thrust under the crest to catch the fish.

This is it, Aristotle says in the *Poetics*[14]: when we see "images" imitated from reality (*eikonas*), we feel pleasure, because we learn something and discuss what each image represents, and then, in a wonderful shock of recognition, we conclude: "this is that," *outos ekeinos*. Mimesis coexists with sublimity, authenticating it: the shock of recognizing, of relearning and making ours what we have seen. Only then do we really know, since before this we had only watched and perceived, distractedly. Now, as we behold the image, that thing, that flight, sinks into our consciousness, becoming part of us. And here, in Homer's sequence, the sublime nestles within "the rush of gusting winds" that accompany Hermes from the crest of the waves "down the deadly gulfs of the barren salt swells," in the sequence that shows the closely-skimmed surface (as in the case of Poseidon) and the depths that open up below, as if to embrace *all*. But this all-seeing sublimity is mimesis, for it brings to each person's consciousness what we already know about the sea: spray and whirlpools, surface and depths, ecstasy and terror.

Mimesis and sublimity then head toward metamorphosis. For the ever-glowing gold of Hermes' sandals shines through the blue-green-white crest of the waves and the wine-dark color of the sea. For an instant, as if changing into each other, sandals and wings are almost interchangeable, as though one and the same. And all these qualities merge into something else. Hermes *skims*, and by skimming crest after crest he becomes the god of lightness and speed—of *quickness*. Calvino describes him thus:

> But all the subjects I have dealt with this evening . . . might indeed be united in that they are all under the sign of an Olympian god whom I particularly honor: Hermes-Mercury, god of communication and mediation, who under the name of Thoth was the inventor of writing and who—according to C. G. Jung in his studies on alchemical symbolism—in the guise of "spirit Mercury"

also represents the *principium individuationis*. Mercury with his winged feet, light and airborne, astute, agile, adaptable, free and easy, established the relationships of the gods among themselves and those between the gods and men, between universal laws and individual destinies, between the forces of nature and the forms of culture, between the objects of the world and all thinking subjects.[15]

Homer's sublimity seems to me a "proposal" for literature, both for the first millennium of the ancient era and for our own third millennium. Indeed, it is actualized and self-conscious poetry. Pieria, the mountain north of Olympus to which Hermes first swoops down in the passage examined above, was already associated with the Muses: an explicit association emerges only with Hesiod's *Works and Days* and *Theogony*. And the poet of the *Odyssey* has Alcinous say that the gods spin "threads of death through the lives of mortal men" so as "*to make a song for those who come.*"[16] When Pindar, Virgil, Tasso, or Milton read *Odyssey* V, the image of poetic inspiration must surely have arisen in their minds immediately, alongside the sandals, the whip, and Hermes' flight across the waves. "As Hermes once took to his feathers light," sang Keats, dreaming not of Mount Ida or the Tempe grove but of the second circle of hell where Paolo and Francesca are buffeted about and battered by whirlwinds. Flying from Homer to Dante, therefore, for poetry also urges us on to other poetry.

Finally, I would like to point out that the passage from Homer is by no means "pure," inhuman, or superhuman. It is primarily narrative, and as such it describes the movement of a deity, but in relation to the *human*. As Zeus says in the *Iliad*, Hermes likes to escort human beings, to "listen to the wishes" of those he favors. As we have seen, Hermes' missions in the *Iliad*, the *Odyssey,* and the "Hymn to Demeter" are an expression of divine pity for men: for Priam and Hector, for Odysseus, for human life blighted by famine. This mercy is ready to defy and overcome even the love of a goddess, Calypso, and the terrible might of Hades. Hermes is simply the "minister" or "messenger," the *diaktoros* of Zeus. And he is the first in a long series of messengers—*angheloi* or angels—to come to the rescue of humankind in literature.

∽੦੶

The flight of Hermes, already a stock passage in Homer, eventually became a topos of Western literature. Rather than explore its entire history, I will examine three important variations. The first, as one might expect, comes from Virgil. In *Aeneid* IV, Jupiter decides that Aeneas is spending far too much time with Dido in Carthage. His duty and fate is to go on to Italy and found Rome, or prepare the terrain for its founding, and love for a woman should not stop him. Jupiter then sends Mercury to Africa to convey the rather threatening message to the Trojan hero.[17] Mercury puts on his golden sandals, "which with the wings, sped on by the wind, bring him high over the earth and the sea"; he then grasps the magic wand (which, as Virgil specifies, he uses to draw "the pale ghosts" from the underworld or to drive them there, to give sleep and take it away, and to restore to light the eyes of the dead). Thus armed, he moves the winds and crosses the turbulent clouds, reaching in an instant the summit of "harsh Atlas, which with its top supports the sky."

Virgil then pauses for four lines to describe Atlas, the mountain range of northern Africa that takes its name from the Titan (father to Calypso) condemned to bear the vault of the sky on his shoulders. Atlas's head, crowned by forests of pine trees, is bound with black clouds, beaten by rain and winds, his shoulders white with snow. *Tum flumina mento / praecipitant senis et glacie riget horrida barba*, "from the old man's chin rivers fall down / and his horrid beard stiffens with ice." Mercury stops on the highest peaks of Mount Atlas, hovering with outspread wings. Finally, he plunges "with his whole body" down towards the waves,

> like a bird which round the shores, round
> rocks full of fish skims the waves:
> like this the Cyllenian god flew between earth and sky
> and plowed through the winds to the sandy shore
> of Libya, coming from his mother's father.
> [avi similis, quae circum litora, circum
> piscosos scopulos humilis volat aequora iuxta:
> haut aliter, terras inter caelumque, volabat
> litus harenosum ad Libyae ventosque secabat,
> materno veniens ab avo Cyllenia proles.]

In the simile with the fishing bird and with the emphasis on speed, Virgil is imitating *Odyssey* V, but the passage makes a rather different impression on the reader. For one thing, the mimetic directness and immediacy of Homer's tern dipping its beak into the water and diving for fish have been replaced by a more distant, and circular, kind of mimesis: *circum*—a bird (not *that* type of bird) flying round and round. Secondly, the "cosmic distances" of Longinus have been cut down to size: earth, sea, and sky are still present, but their width, height, and depth are geographically located. Mercury is flying through the *orbis terrarum* as known between Homer's time and the Augustan age, from Mount Olympus in Greece to the Atlas range and on to Libya and Carthage. The sublimity Longinus had in mind is gone. Virgil aims at it in a different manner, by presenting the reader with a description of Mount Atlas as an old man, contrasting this with a view of the sandy shores of Africa. The awe (perhaps even the horror—"horrid beard") the mountain inspires is set against the sense of peace and fertility evoked by the beaches and the rocks full of fish, rather like in Roman frescoes of the Augustan age.

What we are looking on is thus a rather "romantic" landscape, dominated by a terrible giant of a mountain. The metamorphic quality (the mountain as an old man whose chin produces rivers and whose beard turns into ice) fires the image with extraordinary power, but what strikes the reader is that immovable mass of "hard" stone (*Atlantis duri*) tied to the earth and forced to support the entire heavenly vault as though it were sculpted from marble by Michelangelo, the *rigor* of ice and body (*riget*): the way in which the myth of Titan translates into the immense, geological age of the old man. This is certainly poetry not of lightness but of bulk and heaviness. Even Mercury plunges down *toto corpore,* as if he too were a piece of rock. Yet immediately afterwards, Jupiter's messenger moves lightly through the winds, flying low just above the water's surface and resembling a bird that circles around the cliffs and shores. Virgil plays on contrasts, alternating between heaviness and oppression on the one hand, and lightness on the other.

If we wanted to unearth the roots of both, I believe we should look for them in the message that Jupiter has ordered Mercury to take to Aeneas: leave Dido, with whom you have fallen in love, and obey fate and duty. Jupiter's words to his messenger are not so straightforward, but recall Venus, Aeneas's mother, and her entrusting of her son to the gods for a sacred mission. The solemnity of the message lies in the epigraphic, sculpted quality of the original Latin text:

> Not such his beautiful mother (Venus) promised him to us,
> nor for this she twice saved him from the arms of the Greeks,
> but so that he might rule Italy pregnant with empire
> and fired with war, propagate the noble blood of Teucer,
> and submit the entire world to law.
> [Non illum nobis genetrix pulcherrima talem
> promisit Graiumque ideo bis vindicate armis;
> sed fore qui gravidam imperiis belloque frementem

Italiam regneret, genus alto a sanguine Teucri
    proderet ac totum sub leges mitteret orbem.][18]

Mercury's flight is light since it prefigures the exultance for the future glories
of the Romans. But it is also heavy because it bears the weight of the whole
Roman Empire, the law of war, conquest, and order. Anyone who hears a
distant announcement of the white man's burden as celebrated in poems and
novels of subsequent empires would not be altogether mistaken. The burden
of politics and history loads poetry down.

ᔥᲿᲿᔦ

My next example comes from the late sixteenth century, from Tasso's *Gerusalemme liberata*. In canto 9, spurred on by Alecto the infernal Fury, Soliman
leads the Arabs on a sudden attack against the Christians in Jerusalem.
Under the blows of Clorinda and above all of the mighty Argantes, inspired
by a "hellish flame," the Christians flee. Watching the battle from Heaven,
God orders the archangel Michael to go bid the "impious band of Avernus"
leave the war to soldiers. Bowing to the Supreme King, Michael spreads his
golden feathers and flies down to the earth "as swift as thought." Since we
are in a Christian and pre-Copernican universe, the archangel does not fly
from Olympus, but from Heaven, and instead of going via Pieria or Atlas,
he dives through a medieval cosmos: first through the fire and light of
the Empyrean, where the blessed have their seats, then through the ninth
Heaven, the *caelum crystallinum* or *Primum mobile*, "the mover first and circle
crystalline"—as Fairfax puts it in his translation of Tasso[19]—and after that
"the firmament where fixed stars all shine." He leaves on his left hand Saturn
and Jupiter and the other stars (wrongly called "errant," namely, planets,
since they are inspired and moved by *angelica virtù*, the power of angels).
Abandoning the "joyful fields inflamed by eternity," the archangel enters
those of rain and snow, "where the world feeds and consumes itself, and in
its own wars dies and is born again." As Tasso says, he now flies, dispersing
with his wings "the horrid darkness and the shadows dun," while the light
from his eyes makes the night golden. The final simile is double, inspired by
both Virgil and Dante:[20] Michael spreads his rays of light like the sun after
the rain, and descends toward the earth like a falling star:

Here He fell silent and the winged warriors' chief
    reverently bowed down to his divine feet;
    then spread his golden feathers to the great flight,

so swift that he exceeded even thought.
He passes light and fire, where the blessed
hold their unmoving, glorious seat,
then he beholds the pure crystal and the circle
that turns and turns jeweled with stars.

Then on the left Jupiter and Saturn
revolve, unlike in working and in shape,
and the other planets which cannot be called errant,
since angels' power moves and informs them;
then from eternity's happy, flaming fields
he comes to the sky where rain and thunder form,
where the world destroys and feeds itself
and in its constant war dies and revives.

He comes dispersing with his eternal feathers
the thick darkness and the horrors dun;
the night grew golden at the light divine
which his gleaming visage spread forth.
So does the sun through the clouds display
after the rain its wondrous color, so
does a star, cleaving the liquid air serene,
fall into the bosom of Great Mother Earth.[21]
[Qui tacque, e 'l duce de' guerrieri alati
s'inchinò riverente al divin piede;
indi spiega al gran volo i vanni aurati,
rapido sì ch'anco il pensiero eccede.
Passa il foco e la luce, ove i beati
hanno lor gloriosa immobil sede,
poscia il puro cristallo e 'l cerchio mira
che di stelle gemmato incontra gira;

quinci, d'opre diversi e di sembianti,
da sinistra rotar Saturno e Giove
e gli altri, i quali esser non ponno erranti
s'angelica virtù gli informa e move;
vien poi da' campi lieti e fiammeggianti
d'eterno di là donde tuona e piove,
ove se stesso il mondo strugge e pasce,
e ne le guerre sue more e rinasce.

Venia scotendo con l'eterne piume
la caligine densa e i cupi orrori;
s'indorava la notte al divin lume
che spargea scintillando il volto fuori.
Tale il sol ne le nubi ha per costume
spiegar dopo la pioggia i bei colori;
tal suol, fendendo il liquido sereno,
stella cader de la gran madre in seno.][22]

This is of course literally cosmic poetry, which goes through the immaterial and material spheres of the universe to finally land in the sublunar world of the atmosphere and the night sky. The speed seems to have decreased, however: Michael's downward flight appears as a silent, majestic gliding rather than a swooping down "with the rush of gusting winds." There is in fact (and rightly so) no wind, and the universe itself seems to be either completely still, as with the Empyrean where the blessed have their *immobil sede* (literally, "unmoving seat"), or circling slowly as with the *gira* of the heaven of fixed stars and the *rotar* of Saturn and Jupiter. This is an orderly, resplendent cosmos, Ptolemaic and Neoplatonic, where Michael's "golden wings" shine out against the background of the fire and light of the Empyrean, the "pure crystal" of the ninth Heaven and the starry gems of the eighth (*di stelle gemmato*)—a universe dominated by *angelica virtù* and the joyful, flaming fields of eternity. For one-and-a-half stanzas it is like being back in Dante's *Paradiso:* more than four hundred years away from the eternal silence of infinite spaces that we will see only with Pascal and with the profound, unfathomable darkness of the post-Copernican cosmos.

When Michael crosses down from Heaven into the sky, a sudden crisis bursts onto the scene. From the luminous gyres beyond time we move on to thunder and rain, and then to the wonderfully dense image of mutability in which the world consumes and nourishes itself, both dying and being reborn in its wars: *ove se stesso il mondo strugge e pasce, / e ne le guerre sue more e rinasce,* translated by Fairfax rather freely as "where heat and cold, dryness and moisture strive, / whose wars all creatures kill, and slain revive." The image evokes a continuous changing of one element into another; corruption and generation out of corruption; a struggle between life and death, with life rising again out of death—this is the nature of our world, summed up in the self-destruction and self-feeding of the first line. *Strugge:* the world literally liquefies, melts, like a candle under heat; then, figuratively, it slowly consumes itself, inflicting pain upon itself. In Tasso's reflexive form, *se stesso,* it consumes itself in longing, passion, desire, or grief.

This is not heavy poetry, but poetry of Heaven versus poetry of Earth, the Great Mother of the last stanza. Unlike Virgil, Tasso does not present a hard, stony mountain, but a world that melts and wanes in a sigh and then waxes again, feeding on itself: a Lucretian world, endowed with a human soul and just a shade of Christian sentiment. A world of metamorphosis, too; not as in Homer's passing freely from divine to natural—from god into gold and wave and fish—but in being confined to a nature whose components themselves are at war with each other and are generated by each other's death. As Heraclitus is reported to have said, "the death of fire is the birth of air, and the death of air is the birth of water"; and again, "for souls it is death to become (*genesthai*) water, for water it is death to become (*genesthai*) earth; out of earth water arises (*ginetai*), out of water soul." This is the succession of life and the changing of bodies and the continuous renewal of the world.[23] Tasso's poetry here is precisely this: a poetry of *becoming* encapsulated by a poetry of *being*.

A perfect and immutable being belongs to Heaven, and it is the archangel who brings it with him down to the world: with his "*eternal* wings" he disperses the "dense, dark fog" and the "dun horrors."[24] When being and becoming meet, however, the darkness of night preserves a trace of divine light, a golden aura spreading forth, as it were, from Michael's scintillating face. We are not so far from Rilke's contrast, in the second of the *Duino Elegies*, between the angels as *Gelenke des Lichtes* and *Räume des Wesens*—as "joints of pure light" and "space formed from essence" on the one hand— and us humans who "evaporate and breathe ourselves out and away" on the other.[25] Tasso sees the metaphysical mirrored in the physical: *s'indorava la notte al divin lume / che spargea scintillando il volto fuori* (night became golden before the divine light which his visage, scintillating, spread forth). Here, borrowing from the *Aeneid* but pointedly changing the terms of the simile,[26] Tasso describes the archangel's final descent to earth like a sun spreading beautiful colors, in an image tightly poised between the rainbow effect and the golden rays of light emerging from the clouds after a storm. Finally, conflating similes from Virgil and Dante, Tasso crowns his piece with the star falling into the Great Mother's (earth's) bosom as it glides downward, plowing through the *liquido sereno*, the liquid serene night air.

Supreme peace reigns for an instant as the metaphysical and the physical join together, as mimesis makes the supernatural touch down to be embraced by and absorbed (not metamorphosed) into the bosom of Mother Earth. This peace will soon be broken by Michael's words and spear driving the demons back to Hell, but for a moment Tasso touches the essence of the appropriate and fitting, enabling us to feel and contemplate what these are. This is precisely *how* it is, we think peacefully to ourselves when we see a falling star streak through the sky and lose itself among the tree tops on a summer's eve: this is how a deity would pass among us, and it would be just as well, for our minds thus perceive the reciprocity of being and becoming. Tasso's poetry seems a proper measure of this: it becomes *liquid* and fit, the very icon not of sublimity but of perfect *beauty*.

〜⚬〜

This was Hermes, via Mercury and Iris, as the archangel Michael. In my next passage, he becomes another archangel, this time Raphael. Indeed, Homer, Virgil, and Tasso all inspired Milton in his description of Raphael's flight to Earthly Paradise to warn Adam and Eve of the impending danger that Satan represents. The passage in *Paradise Lost* V[27] is far more complex than anything we have yet encountered, as Milton tries to combine a rewriting of Scripture with a rewriting of classical myth, and a rewriting of Italian poetry with a new mimesis derived from Italian science.

Standing "veiled with his gorgeous wings" among the other angels, Raphael begins moving—"up springing light"—"through the midst of heaven." The angelic choirs part to give him way, and the gate of Heaven opens automatically to let him through, as it did for Hera and Athena in *Iliad* V (one of our first passages) and for Saint Peter and the angel in the Acts of the Apostles.[28] Here, Raphael beholds the universe:

> From hence, no cloud, or, to obstruct his sight,
> Star interposed, however small he sees,
> Not unconform to other shining globes,
> Earth and the garden of God, with cedars crowned
> Above all hills. As when by night the glass
> Of Galileo, less assured, observes
> Imagined lands and regions in the moon:
> Or pilot from amidst the Cyclades
> Delos or Samos first appearing kens
> A cloudy spot.

Raphael's sight is, as Dante puts it,[29] *non interciso*, not intercepted by any object, neither cloud nor star. However small (though "not unconform to other shining globes"), even the Earth, with the Garden of Eden and its trees, is actually visible to him. His view is more-than-telescopic: Galileo's startling, human instrument[30] forms the basis for Milton's first simile here, but the telescope, pointing up at the moon from the earth, is "less assured" than a seraph's almost godlike eyes (there is an optical inversion, since Raphael looks either downward or horizontally), so that Milton can play on a second simile, this time classically inspired: that of the pilot glimpsing a distant island on the horizon as "a cloudy spot." The distance, cosmic in the first simile, becomes nautical and human in the second, while maintaining its sense of remoteness through time: the Cyclades, Delos, and Samos are as far removed—in the ancient past of classical literature—from the ordinary experience of a seventeenth-century Englishman as the "imagined lands and regions of the moon" are to anyone who does not use "the glass of Galileo."

Whether the universe envisaged here by Milton is Ptolemaic or Copernican, and whether Raphael's "preternaturally acute vision" takes its inspiration from Flemish landscapes or from Italian frescoes such as Michelangelo's Sistine Chapel, Raphael's Creation scenes in the Vatican Loggias, or the early baroque Heavenly Triumphs,[31] the fact remains that Milton's poetry relies on the shock of *wonder* and *astonishment* a reader of the day would have felt when invited to peer through a telescope or to squint in order to spot Delos or Samos as an ancient Greek sailor might have done. In short, the blind Milton relies on the imagination as much as the blind Homer relied on mimesis and experience and on the imagination of the nonvisible.

Moreover, Milton goes further than Tasso in attempting to reconcile the two dominant mythologies of his poem, Christian and classical. Delos and Samos, birthplaces of Apollo and Diana, respectively, and of Hera, represent a mythic analog to Eden. In the end, Milton goes back to Tasso and Virgil for Raphael's actual flight, for until now we have only had a overview introducing it. Although the simile with "Maia's son," the key to Milton's sources, comes only at the end of the passage, we know right from the start that we are back with Virgil's and Homer's birds. Indeed, in a sense we are beyond them, with an immense panoply of birds and birdlike beings: "towering eagles," "all the fowls," the phoenix, and the "seraph winged." A twenty-three-line-long metamorphosis unfurls in four stages before our astonished eyes, resorting to the lore of Tobias, Isaiah, and Pliny, while covering "ethereal" distances "between worlds and worlds," "polar winds," ancient Egypt and Eden, and displaying a rainbow of colors and multitude of shapes that even include a medieval knight.

In this marvelous passage, Raphael first flies quickly down through the broad skies "between worlds and worlds." When he reaches the eagle, all the birds take him to be the phoenix that flies to Thebes to bury his relics. Upon his arrival at the "eastern cliff of Paradise," he puts on his own angelic form once more, with three splendid pairs of wings. Finally, he stands "like Maia's son," shaking his magnificent and fragrant divine feathers. Thus, we have four stages

(1) Down thither prone in flight
He speeds, and through the vast ethereal sky
Sails between worlds and worlds, with steady wing
Now on the polar winds, then with quick fan
Winnows the buxom air; (2) till within soar
Of towering eagles, to all the fowls he seems
A phoenix, gazed by all, as that sole bird
When to enshrine his relics in the sun's
Bright temple, to Ægyptian Thebes he flies.
(3) At once on the eastern cliff of Paradise
He lights, and to his proper shape returns
A seraph winged; six wings he wore, to shade
His lineaments divine; the pair that clad
Each shoulder broad, came mantling o'er his breast
With regal ornament; the middle pair
Girt like a starry zone his waist, and round
Skirted his loins and thighs with downy gold
And colours dipped in heaven; the third his feet
Shadowed from either heel with feathered mail
Sky-tinctured grain. (4) Like Maia's son he stood,
And shook his plumes, that heavenly fragrance filled
The circuit wide.

The passage overwhelms, feeling almost unbearable, as the cosmic, clear sublimity of the first five lines is smothered, as it were, in the next five lines by the number of birds and the "relics" of the phoenix, with its Christ-like, resurrection symbolism and its allusion to the solar shrine. The sublime then flies, literally, on biblical wings, when the story of Tobias and the description of the seraph's wings in Isaiah are echoed in the following eleven lines.[32] But Milton rewrites Scripture, embroidering upon it by means of the Pliny-derived colors and texture of the phoenix,[33] the image of the "starry" girdle inspired by Revelation,[34] and the angel-knight's armor. Then, out comes a Virgilian Mercury, shaking his wings like Gabriel in Tasso's *Gerusálemme liberata*, and shedding "heavenly fragrance" all around.[35]

The entire passage is cast with phenomenal vision, starting from the simile of Galileo's telescope. Milton imagines the cosmos as an almost infinitely magnified universe "between worlds and worlds," where Raphael "sails" just like the explorers of the day. But he also imagines it as a terrestrial globe suspended in the "vast ethereal sky" where polar winds blow, surrounded by soft air. This universe is reflected also in the seraph's clothing: in the "starry" girdle around his waist and in the heavenly colors adorning his legs and feet. The wings on which Raphael flies through the worlds and winds give rise to the image that then follows, in which the archangel seems "to all the fowls" like a phoenix, the mythical eagle-like creature which every five hundred years is sacrificed on a pyre, arising from its ashes to go to Heliopolis, city of the sun, to bury its relics. The phoenix is a loyal friend to humankind, an emblem of virtue, symbol of Christ and the Resurrection: an appropriate mythical correlative to the archangel who must warn Adam and Eve of Satan's doings. With the phoenix, we have of course moved beyond the vision of the cosmos, and the angel returns to its own form, complete with Isaiah's three pairs of wings, but with Pliny's purple and gold, and the addition of the sacred blue of God's shrine.

Although the visionary nature of the passage is inspired by the prophetical books of the Bible, it functions as a gradual metamorphosis in which each stage takes up, modifies, or reflects elements of the previous one, as in a kaleidoscope: cosmic flight, birds, phoenix, seraph, Mercury. What characterizes Milton's poetry, however, is a new baroque sublime of accretion and concretion, as in the churches of the Gesù and Saint Ignatius in Rome. Even more so than in Tasso, this is the poetry of exegesis and *interpretation*: the poetry of some twenty-five centuries of tradition and re-Scripture.

∽०∾

In a swish of Ockham's razor, the Ptolemaic cosmos was superseded by the Copernicus-Kepler system. Perhaps this is why Gabriel's flight from the Mount of Olives to Paradise in Klopstock's eighteenth-century *Messias*[36] is so straightforward and immediately captivating. On earth to serve Jesus, Gabriel lies prostrate in the dust while God the Father and Christ plan the Passion as a way to redeem humanity. The all-comprehending seraph rises in astonishment, and a blinding light shining from him lights up the whole mountain peak. Jesus, however, orders him to veil his light, which is to shine again only in Paradise after he has delivered his message: it is now time, and he is ready. Gabriel rises, hurrying toward the boundaries of Heaven *wie ein Morgen empor*, "as morning rises"—the level, humble, and peaceful style of utmost piety, an almost Homeric purity, a pre-Rilke dawn. He might even be one of the angels of the second of the *Duino Elegies*, "joyous first creation, mountain peaks at dawn."

The world Gabriel passes through is equally pure. In Klopstock this space on high is filled only by the suns, whose brightness surrounds Heaven like a veil interwoven with rays of light. The inhabited earth flees into the distance below. Tiny and almost invisible, like specks of dust under a pilgrim's feet, the worm-infested worlds crawl round, then disappear in swarms. Around the immensity of the skies, a thousand paths open up, endlessly long and surrounded by suns. One of these paths, leading toward the earth, was once illuminated up by a ray of divine light, after the Creation and before the Fall. Here, or on the ground lit up by the hues of the rainbow or by the dawn, God and the angels would come to talk with humankind.

There are no wings here, nor seas and sailing: no Hermes. But there are lights, dawn, stars, and endless orbits, all of which enable the poet to place his myth within them: the primordial path between humankind, angel, and God is almost a Jacob's ladder transformed into a ray of light, delivering Christ's message immediately to the suffering. Those who hear in this enchanted sublimity an echo of Bach's *Saint Matthew Passion* or Handel's *Messiah* are simply detecting the music already contained in the work: "as morning rises."

∽०∾

Scripture itself presents only two flights worth mentioning in this context of divine beings. The first occurs at the very beginning of the Bible, when, "in the beginning," God creates the heaven and the earth. *Before* (if this is the word) actual creation, the earth is formless and void, and darkness lies upon the face of the deep. In that "between time," before time, *ruah 'elohim merahepet 'al-pene ha majim*: "the Spirit of God moved upon the face of the waters," or "the breath of God hovered over the waters."[37] *Merahepet* contains the sense of "fluttering" wings, which some traditional interpretations translate with *volitabat*. Hovering over the primal waters, the "awesome wind" (if we opt for this translation of *ruah 'elohim*) crowns the description of the "beginning of the beginning." The breath, or Spirit, of God (if we decide in favor of this reading of the same expression) skims the surface of the pristine ocean preparing for—as if "brooding," another early interpretation—the Creation, which begins in the following line with "And God said, Let there be light: and there was light." The desolate, empty earth and the darkness of the primordial ocean have long been read as icons of either chaos or nothingness, but I suspect that the recent interpretation below evokes more closely their actual meaning:

> All the elements of the first verse recur in the second verse as phenomena which are not yet present: God does not yet create, the heaven is still *tehom*, the earth is still *tohu wa-bohu*. This is the primal situation: not "nothing," far less a chaos which has to be ordered, but a situation of "before everything" or "not yet" in respect of what has to come. Even God is not yet the creator God, but still hovers over the waters as an indeterminate spirit of God.[38]

Let us recall the definition of the sublime by Longinus presented at the beginning of this chapter in connection with the Creation of light in Genesis: "The law giver of the Jews, no ordinary person, for, having formed a high conception of the power of the Divine Being, he gave expression to it." If we applied his idea to the verse from Genesis above, we would have to say that nothing is simpler, more profound, or more sublime—or more modern— than the picture of *indeterminacy* and *potentiality*, of *non-presence* conveyed by the hovering of the divine spirit over the waters. It is worth noting that only one Western writer has been able to recapture such an absolute and abyssal simplicity: Dante. As Beatrice declares when recounting the Creation of the angels, heaven, and prime matter, "before" and "after" did not exist until the *discorrer di Dio*, God's moving upon the waters:

> Nor did He lie, before this, as if languid;
> there was no *after*, no *before*—they were
> not there until God moved upon these waters.
> [Né prima quasi *torpente* si giacque;
> ché né prima né poscia procedette
> lo *discorrer* di Dio sovra quest'acque.][39]

In Exodus, the divine wings finally spread out. Three months after leaving Egypt, the children of Israel enter the "wilderness of Sinai" and camp at the base of the mountain. Moses goes up "unto God" and the Lord calls to him "out of the mountain," saying: "Thus shall you say to the house of Jacob, and shall you tell the Israelites: 'You yourselves saw what I did to Egypt, and I bore *you on the wings of eagles*, and I brought you to Me.'"[40] God has indeed chosen Israel: in the next two verses, offering the covenant, he consecrates his people as a "treasure," a "kingdom of priests," and "a holy nation." Here, however, he reminds the children of Israel of what he has already done for them: he has not only delivered them from Egypt, but also brought them "to himself." He has made them his "children," elevating them to his height, welcoming them to his trust. The eagles' wings—to which I shall turn in a later chapter—with which God bears Israel unto himself are, therefore, a powerful and uplifting icon of salvation and grace. God bends down to Israel to preserve and care for it: there may well be a threatening note in the eagle image, but this is decidedly overshadowed by the protective one. As the Song of Moses splendidly proclaims in Deuteronomy:[41]

> He found him in the wilderness land,
> in the waste of the howling desert.
> He encircled him, gave mind to him,
> watched him like the apple of his eye.
> Like an eagle who rouses his nest,
> over his fledglings he hovers,
> He spread abroad His wings, He took him,
> He bore him on his pinion.
> The Lord alone did lead him,
> no alien God by His side.

The sublime here is God's *love*. Human hope has only to respond to it, as in Isaiah: "They that wait upon the Lord shall renew their strength; they shall mount up with wings as eagles."[42]

The New Testament interprets this by replacing the eagle with the dove and shifting the moment of its epiphany to the very beginning of the universe. When Jesus is baptized by John the Baptist in the Jordan, the heavens are opened "unto him" and he sees "the Spirit of God" (*pneuma tou theou*) "descending like a dove, and lighting upon him."[43] A voice from heaven is then heard proclaiming Jesus "my beloved Son, in whom I am well pleased," echoing Isaiah's prophecy about the servant of the Lord.[44] The Evangelists obliquely rewrite Genesis. The *ruah 'elohim* moving upon the face of the waters had already been envisaged in Jewish tradition as a dove "with mighty wings outspread"—as Milton was to put it—"brooding on the vast abyss" to make it "pregnant."[45] The Gospels appropriate this tradition, reading the Hebrew *ruah*, in the interpretation sanctioned by the Greek Septuagint translation,[46] as *pneuma tou theou*, the Spirit of God. The baptism of Jesus in the Jordan represents the prologue to a new Creation. The fourth Gospel, traditionally attributed to John the Evangelist, makes this absolutely clear by opening its account with the *arkhe* of Genesis ("In the beginning was the Word, and the Word was with God, and the Word was God"), by inserting the baptismal dove image into its first chapter, and by concluding it with the vision, from Jacob's dream of the ladder in Genesis 28, of "the angels of God ascending and descending upon the Son of man."

∽○∾

We have come a long way from Hermes' flight across the countless waves of the Mediterranean to the primordial sea before Creation, from Mount Olympus to Atlas and Sinai, from tern to eagle and dove. But have we really travelled cosmic distances? Hermes' missions, as we have seen, are directed towards helping (and sometimes deceiving) mankind. The God of Israel is doing nothing different, but he does it in a different manner and in a different spirit. He creates a whole universe and fills it with being. He does not deceive, but takes it upon *himself* to rescue and feed his children and bring them to himself. The Christian God will become flesh, be baptized and re-create the world and humankind. With Zeus behind him, Hermes can help Priam, restore Odysseus to his long-lost home, spur Aeneas to fulfill his duty and fate. They *pity* and *command:* the God of the Bible *loves.*

All of them, however, fly, hover and flutter, and above all *skim* the surface: they move, *discorrono,* as Dante would put it. Such is the measure of the divine as it passes among us. This is what distinguishes it from evil, whose passage is always clumsy and heavy, its flight unfolding with difficulty, in slow whirlpools. There goes the monster, the filthy image of fraud, flying in Dante's hell: the beast Geryon, with its human face, reptilian body, lion's claws, and poisonous forked tail. This sluggish machine and soulless vessel is the forerunner of the airplane. When Dante and Virgil mount it to descend to the depths of the universe, the beast moves like a small boat slowly leaving the port, backing out *in dietro in dietro,* little by little. Once free to move, it points its tail toward the shore, moving it stiffly like an eel, clutching at the air with its claws. Finding himself engulfed in air and seeing only the beast, the living passenger is more afraid than Phaethon and Icarus. But the beast *sen va notando lenta lenta; / rota e discende,* "it goes swimming slowly on, wheeling and descending," although the unsuspecting Dante would have remained oblivious to this movement were it not for a breath of wind on his face and from below. Finally the circling vessel prepares to land: like a falcon *assai su l'ali,* that has been flying for some time neither hearing the hunter's call nor seeing prey, it descends to the place from which it departed, now tired, bad-tempered, and angry, circling slowly and endlessly in a hundred circles, *per cento rote.* Thus Geryon lands Dante and Virgil in the depths of the universe, finally to disappear like an arrow from a bow, *come da corda cocca.*[47]

The speed is in the disappearance alone. But the *messo*, the heaven-sent angel who comes to that same hell in the guise of Mercury with his wand and throws open the gates of Dis, crosses the Styx *con le piante asciutte*, with dry feet. And with an even more supreme lightness: the angel who arrives at the shores of Purgatory, leading the sinners to the mouth of the Tiber, suddenly appears as *sorpreso dal mattino, / per li grossi vapor Marte rosseggia / giù nel ponente sovra 'l suol marino:* "just as Mars, when it is overcome / by the invading mists of dawn, glows red / above the waters' plain, low in the west." He hovers above the sea, like the earth at dawn, and is seen first as a swift light on the water, growing bigger and brighter until a white light appears beside and beneath him. Finally, the light at his sides materializes into wings. Nothing announces the divine more evocatively than this silent *anghelos*, its white robes like those of the young man sitting to the right of the tomb on the day of the Resurrection.[48] Scorning human instruments, Dante's angel needs neither oar nor sail other than his own wings, and fans the air with these eternal plumes. This *uccel divino* comes closer, shining so bright now that it is no longer possible to keep one's gaze upon it. It reaches the shore with a vessel so swift and so light—and this is the point—that the water does not even touch it, *l'acqua nulla ne 'nghiottiva*. And while the spirits sing *In exitu Israel de Aegypto*, the psalm celebrating liberation and the Exodus, we understand why, much later on in the poem, God "discorre," moves above the primordial waters.

Halcyons   4

Halcyons—also called "kingfishers" in English—are seabirds. They have small, stumpy bodies, short wings, long and curving spearlike beaks, and brightly colored feathers tinged with glistening metallic hues. From afar, they resemble terns or gulls, to whose flight Homer likened that of Hermes in the *Odyssey*. The male of the species is known to the Greeks as *kerylos*, "cerylus." In the latter half of the third century B.C., Antigonus of Carystus, author of a volume of *Marvels* and perhaps also an artist and sculptor working in Pergamum, wrote of a curious habit to which kingfishers are prone when old and weak. No longer able to fly, they entrust themselves to the halcyon hens, flying aboard their wings. Antigonus also tells us that Alcman had something similar in mind when referring to himself as an old man no longer able to fly in dance along with the chorus of young women:

> No longer, honey-toned, strong-voiced girls,
> can my limbs carry me. If only, if only I were a cerylus,
> who flies along with the halcyons over the flower of the wave,
> with resolute heart, strong, sea-blue bird.[1]

Alcman is a poet of choral lyrics: he leads the dance singing the song which he has composed for the occasion. His inability to take part in the dance implies for him relinquishing the *performance* of his poetry, the ritual and sacred moment when it becomes public movement and voice: it means losing at least half the resonance that the poem has for him. For this reason he desires to be at least like the kingfisher, which, when carried by the hen of the species, can continue to skim the sea foam. Flying over the flower of the wave like the cerylus means taking the fragility of old age back to a youth now past but still accessible through the young women of the chorus; it means becoming strong and resolute once more: a bird "of the first life," and in this sense "of spring." It means regaining the "purple-blue" color of the sea depths, caressing the sea surface, carrying the reflection of the ocean. Thanks to the female kingfishers, it means being present to poetry at least, still possessing its light; composing it, as though skimming across the water. Not a movement denoting possession and strength, it is but a swift gesture, a delicate and somewhat modest moving in and pulling back without contact.

Alcman was a poet of the late seventh century B.C. It is uncertain whether he was from Sparta or from Sardis in Asia Minor. It is clear from his few surviving fragments, however, that he paid considerable attention to birds, as Aristophanes was well aware in *The Birds*, which echoes the lines quoted above.[2] Another fragment by Alcman, describing the night and sleep of all beings, closes with birds, and probably continued with "but I lie awake out of love, out of desire for my woman." The twentieth-century Italian poet Salvatore Quasimodo rewrote these lines as follows with a fine sense of rhythm, reproducing the hypnotic quality of the original:

> Dormono le cime dei monti
> e le vallate intorno,
> i declivi e i burroni;
>
> dormono i rettili, quanti nella specie
> la nera terra alleva,
> le fiere di selva, le varie forme di api,
> i mostri nel fondo cupo del mare;
>
> dormono le generazioni
> degli uccelli dalle lunghe ali.

An English translation attentive to the Greek original might read as follows:

> Asleep are the mountain peaks and the ravines,
> And the headlands and the torrent beds,
> All the creeping things the black earth nourishes,
> The mountain beasts and the race of bees
> And the monsters in the depths of the purple sea;
> Asleep are the tribes of the long-winged birds.

Alcman is particularly knowledgeable about birds, possessing a familiarity nourished by song and music. In one fragment he says, "I know the tones of all birds"; he knows the *nomos* of birds, their melodies, the rhythmical "laws" governing their song, and the secrets of nature, which birds have always known. The prophet or soothsayer may divine and prophesy by interpreting the flight of birds, but the poet knows how to listen to them, learning to create poetry from them. Another famous passage from Alcman tells us, "Alcman discovered these words and melody by observing the tongued cry of partridges." *Heure*, proclaims the poet proudly: he "found," "discovered," "invented." This discovery of words and music, however, is related to the cry of partridges, a cry literally endowed with a tongue (*geglossamenan*). Alcman chooses a humble bird, like the pheasant, which in Wallace Stevens's *Adagia* disappears into the brush—hardly a noble paradigm of song like that of the swan or nightingale deployed by the philosopher Democritus.[3] Alcman's choice is a bird who chirps shrilly, and it is precisely this chirruping sound that he observed, "articulating" (*synthemenos*) it in poetry. Words may already have been mysteriously "winged" for Homer, but Alcman has not simply "imitated," as Democritus would have it and as his Roman disciple Lucretius advocated.[4] He learned to sing by attending to that tongued cry, which he then "arranged" into human rhythms.

Alcman is not naïve, for, as he says elsewhere, he knows perfectly well that in order to celebrate the beauty of Agido and Hagesichora, the splendor of Castor and Pollux, or the intricate beginning of the cosmos, he needs the Muses, daughters of Zeus and Mnemosyne goddess of Memory, and particularly Calliope, to lend "desire" to his song. He compares the Muse to a Siren, one of those creatures of "sweet song" from the *Odyssey*, who promise pleasure, wisdom, and the shadow of death.[5] Alcman knows the power and turmoil of the divine inspiration from which poetry stems and the bewitching enchantment it produces in those who compose and listen to it.

The Sirens in ancient Greek vase painting are depicted as birds, and so it is not impossible to conclude that Alcman considers birds in every sense at the beginning and end of poetry. He also places them in the middle, in poetry's very center: like the kingfisher flying over the flower of the wave. Alcman has in fact become a Hermes: like him, he descends upon the Mount of the Muses at Pieria; like him, he plunges down and glides over the foaming surf. Hermes may have invented the lyre, but it was Alcman, by studying the melodies of birds, who discovered how to use it and to what end.

☙

We should, however, ask ourselves what the real subject of Alcman's poem is. It may simply be about lovely young girls dancing together: a concrete and aerial image, simultaneously one of beauty and holiness. It is equally feasible that the poem obliquely celebrates itself. With poetry, however, one constantly wonders what lies *beyond*, what might be its remotest or most ungraspable object that nonetheless has the incomparable ability to shower its light through and upon us. Beyond Alcman's kingfisher and halcyons there is something else that enchants and challenges us, making us rise in flight along with them. It is not only the indescribable elation that grips us when we see those sea colors hovering above the crest of the wave. That fleeting vision, so we intuit or recognize, has deeper and more solid roots within us and within the poet's world. We have seen that in the *Iliad* and *Odyssey* Hermes' flight heralds a message: the pity of the gods (and men) for Priam, for Hector, and even for Achilles; the liberation of Odysseus. In the case of the *Odyssey*, Hermes' flight announces the return of the hero: a return homeward and to being a man once more, his reentry into time and mortality, a return to his woman, his wife Penelope. What news does the flight of the halcyons herald?

Pliny maintains that the halcyon is rarely seen, and in any case only at the two solstices and when the Pleiades set.[6] Does its flight therefore fall within the light of the longest or the shortest day? And, following Robert Graves, are we to think that the halcyon originally was "a manifestation of the Moon Goddess who was worshipped at the two solstices as the Goddess of alternatively Life-in-Death and Death-in-Life"?[7] We may be on the right track here. In actual fact, the only person to have provided a poetic answer to this question is a Roman from the age of Augustus, namely, Ovid. In his distant and mysterious exile on the shores of the Black Sea, he composed a book as large as the universe, starting with the beginning of the world and swiftly narrating its "indistinct confines" and continuous changes, the *Metamorphoses*. In book XI, he tells the story of Ceyx and Alcyone. It is a tragic tale but has a surprising consolatory ending, for in death the two spouses are returned to each other, changed into kingfishers.

Let us start at the beginning. Alcyone, daughter of Aeolus, king of the winds, marries Ceyx, son of Lucifer (the morning star) and king of Trachis in Thessaly. Ceyx decides to go on a sea voyage in order to consult an oracle. Alcyone tries to dissuade him. She fears the sea, the "dismal ocean," the shipwrecks whose ruins she sees constantly on the shores, the named and empty tombs of those who have drowned at sea. Not even her father Aeolus can save her husband, for, once unleashed, the winds take hold of the sea, destroying everything in their path. If Ceyx must depart, he should at least take her with him. Though moved by her words and burning with love for her, Ceyx wishes neither to forego his journey nor to expose her to the risks of a sea voyage. Promising to return before two months have passed, he sets sail. The trembling Alcyone follows his fading outline, then watches his ship as it vanishes into the distance. When the sails too have disappeared, she runs to her room in anguish and throws herself on the bed, weeping desperately.

Meanwhile, Ceyx and his men continue on their voyage, until suddenly a dreadful storm approaches their ship and catches it full blast. Ovid describes it at length and with astounding precision, moving his lens from the details of gesture, movement, and the words spoken by the sailors, to the tenebrous appearance of the elements in turmoil:

> The sea rises up with its surges and seems to meet the sky
> and with its spray to sprinkle the lowering clouds.
> At one point, when from the bottom it raises the yellow sand,
> it becomes like it in color; at another it is blacker than the water of Styx;
> at yet another it lies flat and looms white with seething foam.
> [Fluctibus erigitur caelumque aequare videtur
> pontus et inductas adspergine tangere nubes,
> et modo, cum fulvas ex imo verrit harenas,
> concolor est illis, Stygia modo nigrior unda,
> sternitur interdum spumisque sonantibus albet.][8]

The waves pound against the heaving ship one after another, increasing in strength and destructiveness; the darkness of the night and the storm engulf everything around, amid flashes of lightning. After attempting to lower the sails and drain the deck, the men fall into a state of total frenzy: some weep, while others pray or think of their loved ones. Ceyx invokes Alcyone: he would like to turn homeward but he no longer knows which direction that might be. The lashing whirlwind snaps the mast and smashes the rudder, and an enormous wave surges over the vessel, sinking it. The men go down along with it. Ceyx grasps hold of a piece of debris, praying to Lucifer and Aeolus, but his foremost thoughts are of Alcyone; he hopes the sea will carry his body to her, and whispers her name into the waves. Finally, a black wall of water rises over the waves, crashes down upon his head, and the sea closes over him.

Meanwhile, unaware of what has been going on, Alcyone prays to the goddess Juno for her husband's safe return. Annoyed at being invoked for the sake of a dead man, Juno bids the messenger goddess Iris to instruct Hypnos, god of sleep, to send Alcyone a dream in which the appearance of the dead Ceyx may explain to her what has happened. Thus commences a powerful secondary scene within the narrative in which Ovid masterfully describes the dwelling place of Hypnos near the land of the Cimmerians. His home is a cavern deep in the hollow of a mountain, immersed in mists and a vague twilight. *Muta quies habitat*: here there is only silence and peace, and the sound of the Lethe trickling over the pebbles, lulling to sleep. The god lies sleeping languidly on a feather bed, surrounded by "empty" dreams that are as countless as the grains of sand upon the seashore. Iris enters, managing to rouse Hypnos enough to convey Juno's request and make him send his son Morpheus to Alcyone. Morpheus is the artist of form, *artificem simulatoremque figurae*, the perfect imitator of every shape, incomparable in his ability to imitate human expression, speech, movement, and way of dressing.

Morpheus transforms himself into Ceyx, and appears before the sleeping Alcyone, a bruised and naked corpse with sodden beard and dripping hair, asking if she knows him, pleading with her to recognize him, telling her of his drowning at sea: "Do you recognize Ceyx, my most miserable wife? Or has death perhaps disfigured me? Look at me: you shall recognize me, but instead of your husband you shall find your husband's shadow . . . It is me, me, now drowned, who tells you of my death."[9]

Still asleep, Alcyone weeps and tries to embrace her husband's body; she wakes up and looks around for him, tearing at her clothes and hair. She cries out to the nursemaid who rushes in at all the commotion: "Alcyone is no more—she is nothing! She died together with her Ceyx. Do not try to console me; he has perished in a shipwreck. I saw him, recognized him, stretched out my hands as he left me, and tried to hold him back. He was a ghost, but even so, clearly and plainly the ghost of my husband."[10] By this time it is morning. Alcyone goes to the seashore, to the place from which she had watched her husband set sail. She is recalling the details of their farewell when suddenly she sees something floating on the water, although she cannot quite make out what it is. When the floating object is carried closer on the waves, it becomes clear that it is a body. Alcyone is horrified and saddened. The body drifts even closer: in utter bewilderment she recognizes her husband. She cries out: *Ille est*—it's him—and reaching out her trembling hands to him says: *Sic, o carissime coniunx, / sic ad me, miserande, redis?* "Like this, my dear husband / like this, poor man, you return to me?" There is a jetty nearby. Alcyone leaps onto it, but hers is no human leap: she is now flying, "beating the light air with newly budded wings, she flew, a poor bird, over the crest of the waves." From her mouth comes a harsh and plaintive sound, a melancholy moan. When she reaches the corpse, she takes it in her wings and with her now hard mouth, a bird's beak, tries to shower it with kisses. Perhaps Ceyx feels those kisses, or perhaps it is the movement of the waves that makes it seem as though he is raising his face toward hers. Yes, he feels them: *superis miserantibus*—through the pity of the gods—both of them have turned into birds. And their love continues, even now that they are birds: the marriage vow, *coniugale foedus*, remains unbroken. The halcyon and the kingfisher mate and breed: for seven days, at the beginning of winter, the halcyon broods on her nest on the sea, wings outstretched. "And then even the waves are calm: Aeolus keeps the winds in check, forbidding them to blow, so as to provide his descendants with a tranquil sea."

And so we find the kingfishers once more, and their soft flight over the crest of the waves. "She flew and, fluttering through the yielding air on sudden wings, she skimmed the surface of the water."[11] Or rather, we have identified the mythical roots of the kingfisher's flight. To some extent, Ovid's extraordinary account actually aims at implanting these roots, based as it is on the etiology of the halcyon days in early December, which enable the kingfisher to build its nest.[12] But we must examine the myth as narrative, and in this connection, one can only say that the flight of the halcyon stems from desperate grief, from the separation by death finally recognized *in corpore vili*, while the flight of the male and female—that is, of the kingfisher as species—stems from a love lasting beyond death. As we have seen, Ovid's account frequently emphasizes the love between Ceyx and Alcyone. It is a love that binds two human beings and two elements: the light that announces the coming day—the morning star, Lucifer, father of Ceyx—and the reign of the wind—Aeolus, father of Alcyone. And the flight soars into the air, between light and wind.

The narrative, however, is more complex and at the same time simpler than such an allegory can hope to reveal. At the outset, Ceyx departs from his wife. In spite of the emotion that seizes him upon hearing her words, he leaves her in order to consult an unspecified oracle. He breaks his marriage vows in order to satisfy a vague thirst for knowledge. His existence, however, is solely as Alcyone's husband: as soon as he leaves her, he dies. Nonetheless, the terrible storm in which he drowns is also regenerative:[13] through it, through the metamorphosis dictated by love and by the pity of the gods, Ceyx reemerges as a kingfisher. In this sense, the terrifying Ovidian gale is the ancestor, the *typos*, of the Shakespearian storm: in *Twelfth Night*, *Pericles*, and *The Tempest*. But, as Alcyone declares, neither can she live without her husband, for she too must experience death in order to be reborn as a bird. Actually, Alcyone has to descend into the depths three times: first, in the premonitory anguish she experiences right from the start at the idea that her husband is to embark upon a sea voyage; secondly, when in the dream Morpheus appears as the drowned Ceyx; and finally, as his corpse slowly floats ashore.

Alcyone's necessary recognition of death is twofold: first there is the shadowy figure in her dream, the likeness of her husband impersonated by Morpheus, creator of forms. Then comes the reality, the dead body. Moreover, Alcyone's dream is the equivalent of Ceyx's storm: here, he continues to gurgle words to her; there, she weeps as she speaks to him. Both dream reality and event are presented on the same level, but while the storm brings life and events themselves to an end, the nightmare generates actions that will lead to metamorphosis. Each reality is thus linked to and continues the other.

Ovid's story is in effect a mirror sequence, a narrative in which the two central characters, bound together by great love and so potentially one and the same thing, diffract in a mirror, which in turn reflects their image onto another mirror, and so on until the moment in which everything is about to be shattered. Alcyone leaps onto the jetty with the obvious intention of casting herself into the sea to join her husband's lifeless body. In that precise instant, she is transfigured: the suicidal leap becomes—*mirum*, a marvel!— flight, and flight as a condition of being. *Volabat, stringebat*: the imperfect verbal forms suggest an enduring state. Nonetheless, Alcyone's human feelings are preserved intact: though already a bird, she looks for Ceyx, explores his body, embraces him in her arms-cum-wings, and tries to kiss him. And the kiss brings him back to life, transforms him—as Shakespeare would put it—"into something rich and strange." Ovid is extremely careful about the crucial point: *Senserit hoc Ceyx, an vultum motibus undae / tollere sit visus, populus dubitabat*. The spectator suddenly evoked on the scene, like the public (*populus*) in a theatre, is in doubt as to whether Ceyx really felt those kisses, or if as a result of the movement of the waves it only seemed as though he raised his head.

This is the second point at which everything might disintegrate. *At ille senserat*, replies Ovid, with enormous faith in the redemption that poetry can suggest: but he *did* feel them. Beyond death and his undoing, beyond the sharp beak of the bird, Ceyx can feel. This swollen and broken bulk, this shapeless no-longer-being, perceives her presence and love. The mirror is reconstructed as a living creature. In the dream, Morpheus had made the bruised and naked corpse say: *ipse ego fata tibi praesens mea naufragus edo*; it is I, really I who am present, though drowned, telling you of my fate. Now, after their metamorphosis, their love remains and continues to bond them in one and the same fate: fatis *obnoxius isdem / tunc quoque* mansit amor.

It is precisely this which lies at the root of the myth as narrative: the flight of the kingfishers holds an extremely simple and powerful message. It celebrates the union between male and female—between man and woman—and the continuation of the species. It exalts the ability of the female, of woman, to nourish and save the male. There is nothing, for humanity, for every living creature, which comes closer to the heart of congenital instincts. The flight of the halcyons sings the song of *life*. It may be the poetry of small things, perhaps even consolatory poetry, but it is truly *human* poetry.

And perhaps something more, for it celebrates the continuation of life beyond death, thanks once more to the female. The dream or the metamorphosis may be both intimately and radically necessary for the artist to create his forms as Morpheus does, but they both suggest a continuity: in the psyche on the one hand and in the body on the other; in both the spirit and the flesh. The medieval allegorists—*Ovide moralisé* and Bersuire—certainly got the point when they spoke of the soul as Christ's spiritual bride. As Bersuire says, "When the soul sees her husband embark upon the ship of the cross on which he submits to storm and dies; when she sees him and thinks him dead, then she too must enter the sea, out of devotion in the bitterness of penitence and confession; and when he becomes a bird in resurrection and ascension, then she too must be renewed, and ascend and fly by means of contemplation."[14]

In any case, the message that transpires from Ovid's account is clear: the love that unites man and woman is celebrated, through Alcyone and Ceyx, by Chaucer, Gower, and Christine de Pisan in the Middle Ages, by Dryden at the end of the seventeenth century, and by Maurice Ravel at the start of the twentieth century. Even Coleridge consecrates it as an icon of domestic peace.[15] In the ode "On the Morning of Christ's Nativity," Milton singles out the "birds of calm," the kingfishers, as the very announcers of the peace and the enchanted, silent moment that reigned on earth when the "Prince of Light" was born.[16] Keats, who in a sonnet composed just before he began *Endymion*, exalts the laurel crown that Leigh Hunt has given him and pronounces only the "dewy birth / Of morning roses, ripplings tenderly / Spread by the halcyon's breast upon the sea" superior perhaps to the bay wreath, returns to the kingfisher in *Endymion*, when he invokes the source itself of his inspiration, Sleep, and sees it as the "comfortable bird, / That [broods] o'er the troubled sea of the mind / till it is hushed and smooth."[17] And D'Annunzio in his *Alcyone* (though the title of this collection refers to a different Alcyone, one of the Pleiades), where he exalts the superhuman flight of Icarus, is spellbound by the peace of the *albàsia*, the dead calm that placates the sea during the days when the bride, Alcyone, builds her nest.[18]

⌇∽⌇

In the form of a proto-film show, the story of Ceyx and Alcyone becomes the starting point of the quest for Ovid carried out by his friend Cotta in the town of Tomi on the Black Sea, in Christoph Ransmayr's evocative novel *Die Letzte Welt*, a metamorphic rewriting of the *Metamorphoses*.[19] Here, decorating Fama's shop door is a poster featuring the Roman actress Antonella Simonini, who has become famous beyond the empire in her role as Alcyone. Above all, Cyparis the projectionist makes "flicker" on the slaughterhouse wall at Tomi a "melodrama" that stages the story of Alcyone. The last scene is described thus:

> As if demented, she [Alcyone] stood up and began to run along the cliffs, the reefs. At last her mad racing had a goal. She leapt, she bounded, skipped from stone to stone and over the crevices in the rocks, flew past the shore boulders. And then the fog bank drifted farther and clouded the view. The audience lost sight of the frantic woman for one gasping moment and in the next saw only a bird launching itself above the cliffs, a kingfisher that hovered above the breakers, gave several graceful flaps of its wings, was above the corpse now, and eased down upon the breast torn open by scavengers. Ceyx. His closed eyes bore rings of salt, and petals of salt had formed at the corners of his mouth. The kingfisher's pinions seemed to caress the ragged cheeks, the brow, the face that beaks had slashed. And suddenly something small and glistening sprang to life in that ravaged face, suddenly the purple and black of corruption faded, the putrid foam in the hair was now only a wreath of downy feathers— white, fresh down. Pearl eyes sprang open—eyes. From the surface of a sea engraved by a gentle breeze, a dainty head lifted, jerking to gaze about as if in amazement. A small, feathered body sat up fluttering its wings and shook off the water, the petals of salt, and the scabs. And the audience, seeing neither corpse nor mourning wife, but only two kingfishers soaring aloft, understood. Many of them laughed in relief, too, and clapped their hands.[20]

The spectators *understood*: the *populus* barely glimpsed in Ovid has here become a proper *audience*, as in the primitive open-air cinema in which Cyparis the projectionist creates a metamorphic screen on the slaughter- house wall. All the movements of Ovid's text are reiterated, broken down into minimal gestures, filled out with magical details; the salt around the eyes and at the corners of the mouth of the dead Ceyx, his face scratched by the pecking beak; the fading hues of death; the foul-smelling sea foam that turns into a white-feathered crown; the very sea is "engraved" by a light breeze. The metamorphosis becomes a mimetic marvel (*mirum*), a fantastic miracle, baroque and postmodern, modeled on an imaginary and deceptive reality (the film: the cloud of mist, the apparent winged caressing of the corpse), yet flashing with "real" details—the salt, the purple, the black, the surf. What first appears as a mere dot, a *something*, a minimal bloom of light and *life*, after only an instant becomes a bird's head. Not only have the spectators understood, but so has Ransmayr. At the culminating moment of the metamorphosis, when the new creature's eyes open, they are like pearls, *Perlenaugen*. "Those are pearls that were his eyes," sang Ariel to Ferdinand about his shipwrecked and apparently drowned father in Shakespeare's *The Tempest*: "Those are pearls that were his eyes; / Nothing of him that doth fade / But doth suffer a sea change / Into something rich and strange."

Like Ovid, Ransmayr goes beyond Ariel's riddle: out of Alcyone's grief and the dead weight of Ceyx comes lightness: *flight*. Out of the last world—the world of history, in which Ovid died on the distant shores of the Black Sea—a tiny feathered body rises into the air, upon a screen, beating its wings and shaking off the signs of death: petals of salt, water, and scabs. What Cotta and the other spectators see is the birth of poetry (as cinema), its primal, minimal traces, the new, tiny, living body, the vanishing yet still present marks of death. Whether Ovid is dead or has disappeared, the memory of the stories he composed remains, a projection of their essence, a flickering film, a shadow of poetry. For poetry—the poetry of the halcyons and the cerylus, of the kingfisher—is a "small thing" indeed,[21] a fragile coming together of time before and time after in the living flesh, at the "right" moment, the instant in which a new flight begins.

∽o∾

The appearance of the kingfisher thus signals hope, the beginning of cheerfulness. Even a writer as pessimistic and paralyzed as Eugenio Montale, the greatest Italian poet of the twentieth century, who in his first collection, *Ossi di seppia*, reacts strongly against D'Annunzio's superhuman proclamations, preferring bare cuttlefish bones and humble lemon trees to eagles and laurels, finds respite in the flight of birds. Of course, he writes, "there is greater joy in waiting," but there is also a "glory of expanded noon / when the trees give up no shade, / and more and more the look of things / is turning bronze, from excess light."[22] Here, in *Ossi di seppia*, Montale finds the day that "is not yet done" for him, when the sun is high and the shore dry. The finest hour is yet to come and will appear over the wall in a pale sunset. But now, as the burning heat grasps hold of everything, here is Alcyone once more, a kingfisher hovering over that "something life has left" that is Ceyx: "L'arsura, in giro; un martin pescatore / volteggia s'una reliquia di vita." The good rain will be "beyond the barrenness." Yet the kingfisher's flight leaves a trace between air and sea, a slight presence, a faint promise in the immense epiphany of the sun, in that glory with its dark yellow hues, light upon dazzling light: the only living creature.

Throughout his work Montale displays an unrivalled poetic ornithology,[23] and for him the lost lapwing, the two jays, and the high-flying hawk are symbols of eagerness, premonitions of miracle, prodigies revealing "Divine Indifference." It is certainly no mere chance, therefore, that he returns to the kingfisher in a poem such as "Crisalide," where the poetic "I" reaches out for a "sunlit occurrence" which the poet contemplates from the shadow, retracing the steps leading back to his own childhood, to the "brief hour of human fervor" that springtime leaves in April's breath with its pity for the "greedy roots."[24] Beyond the bars imprisoning the poet within his pessimism, the sea surge "sometimes speaks of salvation," and illusion arises "nimbly":

> They spiral out over the sea,
> then gather on the horizon, shaped like schooners.
> One of them takes off silently,
> skimming the leaden waters like a kingfisher
> in flight. The sun hides in the clouds;
> the shaky hour of fever ends.
> [Vanno a spire sul mare, ora si fondono
> sull'orizzonte in foggia di golette.
> Spicca una d'esse un volo senza rombo,
> l'acque di piombo come alcione profugo
> rade. Il sole s'immerge nelle nubi,
> l'ora di febbre, trepida, si chiude.][25]

It is then that a "showy, soundless breathlessness / rises in the throats": for in the sweltering afternoon heat "the bark of salvation" appears or, rather, has arrived. It is awash "among the shoals," letting down a longboat "which makes for the gentle breakers," and "awaits us there." The "fleeing," "refugee" (*profugo*) kingfisher announces the moment of illusion and harmony: its silent, skimming flight is "a staring around of eyes that now can see."[26]

∽∾∾

But there is more poetry of the kingfisher, a little less uncertain, a little more confident. In *The Waste Land*, T. S. Eliot has the modern-day prophetess Madame Sosostris utter the line from *The Tempest* ("Those are pearls that were his eyes. Look!") when she sees in a pack of tarot cards the future of the drowned Phoenician sailor, later identified as Phlebas. In doing so, he opens up the poem to an ambiguous salvation. In the original manuscript draft of *The Waste Land*, however, the fourth section, "Death by Water," tells the full story of Phlebas's shipwreck. Here, Eliot has this modern-day Dantean Ulysses set sail toward the rocks of the Dry Salvages in a soft breeze, with the sails at full mast billowing in the wind:

> Kingfisher weather, with a light fair breeze,
> Full canvas, and the eight sails drawing well.
> We beat around the cape and laid our course
> From the Dry Salvages to the eastern banks.[27]

A time of peace and of good hope, therefore, which soon after changes to storm and disaster. Eliot returns to the Dry Salvages and to the halcyon days with an altogether different sort of consciousness in the *Four Quartets*. Here, universal and personal history are united in a meditation on experience, the point of intersection between the timeless and time, and incarnation. In the second movement of the third quartet, "The Dry Salvages," Eliot looks at the past with the eyes of an old man: a different "pattern" thus obtains, and it is no longer a mere sequence. The moment of true happiness, the "sudden illumination," has indeed been experienced in the past, but its meaning was not understood. For, past experience "revived in the meaning" is not the experience of one life only, but that of many generations, as far back as the "primitive terror" of prehistoric humanity: the experience of history and of the species. When old, one discovers—and all the more clearly in the experience of others—that the moments of suffering are equally "permanent": "agony abides." Thus, time the destroyer is also time the preserver, as we learn from the river (the Mississippi of Eliot's childhood, symbol of time flowing like blood) and the rocks in the sea (the Dry Salvages of the poet's youth, planted in the ocean which surrounds the earth just as eternity surrounds time):

And the ragged rock in the restless waters,
Waves wash over it, fogs conceal it;
On a halcyon day it is merely a monument,
In navigable weather it is always a seamark
To lay a course by: but in the somber season
Or the sudden fury, is what it always was.[28]

We thus move beyond the halcyon days that bring Ovid's narrative to an end. We are on the rocks, perhaps the very ones where Alcyone's metamorphosis started, certainly the *trois sauvages*, the "three savages," which emerge above the perilous shipwrecking waters off the coast of Cape Ann, Massachusetts. Thanks to their lighthouses, they have become "dry salvages," leading away from disaster, toward safety. These rocks *are*: monuments, navigation markers, entities that ships crash into. Eliot repeats no fewer than three times the "is" that connotes this being, and twice he adds "always." Times change—the dead calm of the halcyon days in early December, the spring and summer weather, the bleak autumn season, the sudden winter storm. Just as the seasons pass, so the temporary nature and purpose (the "final cause") of *being* change: in other words, it *becomes*. Yet now and forever, it "is what it always was." We thus discover that through the kingfishers poetry sings, as it did with Alcman and Ovid, of time that destroys as time that preserves: of being in becoming.

Eagles 5

"Whoever seeks to emulate Pindar," wrote Horace in his *Odes*, "takes flight on wings whose waxen fastenings / Daedalus might have thought of; like Icarus he / will leave his name on the waters of some sea."[1] With this image in mind, we now return to the story of Icarus, which opened this book. Note, however, that Horace speaks of an Icarian fate only for those imitating Pindar, while Pindar himself flies with wings made "by Daedalean craft." Daedalus does not plunge into the sea but flies on from Crete until he reaches Sicily. He is the supreme craftsman and artist of ancient Greece, the inventor of carpentry, the saw, the axe, and glue, the first to give ships mast and boom, the creator of the cow for Pasiphae, the labyrinth, the first dancing place (*khoros*), and automata. As well as being architect and sculptor, Daedalus was the first to make human flight possible. Likening Pindar to him is not without significance for Horace, since Pindar too was a unique innovator, an unprecedented craftsman of verses and an architect of unparalleled poetic structures. Like Daedalus, Pindar *flies*, as recognized by ancient and modern poets alike. In his early poem "Mein Vorsatz" ("My Resolution"), Hölderlin—future translator and renowned rewriter of the Theban poet—exhorts himself to aim ever higher in an attempt to reach the unattainable "flight of the great, hovering over the worlds," and declares his desire to leave human company behind as he thirsts for virile perfection and pursues a burning desire for the greatness of Klopstock—the poet of the *Messias* we encountered in chapter 3—for a *schwacher Schwung nach Pindars Flug*, a "gentle rush towards the flight of Pindar."[2]

"When the Dircean swan thus takes his rapturous flight / He's carried up by music flying high / As the highest clouds are high," says Horace of Pindar in the ode cited above, after likening him to a torrent gushing down and overflowing its banks. Pindar, however, appears to imagine himself as an eagle. In the fifth *Nemean*, he declares that he is not a sculptor of statues that stand motionless upon a pedestal: "I take my sweet song aboard a weightless ship flying towards Aegina; if my resolve is to praise wealth, or the strength of hands, or iron-clad war, then mark off a long jump for me: I have a light spring in my knees: eagles swoop beyond the sea."[3] The athlete and the poet are, in a sense, one and the same. Dedication to sport and the composition of poetry both derive from *agon*, a struggle or contest, and in the Greek context, their principle aim is victory. Most of Pindar's compositions, and certainly the most beautiful, are epinicions, odes celebrating victories in the Olympian, Pythian, Nemean, and Isthmian games. Even when victory is a statue—such as the famous Nike of Samothrace in the Louvre—it is always winged. So too with poetry, which is not static like a statue but moves rapidly: a ship riding the waves, a bird in flight, a javelin soaring towards its boundary, an arrow shot at its target, "a winged song of praise."[4]

The flight of the eagle, the bird of Zeus, is one of Pindar's favorite images for his own poetry. In his third *Nemean*, he juxtaposes eagle and jackdaw. "Swift is the eagle among birds, / which suddenly seizes, as it searches from afar, / the bloodied prey in its talons, / while the cawing jackdaws range down below."[5] Pindar's view is that a great poet, like a great athlete or politician, is a majestic, sharp-eyed, and fast-flying *bird of prey*: other poets are mere jackdaws or crows in comparison. In the second *Olympian*, this icon is superbly merged with that of the arrow: the real poet—*sophos*, he who knows by nature—is different from those who need to learn, who talk too much and squawk at the bird of Zeus (a pair of crows identified by ancient commentators as Pindar's peers Simonides and Bacchylides: the latter likened himself to an eagle and a nightingale):

> I have many swift arrows under my arm,
> in their quiver,
> that speak to those who understand, but in general they need interpreters.
>   Wise is he who knows many things
> by nature, whereas learners who are boisterous
> and long-winded are like a pair of crows that cry in vain
>
> against the divine bird of Zeus.
> Now aim the bow at the mark, come, my heart. At whom

do we shoot, and this time launch from a kindly spirit
our arrows of fame?[6]

With his instinctive nobility of intellect, Pindar is a poet of the aristocracy:
thus the eagle befits him as it does Heracles, to whom it is sent by Zeus
himself,[7] just as it befits the temple and the stadium, places of devotion
and competition where divine and human meet. We should remember that
although the Corinthians were the first to place an eagle upon the two pin-
nacles of their Doric temples as the highest symbol of human achievement
dedicated to the divine (a detail Pindar recalls in the thirteenth *Olympian*
when he mentions the Corinthian "inventors"), the gates of the stadium in
Olympia opening onto the track were mounted by an eagle and a bronze
dolphin that flew upward and downward, respectively, when the gate mech-
anism was set in motion.

Pindar is both eagle and dolphin. Beyond his self-imposed restraint and
in order to avoid boring his audience, Pindar recognizes only one limit: that
set for the eagle, the dolphin, and humanity—in air, water, and earth—by
"god" (*theos*) who is superior to all things in the universe, however noble they
may be. In the second *Pythian*, while declaring himself different from the
evil-speaking Archilochus, poet of slander, he issues a warning to himself,
the supreme singer of praise, and Hieron, its object, great regent of Syracuse,
lord of the West and champion in the chariot race:

> The god accomplishes every purpose just as he wishes,
> the god, who overtakes the winged eagle
> and surpasses the seagoing
> dolphin, and bows down many a haughty mortal,
> while to others he grants ageless glory. But I must
> flee the persistent bite of censure,
> for standing at a far remove I have seen
> Archilochus the blamer often in straits as he fed on
> dire words of hatred. And possessing wealth that is
> granted by destiny is the best object of wisdom.[8]

Reading Pindar more than two and a half thousand years after the *Odes*
were written (and bearing in mind that during this time we have not *heard*
them sung on solemn occasions as their original audiences did) is at the
very least a dual experience, and doubly astounding. Readers approaching
his poetry for the first time, however many studies, introductions, and commentaries they have consulted beforehand, are overcome (as Horace said) by

the flowing rush of word clusters, images, thoughts, pronouncements, myths, and historical events, with their ever-changing direction and rhythm. Everything unfolds as if viewed by an eagle soaring across mountains, looking down upon the salient features of the landscape and simultaneously pinpointing the tiniest detail: it is a dizzying experience for an ordinary person, unused to flying a plane and unable to adjust his or her eyes to such telescopic vision. Add to this the despairing feeling that the eagle has a specific target, a prey or object that we cannot perceive; and the distant perception of ancient music—it is rather like imagining the sound of wings from below breaking through the silence as they flap effortlessly to make each sudden turn. This may give some idea of the experience of reading Pindar for the first time: the impression is an overwhelming one of alienation, inadequacy, elusiveness: of dull stupor before these so-called "Pindaric flights." After some time spent caught up in these flights—all readers spend a good deal of time struggling with them, although this may vary according to individual intelligence and learning—the moment comes when at last one sees the composition as a whole, its complexity, the logic of its associations and its unexpected and sudden twists; even its internal symmetry, the repetitive and circular structures, the polyvalence, the variation and combination of the words, the intertwining melodies: in a word, its harmony. Then our marvel grows, as if realizing that *this*, then, was how the eagle flew, its journeys made up of immense circles and sudden swoops on *that* object, and that the space crossed had a meaning in time and everything was *right!*

∽○∾

Let us take as an example the first *Pythian*, composed for the Delphic victory of Hieron of Syracuse in the four-horse chariot race in 470 B.C. The ode opens with the famous celebration of the golden lyre, the music that possesses the singer and is possessed by Apollo and the Muses. The entire composition is bathed in a blinding light emanating from this point, and right from the first strophe it dazzles like lightning, quenching even "the warlike thunderbolt of everlasting fire," supreme prerogative of the greatest god. Opening the dance is the lyre, which the bards or poets must obey. Its music lulls the eagle to sleep on Zeus's scepter, thus placating Ares, god of war, and enchanting all the gods.

An opening such as this stuns, making us want to linger over the enchantment of the *khrysea phorminx*, take one more glimpse at the Muses with their violet locks who form the background to the golden aura of the lyre, and come to understand how a lyre might be capable of extinguishing the thunderbolt of the god of the eternal flame, of lulling an eagle to sleep and assuaging all struggle, conflict, or war. Pindar does not allow this, but presses on with the vision of the music and the poetry from, as it were, the other side: as he warns, "those creatures for whom Zeus has no love are terrified / when they hear the song of the Pierians, those on land / and in the overpowering sea." The Muses are truly terrible toward those who do not enjoy the favor of the gods: and especially for Typhon, the one hundred–headed monster who lies in Tartarus, who dwelled previously in a cave in Asia Minor and is now held between the coasts of Cumae and Sicily, where "the pillar of sky holds him down": Etna, the volcano that dominates the island and all the sea to the west of Italy.

Suddenly, from the blinding light of the lyre and the summit of Olympus, we plunge to the hollows of the earth, to the immense mass of mountain that presses down on the land and water and that in turn is weighed down by the air: "snowy Etna, nurse of biting frost all year round." It is an inexhaustible source of fire (thus a flash crosses our minds, the four elements join together at a single *point*, which is at the same time a whole *world*). The second strophe and the first part of the second antistrophe are dedicated to the eruption of the volcano: possibly an eruption of some years earlier, which Pindar may have seen for himself and which left a powerful trace in Aeschylus's *Prometheus*.[9] In this passage the flames turn into liquid fire: by day a river of lava and smoke, by night a crimson stream pouring down to the sea (of which the eagle observes not only the "expanse" but also the innermost depths). The words tumble out like hunks of rock shouldered along by the flames, and the poetry becomes rolling magma and terrible fountain of Hephaestus in the air: the spectacle is a monstrous wonder not only for those who have witnessed it, but also for anyone hearing about it from those who saw it. The bewitching melody of the lyre is now replaced by a tremendous roar, even in the very sounds of the words, while its gold has quite literally taken shape, like that of the first *Olympian*, "like a blazing fire in the night."[10] That flame now shoots up from below the earth: it is not the fire of divine light that we recall being put out by the lyre. It is no longer "eternal," it has become *matter*, almost "prime," primordial matter suspended among the four elements, somewhere between a liquid, solid, and gaseous state, but still "inaccessible" and from "terrible springs":

> from whose depth belch forth holiest springs
> of unapproachable fire; during the day rivers of lava

pour forth a blazing stream
of smoke, but in times of darkness
a rolling red flame carries rocks into the deep
expanse of the sea with a crash.
That monster sends up most terrible springs
of Hephaestus's fire—a portent
wondrous to behold,
a wonder even to hear of from those present—

such a one is confined within Etna's dark and leafy peaks
and the plain; and a jagged bed goads the entire length
of his back that lies against it.[11]

Matter which is *here* and *now*: from the remote recesses of myth—in which Zeus punishes Typhon for his threats to the order of the cosmos by hurling him into Tartarus—it penetrates the geological roots and present of Sicily (where today his bed still "goads" the whole length of his back) and pours out from snow-covered, leafy Etna (which changes from season to season just as the appearance of the eruption changes from day to night) down to the plain and the sea, as far as the city of Etna, founded by Hieron.

Pindar has forced us to use continual parentheses and incidental remarks, which interrupt his flow. To keep sight of him, we are obliged to focus our eyes on continually moving parallel and intersecting lines. Together with Aeschylus in *Prometheus,* he has in effect invented the eruption of Mount Etna for the whole of Western literature. The first-time reader of his poetry undergoes a truly scorching and unforgettable experience. One wonders how poetry can reach such heights. The anonymous author of *On the Sublime* held that Pindar and Sophocles, in their creative transport, set everything aflame.[12] In this case, the claim should in fact be taken literally, for Pindar has created a flaming magma of words.

Ovid, Virgil, Seneca, and the author of *On the Sublime*[13] tried in vain to imitate Pindar. According to the ancients,[14] Virgil fails because he tries to be "more daring and bombastic" than his forerunner, struggling in *strepitu sonituque verborum.* In other words, he exaggerates (for one thing, he has the molten rock of Etna licking the stars), falls short in mimesis, and condenses into a single image phenomena that Pindar describes in sequence. The difference between the two is not insignificant for a poetry scholar. Virgil describes what has become a *topos,* a *literary* eruption, while Pindar describes *this* particular eruption, which in his hands becomes Eruption itself: he creates, as Aristotle would put it, the *tode ti,* the universal manifested in the particular.

The only poet who comes remotely close to him is Lucretius, who dedicates a lengthy passage to Etna in book IV of *De rerum natura*. And Lucretius equals his predecessor precisely because, instead of following in his footsteps, he uses the power of his verses to provide a "scientific" explanation for the phenomenon: like a rising and thundering of the wind that, gathered in the hollow of the volcano, heats, sets alight, and shoots everything out.[15]

⌘

Meanwhile, Pindar has not stopped; with a shorter leap he lands, temporarily, on the Pythian games, which the lord of Syracuse has won, and has the herald in Delphi proclaim him "Etnean." But right in the middle of the second antistrophe, between Typhon who lies below the volcano and Hieron who emerges victorious from the Pythian games and founds his city on the mountainside, comes Zeus, who reigns "over this mountain" and to whom the poet addresses his prayer for himself (as though he were afraid, the scholia say, of the story of the fate that befell the monster) and for the king of Syracuse. Zeus, who tamed Typhon, dominated the opening of the poem with the lightning and the eagle.

We would seem to have reached the event, the chariot race, and the triumph and the glory we have been expecting from the beginning. But no, on the one hand we have only just set out, while on the other we have gone much further and arrived in the future. "For seafaring men," Pindar sings in the second epode, "the first blessing / as they set out on a voyage is the coming of a favorable / wind, since it is likely that they will attain / a more successful return at the end as well." Odd, but psychologically true: at the moment of departure travelers often think of their homecoming; for them, therefore, a favorable wind is *kharis,* grace and joy. Thinking right from the outset of the end and a "more successful return"—a complete journey, a full circle—the poet, like the eagle, looks ahead, into the future. Precisely "in *these* events," given the present circumstances of Hieron's triumph, his words (*logos*) express the wish that in the future the city will be renowned "for crowns and horses, / and its name honored amid tuneful festivities." Already evoked in the first line of the ode, at one with the lyre and the Muses, Apollo is called upon to preside over such a future, as well as the present of the song which opens up and prefigures that future: "pure" lord of Lycia, Delos, and Delphi (and therefore of the entire Hellenic world), god of light and darkness, sovereign of the "Castalian spring" of Parnassus, prophecy, music, and poetry: may he "willingly put these wishes in [his] thoughts, and make this a land of fine men."

One would expect at this point (we are now at the beginning of the third strophe) to return to the magic of the opening, to the lyre, the instrument of Phoebus. But this occurs only indirectly and for a single instant. The third strophe opens, linked to the invocations to Zeus and Apollo in the previous antistrophe and epode, with a maxim or general truth, a *gnome*, which is both metaphysical and ethical, whereby all the human *aretai*—wisdom, agonistic and battle skills, eloquence—have a divine source: "from the gods come all the means for human achievements, / and men are born wise, or strong of hand and eloquent." Only now does Pindar return to poetry, to the song of praise produced by the golden lyre, with the image of the javelin. A true poet does not hurl his verses too far, for he must know the *just measure:* he is to overcome his rivals and win the race as an athlete does, of course, but he must not go "off-track":

> In my eagerness to praise
> that man, I hope
> I may not, as it were, throw outside the lists
> the bronze-cheeked javelin I brandish in my hand,
> but cast it far and surpass my competitors.[16]

Similarly, Pindar hopes that "all of time" will give Hieron prosperity and wealth (but it is the gods invoked at the start of the strophe who will bestow these gifts) and most of all "forgetfulness of his hardships." In the third antistrophe, the poet finally concentrates on Hieron, celebrating him and his enduring soul in battles of war. In these, together with his brother Gelon and "with divine help," he found honor and, as a crowning glory, wealth (the two ideals of the aristocracy), which no other Greek ever obtained, by defeating (the text alludes only briefly to this) the Carthaginians led by Hamilcar at Himera in 480 B.C. Together with the victory at Cumae against the Etruscans mentioned later by Pindar, this was decisive for the control of Italy's seas.

From the magic spell of the lyre, the myth of Typhon, the eruption of Etna, and the games in Delphi, we have arrived at *history*, at that point in time when Syracuse became a superpower of the Greek western world. Pindar immediately offers an equivalent in *myth*, by flying back in time to Philoctetes, the hero decisive in the defeat of Troy and abandoned on the island of Lemnos by the Greeks because of the stench from his wounds. Ailing and perhaps limping like the mythical archer, Hieron "has gone to campaign" just *now*, "in the manner of Philoctetes." The present is thus foreshadowed by the mythical-divine world of the past. According to Pliny,[17] there was in Syracuse at the time of Hieron a famous statue of a clubfooted Philoctetes; and Philoctetes was a cult figure in Sicily. But what is also remembered here is another of Hieron's battle victories, more recent ("now," *nyn*), and probably in Sicily, against the inhabitants of Akragas: "even one who was proud / found it necessary to fawn on him as a friend." In his celebration, Pindar *skims* over historical events, preferring to concentrate on their mythical prefigurations. Banished to Lemnos, Philoctetes is joined by "godlike" Greek heroes: depending on various traditions, Diomedes, Odysseus, Neoptolemus. The episode was to become the subject of great tragedies by Aeschylus, Euripides, and most important, Sophocles. Quick as an eagle and never hurling the javelin beyond the track, Pindar sums it up in six lines, highlighting Philoctetes' terrible wound and ailing body, which remained unhealed until after the defeat of Troy:

> They tell that the godlike heroes came to fetch him
> from Lemnos, wasting from his wound,
>
> Poias's archer son,
> who destroyed Priam's city and ended
> the Danaans' toils;
> he walked with flesh infirm, but it was the work of destiny.[18]

"But," adds the poet with the wisdom of one who "knows by nature," *moiridion en*, "it was the work of destiny": thus the destruction of Troy and the completion of the trials of the Greeks by Philoctetes are sealed by the fulfillment of destiny, as predicted in the prophecy of the Trojan Helenus (according to whom Troy could not have been won without the prodigious bow which Heracles gave to Philoctetes). Just as the hero of Lemnos recovered at the end of the war, so now may the "god" restore Hieron's health and allow him the fulfillment (*kairos*) of his desires. Between the third antistrophe and the third epode, myth has penetrated deep into history, and the gods and the Moiras have ended the ten-year war: in an instant.

A moment later, the Muse is invoked for the fourth time in the ode: so that the poet, riding on her chariot, may also sing a "hymn" to Deinomenes, the son Hieron had made governor (Pindar calls him "king") of the new city of Etna, so that a father's victory may be "no alien joy." Gelon, Hieron, and Deinomenes now arise on the poetical-historical horizon as a real Syracusan dynasty, of fundamental importance to Greece and the Mediterranean.

It is for Deinomenes, continues Pindar in the fourth strophe, that Hieron founded Etna "with divinely fashioned freedom" and in accordance with the laws of the rule of Hyllos, son of Heracles and of Aegimius, that is, two of the founders of the Dorian line that colonized the Peleponnese, and Sparta in particular. Again, with incomparable speed, Pindar depicts in a few lines the Doric conquest of Greece, from Mount Pindus in the north, to Amyclae near Sparta in the south; there, beneath the cliffs of Taygetus, their descendants, highly renowned neighbors of the Dioscuri Castor and Polydeuces "with their white horses," strove to persevere in ancestral laws; and there "the fame of their spears" flourished. After Philoctetes and the mythical heroes of the Trojan War, the genealogical roots and the "ethnic" history of the Acheans are traced. Linked to this are the rules that tradition, customs, and law have laid down for the Dorians and that find their institutional model in "aristocratic" Sparta. Pindar sees such constitutional wisdom applied on foundations of freedom built by the gods and therefore inalienable, even in Etna, which Hieron populated with Dorian settlers. Thus, the first *Pythian* becomes a *political* message: traditionalist, conservative, and oligarchic, but still one of freedom.

Pindar hopes that Zeus (invoked now at the beginning of the fourth antistrophe, for the third time in the ode) will grant good fortune to the citizens and kings of this Sicilian city through "true" reputation, truthful narration: and that Hieron and Deinomenes, by bringing "honor to the people," may lead them to *hesykhia,* internal harmony and external peace, particularly from the Phoenicians and the Tyrrhenians—the Carthaginians and the Etruscans—who were defeated by Hieron "off Himera" and at Cumae, respectively: here the *hybris* of the Etruscans truly suffered, because the Syracusan leader "cast their youth / from their swiftly sailing ships into the sea," delivering Hellas "from grievous slavery." Pindar sees Hieron's triumphs in the West as forming part of a series of events that freed the whole of Greece from bondage to the barbarians. In the fourth epode the poet provides a solemn reminder of the victories in 480 and 479 of the Athenians at Salamis and of the Spartans over the Persians—"the curved-bowed Medes"—at Platea (one sea and one land battle, like those of Hieron against the Tyrrhenians and the Phoenicians.) Yet here too the celebration of such a pan-Hellenic Nike is presented obliquely. *While* praying to Zeus to end "the war cry" of Carthaginians and Etruscans, Pindar is in fact talking *to himself* and saying that he will have his reward from Athens and tell of the battle of the Spartans at Platea "before Cithaeron"; and furthermore that "by the well-watered bank of the Himeras" he will "pay" the tribute of his song (which, in the third epode he had asked the Muse to help him "devise" for Deinomenes alone) to the entire dynasty of the Deinomenides. In other words, Pindar is proposing himself as the singer of all Greeks, as their "winning" poet, on a par with the Greek victories in war.

ᴄᴏᴏᴄ

The fact that the eagle is now observing its own flight, its own poetry, is confirmed by the poet's declaration immediately afterwards in the fifth strophe, in which he presents a poetics of measure, brevity, and compactness in multiplicity:

> If you should speak to the point by combining the strands
> of many things in brief, less criticism follows from men,
> for cloying excess
> dulls eager expectations,
> and townsmen are grieved in their secret hearts
> especially when they hear of others' successes.[19]

Hölderlin's more concise translation is rather closer than this to the pre-scriptions of the first lines in the original: *Das Schickliche wenn du es redest, vieler / Versuche zusammenfügend / In Kürze.*[20] Today, we might render it as follows: if you find the right measure at the opportune moment (*kairos*), outlining many things in brief. The ideal is that of *opportuneness*, implying both time and space: in the first *Nemean*, Pindar claims he has reached the *kairos* of many things (literally: launched into many themes, seizing their *kairos*) without spreading false words.[21] Arriving at opportuneness, however, is like weaving many threads together on a loom to make cloth, where the weaving is compact (*syntanysais*) and at the same time concise.

Poikilia, the art of embroidering with many colors, of skillful entwining, is achieved in lyric poetry through the conciseness favored by the experts, the elite audience for whom the odes are written and to whom the poet adapts: "the law of song keeps me from telling the long tale, / and the pressing hours," says the fourth *Nemean*,[22] and the ninth *Pythian* expresses the idea more explicitly, using the verb *poikillein*, the nominalized adjective *baia* ("few things") and the nouns *sophoi* (the wise, experts, poets) and *kairos*:

> Great achievements are always worthy of many words,
> but elaboration of a few themes amid lengthy ones
> is what wise men like to hear, for deft selection conveys
> the essence of the whole as well.[23]

Seizing the propitious moment, the opportunity, the *kairos*, this is the ideal: everything has its right proportion, and knowing the *kairos*, what is "right," convenient, opportune, is therefore the best thing. But "the opportune moment, for men, has a brief measure."[24] We finally understand why a Pindaric ode is so diverse, complex, tight, variegated, and compact; why the tale of the myths of Typhon and Philoctetes, the description of the eruption of Etna, the allusions to contemporary history and to the ancestral roots of Greece are so brief, so fulminating. It is not only because the slander of men, an unbearable fullness, and the envy of others for the object of praise prevent dwelling on points *en makroisi*, in long discourse, and render selection and flight obligatory: it is also because *kairos*, dominating, determining, and blending in with all this, containing the gist of the whole, is the "brief measure" for humankind.

We have few real chances, rare opportunities, mere instants. And the poet has even fewer, for he has to find the appropriate words for the event, the sporting contest, at that particular time and on that particular occasion, purposely and with the right proportion. The poet must capture *kairos in the kairos* and embroider a dense, multicolored tapestry upon this point of convergence, distilling from it a liquid as sweet as honey and pure and pristine as water, and forging a lyre as shining and precious as gold.

In actions and in words, cling to the beautiful, the just, the true, Pindar exhorts Hieron at the end of the fifth strophe: "do not pass over any noble deeds," "guide your people / with the rudder of justice," "on an anvil of truth / forge your tongue." Even a slight thing becomes important if it comes from him, "the steward of an ample store." Let the words of Hieron be "tempered" like his works, and his nature—the disposition of his soul—blossom and flourish in liberality: "if indeed you love always to hear pleasant things said / about you, do not grow tired of spending." Renown is achieved through munificence. So, Hieron, "like a helmsman," let out the sail to the wind: and like sailors who set sail with the joy of a favorable wind (mentioned in the second epode), you will have a happy homecoming. Thus, while those sailors with their thoughts of return at the start of their voyage referred to both the founder of Etna and to the poet celebrating him and looking forward to the goal and end of his composition, now homecoming is the reward for Hieron's generosity—and it is of course the narrative and the poetry that here and now join past and future, death and immortality:

> The posthumous acclaim of fame
> alone reveals the life of men who are dead and gone
> to both chroniclers and poets.[25]

Poets and *logioi:* Pindar repeats this in the sixth *Nemean,* combining the image of the archer aiming at the center of his target with the invocation of the Muse:

> I hope,
> by making this great claim, to hit the mark head on,
> shooting, like an archer, from my bow.
> Come, Muse, direct to that house a glorious wind
> of verses, because when men are dead and gone,
> songs and words preserve for them their noble deeds.[26]

And while it may seem strange to us that Pindar, singer and poet par excellence, associates the *storytellers* with the praise and divine inspiration of the Muse, we must convince ourselves that in his view anyone who narrates myths or traditional stories, even in prose—for example, Hecataeus, a younger contemporary of Pindar and author of *Histories* and *Genealogies* of this kind—is creating works similar to his own: Themistocles and Pausanias, victorious at Salamis and Platea, will have eternal renown, equal to that of Hieron, among the descendants of such *logioi,* the historians. Herodotus is about to appear on the scene, while Thucydides will himself be "Pindaric."[27]

Moreover, the poet now recalls in the fifth epode, which closes the ode, two historical characters: Croesus, king of Lydia, immensely rich and whose "kindly excellence," generosity, and *pietas* have lived on after him (and open Herodotus's *Histories*); and Phalaris, tyrant of Akragas, whose merciless mind conceived the bronze bull in which he had his enemies roasted: his lasting renown is infamous, "universal execration." The liberal behavior and fair government to which the poet invites Hieron find an illustrious precedent in Croesus, and poets and storytellers can sing the praises of both. Phalaris, by contrast, is a negative model of despicable tyranny and is destined to oblivion:

> no lyres in banquet halls welcome him
> in gentle fellowship with boys' voices.[28]

Thus, at the end of the ode, we have returned full circle to the bewitching image of its opening, the golden lyre. Now the eagle really does end its flight: on a peak, that represented in life by the convergence of success and good reputation, of present joy and future renown: "the man who / meets with both and gains them has won the *highest crown.*"

‰

How many full circles has the eagle completed in its flight? Inside the widest, from the lyre to the lyre, we now begin to see other, concentric ones—from the peace that the art of Apollo and the Muses spreads over Olympus, to the peace in the city of Etna and the whole of Greece; from the fury of Typhon below the volcano, to the barbaric Carthaginians, Etruscans, and Persians conquered at sea and on land; from the prayer to Zeus and the proclamation of Hieron's Pythian triumph in the second antistrophe to another invocation of Zeus and the celebration of Hieron's triumphs at Cumae and Himera in the fourth antistrophe. Apollo and the Muses open the first strophe and come together again at its end; Apollo is evoked once more, implicitly with the Muses, in the second epode; the Muse is invoked in the third. We could go on; words, images, figures, ideas—as we have often seen—are harmonious and discordant, recurring and complementary, rather like in a Bach fugue.

There was a plan in the eagle's flight: a supreme symmetry, a preordained order to be achieved, an incomparable harmony. It was not static, not sculptorial, but constantly reshaping with the quickest of movements. If now, standing still, we can see it in its completeness, it is because the winged creature of Zeus has landed at last on the "highest crown" and the dance and the song are over. We have now drifted off into sleep, into the lyre-induced *koma* into which all people and gods fall, a drowsiness so profound that it cancels even what joins, in the quickest movement known to humanity—the speed of light—that which from eternity enters time, lightning: the warring thunderbolt of eternal fire. Now the eagle sleeps on Zeus's scepter, its wings folded, its eyelids gently closed by the dark mist of the music that possesses it. It breathes the powerful, tranquil rhythm of sleep. This too is poetry, the experience we sometimes make of it.

The terrible eruption of Etna, the ailing Philoctetes triumphant at Troy, Hieron master of the West, the Persian wars, the origins and laws of the Dorians, Croesus and Phalaris—all of this, now, is here: Ares, god of *polemos* and, as Heraclitus would say, of *eris*, of the universal strife that dominates the cosmos,[29] for a moment warms his own heart, setting aside his rough spear point; and all the gods are spellbound by the arrows of the poet and the strings of the lyre. Here and now, where the javelin has reached its target, at the furthest point but still within the track, in the right place at the right time, at Delphi or Etna where the ode was sung in the fifth century B.C., or in Rome, Cambridge, or Toronto in the twenty-first century: a "leaf of songs." Because *kairos* is *within it*—this is the point where sea, land, sky, and abysses of the earth meet; where the eternal encounters the past, the present, and the future; where divine, chthonic, and human mingle: in short, where myth, laws, history, and politics come together.

Khrysea phorminx: the five vowels—as at the start of the first *Olympian*— chant the world. Let us reread the opening strophe and antistrophe of the first *Pythian*, in silence, as we drift off into sleep.

> Golden lyre, rightful possession of Apollo
> and the violet-haired Muses, to you the footstep listens
> as it begins the splendid celebration,
> and the singers heed your signals,
> whenever with your vibrations you strike up
> the chorus-leading preludes.
> You quench even the warring thunderbolt
> of ever flowing fire; and the eagle sleeps
> on the scepter of Zeus,
> having relaxed his swift wings on either side,
>
> the king of birds, for you have poured
> over his curved head a black-hooded cloud,
> sweet seal for his eyelids. And as he slumbers,
> he ripples his supple back, held in check
> by your volley of notes. For even powerful
> Ares puts aside
> his sharp-pointed spears and delights his heart
> in sleep; and your shafts enchant
> the minds of the deities as well, through the skill
> of Leto's son and of the deep-breasted Muses.[30]

In the drowsiness that has overcome us, we relive the great flight of the ode and feel upon us the strength of Zeus "who accomplishes all," to whom everything is due and whose name we hear repeated five times: he has defeated chaos and cast Typhon ashore; he reigns over Olympus and Etna. Everything happens in his shadow: lightning in his hand, the eagle on his scepter, as in Phidias's statue at Olympia. He is *theos*, God: to whom Pindar has dedicated a famous hymn, and whom Aeschylus celebrates as the unique in his tragedies.[31] The divine, so often invoked by the singer, is thus an integral part of this poem, which *enchants the divine.* Together with Zeus, dominating the ode are the *sophia* of Apollo and the song of the Muses: the wise art of he who from birth has the lyre, the bow, and the oracles on his side;

and the melodious and terrible voice of Memory's daughters. The recognition that "from the gods come all the resources for the achievements"—wisdom, strength, speech—means giving to God what is his, realizing that in the universe generally, as in this place and at this moment, there is at work a full being who is both transcendent and immanent, incredibly far off and yet extremely close.

Nonetheless, there also exists in human things, as in the Trojan War, a *moiridion*, a fate that unravels and comes about with time along with human action, alongside Philoctetes with his open wounds bending his bow, and alongside the ailing Hieron's triumph in the race and in battle. These interwoven threads conform at the point of *kairos*, the propitious moment, the right or proper time. This will be the founding of Etna and the "just" laws it makes for itself, the triumphs of Athens and Sparta over the Persians: the *kairos* is *within* history and *within* politics—and perhaps there is something here we modern-day, timid preservers of strictly personal, lyric poetry still have to learn: poetry sings openly, without attempting to hide, because it is actually speech adapted to the occasion. The events continually repeated in Pindar's poetry—the triumphs of the athletes in the games—are transcended only insofar as they come *to the point* thanks to an art that takes off and flies: transported and restrained, light and dark, crystal clear and glittering like gold. According to Leopardi, grand illusions conceived at moments of enthusiasm or desperation contain the most real and sublime truths "and reveal to man as in a sudden flash the most hidden mysteries, the most unfathomable depths of nature, the most distant or secret relations, the most unexpected and remote reasons, the most sublime thoughts." Philosophers try to analyze and synthesize these, but it is the true lyric poet, such as Pindar, who discovers and reveals them, because he is "a man inflamed by a raging fire, his soul in total disorder, a man in a state of fever, out of the ordinary, and as though drunk."[32] Such is the impression this poetry makes on the reader.

According to Pindar's ideal, life is as limpid as water and as glittering as gold, both dark and light. An ethics of the beautiful, the right, and the true renders this immanent, within the short span of a human life on earth: first, oblivion to troubles, and then prosperity and plenty of belongings; finally, the honor that crowns wealth, the enjoyment of success and high renown. When a man finds and takes on (*enkrysei*) both, or when one finds a man who takes on both, this is the truly supreme *krisis*: the *kairos* of life, the "highest crown." Then we may say that *kharis*—grace, beauty, splendor, favor—sustains existence. And with the same dazzling light used in the first

Pythian, we may proclaim, as the first *Olympian* does for Hieron, triumphant this time in the single horse race:

> Best is water, while gold, like fire blazing
> in the night, shines preeminent amid lordly wealth.
> But there too, poetry took immediate possession of the arcane liquid and the
>   golden splendor, aiming at the sun and the stars:
> But if you wish to sing
> of athletic games, my heart,
> look no further than the sun
> for another star shining more warmly by day
> through the empty sky.[33]

Aiming at the sun, as only the eagle can. This, we should note, is poetry. But we should be careful: it is not for everyone (nor is that kind of life); indeed for some, or many, it is dangerous and terrible: "those creatures for whom Zeus has no love are terrified / when they hear the song of the Pierians, those on land / and in the overpowering sea."[34] A "blind, overwhelming terror" grips the enemies of the God when they hear the song of the Muses, wherever in the world they may be. And although, with Pindar, we should identify these beings with the enemies of Olympian order, monsters such as Typhon, we may still wonder: why must those who are unloved by God tremble with fear when listening to poetry? Why does the voice of the Muses become a war cry for them? And what exactly is the *philia* of Zeus, the love of God? We of the twenty-first century are plagued by a deep uneasiness: God's love for us and our capacity to enjoy poetry, and be captivated by it, are bound together in some mysterious way, as though we were in the world of prophecy in the Hebrew Bible. Let us not upset this delicate, precarious balance, for we might find ourselves—what an unbearable fate!—fearing the music that enchants the eagle and lulls it to sleep. Let us remember that for human beings the "right moment" has a "brief measure." And, the passage goes on, "they say that the most distressing thing is to know the beautiful and the good (*kala*) / but to be forced to stand away."[35]

⌇⍜⌇

At the end of the fifth century—taking inspiration from an ode by Anacreon—Aristophanes ridiculed, in an apparently irredeemable manner, those poets who likened themselves to birds, transported in the air toward Olympus on ethereal wings, flying with intrepid spirit through the many and preferably new directions the melody takes them. His portrayal of Cinesias is subtle and savagely ironical. In the imaginary nation of *Birds*, Cinesias sings out: "On the lightest of wings I am soaring on high, / Lightly from measure to measure I fly . . . To be a bird, a bird I long, / A nightingale of thrilling song." He explains to Pisthetaerus that the "noblest dithyrambs" are "but things / Of air, and mist, and purple-gleaming depths, / And feathery whirlwings," and warbles on blithely: "I'll go through the air, dear friend, for you . . . Shadowy visions of / Wing-spreading, air-treading, / Taper-necked birds . . ."[36]

But the poets did not give up: the example set by the *Homeric Hymns*, by Alcman, Sappho, Aeschylus, Pindar, Bacchylides, and Theognis was too attractive.[37] The flight of birds, mysterious and lofty, was such a beautiful metaphor for poetry—an object for divination and interpretation, the point at which heaven and earth, inspiration and words met—that it could not simply be abandoned. It wasn't. Euripides calls the ancient singer-poets "swans," birds of Apollo, using the image also for himself. At the end of his *Republic*, Plato identifies in the swan the being whose soul the poet enters and whose form he takes on. Although preferring *logos* to the Muses all his life, even Socrates, prior to his death, dedicated a song to Apollo and turned some of Aesop's fables into verse: thus, "like a swan and high priest of god," writes Plato in the *Phaedo*, he approached the final step. And while in the image of the swan Socrates sees himself as a thinker, who during his trial had considered philosophy the only form of music possible, now, at the end, sees himself also as a poet: the song of praise to Apollo, his most beautiful, is his "swan song."[38] In the symbol of birds, poetry, music, and philosophy come together, in one of the supreme *kairoi* in the history of Western civilization, as if in ultimate harmony.

The poets continued to liken themselves to the winged creatures that cleave to the heavens. The Greek and Latin traditions are endless: Callimachus, Apollonius Rhodius, Moschus, Ennius, Lucretius, Virgil, Ovid, and Propertius.[39] The icon crystallizes and changes shape a thousand times through the Middle Ages and the Renaissance, to Milton, who opens *Paradise Lost* exalting his own "adventurous song, / That with no middle flight intends to soar / Above the Aonian mount, while it pursues / Things unattempted yet in prose or rhyme,"[40] and on to the Romantics. Keats creates a nightingale that is a "light-winged Dryad of the trees" and sings of summer "in full-throated ease." On the invisible wings of poetry, Keats seeks to fly toward the nightingale, to listen to it while he himself grows gloomy, to grasp its immortal song.[41] Shelley's skylark, soaring ever higher "like a cloud of fire," winging the blue deep and singing unseen, is likened to a poet:

"Like a poet hidden / In the light of thought" who sings hymns unbidden until the world is awakened to unknown hopes and fears and universal suffering.[42]

Baudelaire too, in "L'Albatros"—no doubt inspired by Coleridge's *Rime of the Ancient Mariner*—compares the poet to the albatross captured by the sailors, pitifully dragging its great white wings like oars: at first the winged voyager appears beautiful, then clumsy and sinister, comical and ugly: some hold a pipe under its beak, while others imitate the limping gait of this cripple that once could fly. The poet is just like this "prince of the clouds" that haunts the storm and is exiled on the ground, his "giant wings" preventing it from walking. The bird among men, on earth: the poet unable to fly is a stranger and an exile. In "Le Cygne," too, with Victor Hugo in mind, Baudelaire turns to this theme, describing a swan that has escaped from its cage: it rubs the dry pavements of the new Paris and drags its white plumage along the ground, invoking the rain.[43]

Dedicating his most sublime sonnet to the swan, Mallarmé describes a frozen lake that lies forgotten beneath the "transparent glacier of unflown flights" and is cracked with one beat of the drunken wing of the "virginal, lively and beautiful today." A swan from the past reminds us that, however magnificent it may be, it struggles in vain to be free because it has not "sung the land" to live in "when the tedium of the sterile winter shone." Its whole neck will shake off that white suffering "inflicted by space upon the bird who denies it," but it will not succeed in casting off the horror of the ground in which its feathers are imprisoned. It becomes a ghost assigned to that place by its pure splendor, immobilized "in the cold dream of scorn" in which the swan clothed itself during its pointless exile. A white spirit in a frozen lake, the poet turns to the only thing left to him, the scorn for everything that imprisons him in the world and for his own inability to reconcile fantasy with reality. But the despair that in the first quatrain freezes the brilliant purity, lively vigor and beauty promised by morning; the rhyming *i* and *ui*, sharp as ice needles; the unflown flights and denied space; the white suffering of winter and of the swan—all this becomes visionary in the final tercet, in which the bird becomes ghost and essential swan: the poet covered in glassy frost, certainly pure, but encased in the ice of his pride and isolation from the world. Nonetheless, only the original text allows us to appreciate fully the wonderful variations on the icy lake, the *givre*, the *glacier*, the *blanche agonie*, the *songe froid*; the passage from the drunken wing to the unflown flights and imprisoned feathers; the metamorphosis of the virginal morning into icy transparency, into the winter splendor of *ennui* and finally *éclat*, the dazzling light detaching his pointless exile:

Le vierge, le vivace et le bel aujourd'hui
Va-t-il nous déchirer avec un coup d'aile ivre
Ce lac dur oublié que hante sous le givre
Le transparent glacier des vols qui n'ont pas fui!

Un cygne d'autrefois se souvient que c'est lui
Magnifique mais qui sans espoir se délivre
Pour n'avoir pas chanté la région où vivre
Quand du stérile hiver a resplendi l'ennui.

Tout son col secouera cette blanche agonie
Par l'espace infligée à l'oiseau qui le nie,
Mais non l'horreur du sol où le plumage est pris.

Fantôme qu'à ce lieu son pur éclat assigne,
Il s'immobilise au songe froid de mépris
Que vêt parmi l'exile inutile le Cygne.[44]

Finally, we should not forget William Butler Yeats, perhaps the greatest poet in English between Wordsworth and the Second World War. Yeats uses the swan "symbol" throughout his poetic career, from *The Wanderings of Oisin* and "The Withering of the Boughs" early on to "Leda and the Swan" and "Coole Park and Ballylee" later in his life. But he also entitled one of his most famous collections of his mature years, *The Wild Swans at Coole* (1919), and opened it with a poem of stupefying perfection that bears the same name.[45] The poet who had looked for the Lake Isle of Innisfree has now found his lake, at Coole Park, and an autumn that has kept the beauty of the earlier poems "The Falling of the Leaves" and "The Withering of the Boughs." But everything is calmer and more open to meditation: in the October twilight, the water itself "mirrors a still sky." In this, which is at once his "Tintern Abbey" and "Ode to a Nightingale," the writer returns on the one hand, like Wordsworth, to his past, and on the other, like Keats, to the birds that mark for him the present and the future. Nineteen years have passed since he had first seen them, the "nine-and-fifty" swans, "all suddenly mount / And scatter wheeling in great broken rings / Upon their clamorous wings." Now, with a heart "sore" because of the passing of time, he meets them again: they still "paddle in the cold / Companionable streams" or "climb the air," not weary, but even now "lover by lover." Unlike his, their hearts have not aged, "Passion or conquest, wander where they will, / Attend upon them still." Here they are, still drifting on the still water, "mysterious, beautiful." Where will they build their nests, which human eyes will they delight when awakening one day the poet will find "they have flown away?"

Life, as the traditional topos has it, is but a dream. But it is a true, concrete dream, made up of earth, water, air, trees, swans, wings; and time stops—in this Yeatsean counterpoint to Mallarmé's "Le vierge, le vivace et le bel aujourd'hui"—in a suspended instant, a "moment of moments" where the sky and the water are still.[46] The only thing that shattered the instant, which still shatters it, is the sudden flash of "those brilliant creatures," their moving in the elements—amidst the stones, in the water and air that are their companions as they are each other's lovers—their climbing high and wheeling in great broken rings. The swans are the mirror in which the poet contemplates his changing image, "emblems of the soul," and at the same time, as we have seen, poetry and inspiration, the song that "delights" human beings. Yeats knows this very well and transfigures them into symbols that he will often use with different meanings.[47] For the moment, their main characteristics are those of building their nests and being "mysterious" and "beautiful." "Build": for poetry is this, too—preparing a house, going back to it, feeding the little ones. The swans wander but finally build a nest, and in this errance and settling down—which, as we shall see in the epilogue, is the same movement described by Rainer Maria Rilke in the first of the *Duino Elegies*—lies their mystery and beauty.

It is certainly no coincidence that Giacomo Leopardi, Italy's greatest lyric poet after Petrarch and the author of an "Elogio degli uccelli," a "Cantico del gallo Silvestre and "Il Passero Solitario," should have the "Wandering Asian Shepherd," his protophilosopher and protopoet, sum up the whole *Sehnsucht* of the Western world in his "Cantico Notturno," with words that express his desire to be an ethereal, soaring being, mindful of the mysteries of the universe and at the same time resonating with that same mystery:

Perhaps if I had wings
to fly above the clouds
and number off the stars one by one,
or if like thunder roam from peak to peak,
I would be happier, oh sweet flock,
I would, oh snow-white moon, be happier.
[Forse s'avess'io l'ale
Da volar su le nubi,
E noverar le stelle ad una ad una,
O come il tuono errar di giogo in giogo,

Più felice sarei, dolce mia greggia,
Più felice sarei, candida luna.][48]

∽o∾

But perhaps I am imagining myself as a flying Pindar. Let me land on earth
and focus at this point on a poet who on many counts stands halfway between
the distant days of Pindar and later times: Horace. Horace was no lover of
eagles; he mentions them explicitly only twice in the whole of his poetic
works and prefers to compare even his master Pindar to a swan rather than
an eagle. We have already seen this: in the second composition of the fourth
book of Odes, Horace likens the imitator of Pindar to Icarus, who flies on
waxen wings created by Daedalus and is doomed to give his name to the sea
into which he plunges. Pindar rushes down from the mountain peaks like a
rain-swelled torrent, in a deep voice he thunders out frenzied dithyrambs,
rolling out new words and, free from the laws of rhythm, singing hymns for
the gods, for mythical heroes, the winners of contests: he dedicates a tribute
to them greater than a hundred statues. Horace writes to his fellow poet
Antonius Iullus that the winds blow powerfully when Dirce's swan ascends
the skies. And perhaps Iullus himself will do just this, composing songs of
praise for Augustus, his triumphs, festivities, the public games in his honor.
To be sure, Horace will join with him and, happy for Caesar's return, acclaim
his triumph, singing O sol / pulcher, o laudande, shouting io Triumphe, and
offering up incense to the benign gods. Iullus, poet of the highest inspiration,
will celebrate the great Augustus. But Horace is parvus, a minor and humble
craftsman of verse, who labors untiringly to create his songs like the Matine
bee, which gathers fragrant thyme by the woods and banks of the dank Tivoli:

> I am like the humble bee, painstakingly
> Seeking to find the honey in the thyme
> That grows in lowly fragrant groves and grows
>
> Along the watery banks of Tivoli's stream;
> My songs are made laboriously and slow.
> [ego apis Matinae
> more modoque
>
> grata carpentis thyma per laborem
> plurimum circa nemus uvidique

Tiburis ripas operosa parvus
Carmina fingo.][49]

Horace thus presents himself as a honey-making bee and likens his beloved, rural Sabine Tivoli to the Apulian Matina, close to his native Venosa, but famous—as Horace himself recalls—for the tomb of the great scientist Archytas of Tarentum, inventor of the only flying object of antiquity: the mechanical dove that we caught sight of in the second chapter of this book. To Pindar the swan, the overflowing torrent; to Horace the bee, the woods, and the waters of the fertile Tivoli: the sublime opposed to the humble; reckless nature contrasted with persevering *labor*.

But things are more complex, for the image of the poet as a bee goes back, through Callimachus, not only to Aristophanes and Simonides, but to Pindar himself, who in the tenth *Pythian* combines it, with his genius for surprise, with that of the helmsman:

But to me, no marvel
if the gods bring it about, ever seems
beyond belief.
Hold the oar, quickly plant the anchor in the earth
from the prow as a safeguard against the jagged reef,
for the finest of victory hymns
flit like a bee from one theme to another.[50]

Horace appears on the poetic scene—we should never forget this—five centuries after Pindar: he and the Theban swan are separated by all of classical lyric and Hellenistic poetry as well as at least two hundred years of Latin literature. Moreover, there are no longer commissioning agents such as Hieron of Syracuse or the Delphic games. In Rome there is a sole commissioner, Augustus, who asked Horace to compose a fourth book of odes. And there are the public games, which the city dedicated to Caesar's triumphant homecoming. As we have seen, Horace now shares the enthusiasm for the prince of the world. But his Muse adopts a tone that is neither epic (like Virgil's) nor dithyrambic (like Iullus's): instead, it follows the bee, apparently humble, but actually Alexandrine and *Pindaric*, surpassing Pindar with the art and nature of Matina and of Tivoli, that is, of Magna Graecia and Rome. And in this way Pindar and Horace are precursors of Rilke: by his own definition "bee of the invisible."[51]

Iullus, Horace writes in the last stanza of his ode, vows to offer ten bulls and ten cows to the gods in honor of Caesar. Horace himself promises a newborn calf that, once weaned, grows on rich pastures, and carries on its head a flaming, waxing crescent like that of the moon, one dapple spot of snowy white, the rest all red. The animal Horace promises is full of life and—like the world reborn under Augustus, according to Virgil's *Eclogue* IV—*iuvenescit:* blooms into youth, leaving the ways of the past behind. The tender calf is the wondrous fulfillment of the bee: its head as pure white as the snows of Mount Soractes, but upon it is the silver sign of the crescent moon, and its coat shines golden—like the Pindaric lyre, like that which in the first *Olympian* comes second only to water. And water reappears once again, between the banks of the dank Tivoli. *Secol si rinova,* Dante has Statius say in *Purgatorio,* citing the opening of Virgil's *Eclogue,* "the age turns new again."[52] And to celebrate it there is a *dolce stil novo* of poetry too: the bee and the calf, Greece and Italy—Rome and its kingdom, its poetry: Horace.

Horace is therefore something more and something less than the king-fisher, the swan, and the eagle. In the fourth ode of the third book, for example, Horace deliberately imitates Pindar's first *Pythian. Descende caelo,* he invokes, turning to Calliope, descend from the skies, and play on the flute a lasting melody, sing unaccompanied with a clear voice, or rest on the strings of *Phoebus's lyre.* Perhaps it is fond illusion (*amabilis insania*): Horace feels as if he were wandering through sacred woods, where waters and breezes murmur. As a child, on Mount Vultur's slopes, he adventured beyond his sheltering Apulia and, tired of playing, fell asleep. Then the *fabulosae palumbes,* the doves of fables and of myth, almost as if they were guardian angels, spread a blanket of freshly fallen leaves over him: the people of neighboring villages wondered at the sight of the child, who with the help of the gods slept peacefully, safe from bears and snakes, covered with sacred bay and myrtle.[53]

The variation on the first *Pythian* is astonishing: lyre, *melos,* Apollo, and the Muses are here too, as is sleep; but it is not *koma,* the deep slumber that possesses Pindar's eagle and gods. The *insania* possessing the poet could match Pindar's "charm of the gods," if it were not for the fact that it is *amabilis,* lovely. And in the place of the eagle we have doves. However, Horace the child arrogates to himself a topos common to Greek poets (and to Pindar himself), who believed themselves protected by the gods and marked by the Muses from birth, and crowns himself with bay and myrtle right from infancy. What is more, we can now see him climbing the Sabine Hills towards Praeneste and Tivoli, and then descending towards the crystal-clear sea at Baiae: *vester, Camenae, vester,* "your child, o Muses, your child," he proclaims himself. He too belongs to them, totally and devotedly. Friend to their springs and dances (we are reminded of the dances and the Castalian springs of the

Pythian), he can truly go wherever he wishes. The defeat at Philippi (where Horace fought on the—wrong, as it turned out—side, that of Brutus) has not destroyed him, even though, as he says elsewhere, it clipped his wings. None of the misfortunes that have befallen him have been fatal: his life continues peacefully, under the protection of the gods and the Muses.

With the aid of the Muses, he is even able to set sail and face the turbulent Bosporus, cross the burning sands of Syria, see the wild Britons: in short, visit the length and breadth of the empire through his poetic imagination. Indeed, the Muses revive Caesar Augustus himself, after the terrible campaigns he wages, in some cave of Pieria: they give the prince "mild thoughts" and do so joyously, as Pindar did with Hieron. There is a moment in which government, war, and poetry can meet, provided each recognizes its limits. Horace knows full well that the impious Titans were struck down by the thunderbolts of he who reigns throughout the cosmos, and that the threats and strength of Typheus (Pindar's Typhon), Mimas, and Enceladus were powerless against Minerva's shield. With her were Vulcan, Juno, and especially Apollo, whose bow is always to hand:

> The god who bathes his unbound flowing hair
> In the stream that flows out from the Castalian spring,
> The god who haunts the wood of Lycia and
> The hill on the isle of Delos where he was born.
> [qui rore puro Castaliae lavit
> crinis solutos, qui Lyciae tenet
> dumeta natalemque silvam.
> Delius et Patareus Apollo.][54]

Here Horace comes closest to the first *Pythian,* replicating, almost to the letter, a passage in the second epode. Just as Hieron was presented there in the guise of Zeus, so here Jove, on a par with Augustus (and the inversion of terms is as meaningful as the comparison itself), governs alone and with justice: *imperio regit unus aequo.* Hieron founds Etna, Augustus refounds Rome: while the former refers to the ancestral genealogy of the Dorians, the latter proposes to the Romans the Julio-Claudian lineage of Troy and Aeneas.

The *gnome,* the *sententia* or warning maxim, can therefore follow: brute strength without wisdom falls in ruins under its own weight; strength tempered by wisdom is intensified by the gods themselves, who detest strength that is willfully dedicated to impiety. This is not the ethics of the beautiful, the right, and the true that Pindar proposes to Hieron, but the translation into Roman civilization and the Augustan ideal (*vis temperata, pietas*) of Zeus's triumph over Typhon. The last three lines of the ode contain a warning to the Giants, Orion and Tityos, and to the belly of Etna consumed by swift flames—in other words, to the monsters of chaos who threaten the Olympian order—but the lines are in fact aimed at a closer and more impending figure: Caesar Augustus, lord *urbis et orbis.* Horace does not imitate Pindar, for if he did he would suffer the fate of Icarus; instead, he rewrites, improves, and adapts him to the Roman spirit.

So what kind of lyric poetry does Horace have in mind when he asks Calliope to descend from the skies and touch the strings of Apollo's Pindaric lyre? He is no longer simply the unconventional, wise, and measured poet of the *Satires* or the *Epistles,* nor the lyrical one of love, wine, joie de vivre and everything ephemeral. In the final ode of the second book, Horace had claimed immortality and seen himself as inspired *vates,* a cross between man and bird (*biformis*), to be borne through the liquid sky by uncommon and strong wing: beyond envy, he will not stay long on earth but will leave the cities of people. He, son of humble parents, who must be ready at all times to answer the calls of the "dear" Maecenas, will not die and will not fall prisoner to the waves of the Styx. On the contrary, he can already feel his skin roughening around the ankles and light feathers growing on his back and hands: *et album mutor in alitem.* Horace undergoes a metamorphosis, like so many characters of his contemporary Ovid: he becomes a great white winged creature: a swan.[55] A swan that sings before dying and yet is a symbol of immortality: sacred to Apollo and linked to the Muses and Orpheus, he flies from the northernmost tip of the ocean to the shores of the Mediterranean. White and mysterious: white-haired, like the ancient poets, almost as if from another world, as Socrates says in Plato's *Phaedo,* prescient of the well-being that will come in the afterlife.

A swan: like Pindar, according to the second ode of the fourth book, which we have just read. Immediately afterward, Horace anticipates the Icarus topos: "Melodious bird I'll fly above the moaning / Bosporus, more glorious than Icarus, / I'll coast along above the coast of Sidra / And over the fabled Hyperborean steppes. / The Colchians will hear, the Dacians too, / Who say they have no fear of Roman arms, / And farther still the Gelonians will listen, / The Iberians by the Ebro they will listen, / And those who drink the waters of the Rhone / Will learn to be more learnèd from my song."[56] Now this extends beyond the borders of the empire, amongst the barbarian populations east, south, north, and west: to the edge of the world.

Horace seems to have chosen his poetry. But not quite: he has simply chosen *poetry* and its inherent immortality. The metamorphosis of the ode (derided by the critics for what they see as a comic element) simply points to the difficulty of transformation, of changing from human into winged creature while remaining both: the hardening of the skin and the heart necessary to become both poet and swan, leave the earth behind and hover in the sky; choose countryside rather than city, overcome the envy of common mortals, escape one's humble origins and the constant service of Maecenas as well. Only in this way can one become more famous than Icarus, son of Daedalus. In this there is undeniably the great danger evoked in the second ode of the fourth book: that of plummeting out of the skies one hoped to fly through and plunging into the ocean depths. But *all poets face this danger* when they decide to consecrate themselves to poetry: the risk of failure, of ending up as insignificant, anonymous scribblers. It is no mere chance that Horace says of himself "more glorious than Icarus." Quite simply, as Ovid and Ransmayr know, this metamorphosis, like any other, has its price: an uneasiness, at that moment, with the nature of the new being one is becoming: *iam iam residunt cruribus asperae pellae,* already the skin puckers and wrinkles about one's ankles. It is not easy to become a swan!

Once the transformation into a white winged creature is complete, man can even do without the funeral ceremonies, the *neniae, querimoniae,* and *luctus,* in which he is mourned after death. The immortal poet needs no *conclamatio* before the funeral pyre. Neither does he need a tomb, because, as the last ode in the third book sings, he has completed a work "outlasting bronze and the pyramids of ancient royal kings," and he shall live on in the minds of those who come after him like those who, according to Simonides' famous epitaph, died at Thermopylae: time that all things destroys can do nothing against his memory.[57]

✧

Horace chooses poetry that transforms him into an eternal, singing swan. Yet he has the gift of savoring a little of that immortality during his lifetime. In the third ode of the fourth book he declares that the citizens of Rome, queen of cities, already consider him one of their sacred poets, and that his rivals' envy is now less fierce. It is in this composition that Horace reaffirms his love of the lyric, his antiheroic choices, and his preference for poetry as reflection, as melody that permeates everywhere.

The song begins: *Quem tu, Melpomene, semel / nascentem placido lumine videris* (He whom you looked upon, / Melpomene, at his birth, / with gentle light).[58] The spell is instant: the Muse is called up once again to the birth of the poet, and from the start looks upon him with peace, grace, and favor. Horace goes back, perhaps through Callimachus, to Hesiod in the *Theogony*: "And when the daughters of great Zeus would bring / Honor upon a heaven-favored lord / And when they watch him being born, they pour / Sweet dew upon his tongue, and from his lips / Flow honeyed words . . . And when a lord / Comes into the assembly, he is wooed / With honeyed reverence, just like a god."[59] But the tranquil light that the Muses' gaze pours upon the child is exclusively Horatian, as later lines confirm. He whom the Muse has seen come into the world in this way will not be made "illustrious" (*clarabit*) for boxing in the Isthmian games, nor will he be led in triumph on a chariot in the Greek contests or crowned with laurels on the Capitol for defeating the overblown pride of enemy kings. No, not for Horace the contests of Pindar and Bacchylides, nor the military triumphs of Rome. All he needs are the waters of the fertile Tivoli and its leafy forests. These will make him noble and famous through his song, inspired by the Greeks.

> The nurturing waters
> That flow past Tivoli's fields
> And Tivoli's leafy groves
> Shall bring him to fame for those
> Aeolian songs he sang.
> [sed quae Tibur aquae fertile praefluunt
> et spissae nemorum comae
> fingent Aeolio carmine nobilem.][60]

Aeolian indeed, for Horace knows full well that the Muse is first and foremost Greek, as it had been for hundreds of years. But his inspiration comes from the Sabine waters (water again, as in Pindar's first *Olympian*), from the river, the springs, and the waterfalls of Tivoli and its woods—not from the Tiber or the streets, buildings, and crowds of Rome, brought to life in the lines that follow. *Those* are the places of poetry and of meditation, of dialogue with nature and the Muse: although of Greek origin, she is now Roman in effect thanks to the Apulian Horace, "player of the Roman lyre" who owes everything to the Muse, pleasing as he breathes, and if he pleases it is thanks to Melpomene. The last two strophes of the ode recreate the enchantment of the first. We find in them the return of the swan and Pindar's glistening golden lyre:

> Melpomene, o Muse,
> Knowing how to adjust

And regulate to sweetness
The notes of the golden shell,
You could, if you so chose,
Instruct the silent fish
To sing as well as the swan,

It is entirely by
Your favoring gift that others,
Seeing me in the street,
Point me out as he
Who plays the Roman lute;
It is your gift if I
Should please, if I do please.
[o testudinis aureae
dulcem quae strepitum, Pieri, temperas,
o mutis quoque piscibus
donatura cycni, si libeat, sonum,

totum muneris hoc tui est,
quod monstror digito praetereuntium
Romanae fidicen lyrae;
quod spiro et placeo, si placeo, tuum est.][61]

But now that lyre has been tempered: the music that in Pindar made humans, gods, the Muses and the eagle drowsy, is now sweeter: no longer is it strained like a bow, shot like a javelin or arrow, a celebration of physical contests, "winged word." It is lyrical, personal music of the soul that makes poetry of itself and its wanderings through waters and woods: no longer only a result of toil and *labor,* but also, finally, of the *gift* that poetry is. And, like that of Petrarch, *modern* lyric poetry. Yet—here and now, in Rome, in the time of Augustus—it retains so much of its primal attraction, of that captivating spell that Homer and Pindar called *thelgein,* that it can, if it so wishes, even give to mute fish the music of the swan.

∽o∾

Horace, as must be clear by now, cannot have loved eagles. Yet he was unable to avoid them completely when composing, at the express request of Augustus, his fourth book of odes. He opens the poem (IV, iv) that follows the one we have just read with two epic similes: the eagle and the lion.

The first runs for three strophes, twelve lines in all: it describes the military campaign of Drusus Claudius Nero—son of Livia and Tiberius Claudius Nero and therefore stepson of Augustus—against the Vindelici tribes in 15 B.C., comparing this campaign and Nero's triumph to the flight of an eagle:

> Just as the winged minister of the lightning,
> Whom the king of the gods made king of all the birds
> (Having learned to trust him when he carried up
> From earth to heaven the yellow-haired Ganymede),
>
> Just as this eagle, when he was still an eaglet,
> Impelled by youth and daring, ventured forth
> Out of the nest, fearful and ignorant,
> Not knowing yet what eagles do to be eagles,
>
> Soon was instructed on the vernal winds,
> The worst of the storms of winter being past,
> How to do his eagle best, and soon he dove
> Eagerly down on a sheepfold, and after that,
>
> Hungry for prey and loving it he swoops
> Down on the struggling serpents meant for him . . . [62]

Horace overpindarizes Pindar himself, achieving this incredible feat in ultra-Homeric and ultra-Virgilian style. The ode's sixteen remaining strophes explain why: Rome owes its crucial victory on the Metaurus over Hasdrubal, brother of Hannibal, to the Nerones family, and likewise its current victory over the Vindelici tribes. Hannibal himself is evoked in the poem, where he gives a speech worthy of Livy, praising (no doubt inspired by Virgil) the people of Rome who carried their household gods, sons, and fathers from the ashes of Troy across the tempestuous Tuscan sea to the cities of Italy and, like a flourishing oak tree stripped by heavy axes, grow anew, drawing strength and vigor from their defeats and massacres, "as if by the force of the blow."

In short, the ode celebrates Rome and its amazing capacity of resistance, and the role of the Claudian lineage in this, from the era of the republic to that of Augustus. What, beyond Pindar, could be a better symbol for this epinicion than the eagle? The eagle stands for the Roman legions whose standards it appears on, symbolizing *imperium* and dominance over the world. For two thousand years it has been present in Western iconography (including some

of its most esteemed democracies) and in that of many earthly empires. I
will return to this later, in another context. For the moment, I would like to
highlight the distance we have traveled so far, starting from the eagle lulled
to sleep by the music of the golden lyre on the scepter of Zeus. Poetry also
exists in history and politics. Horace, who preferred swans to eagles, and who
unlike Virgil kept a distance from the center of power, is about to write his
Carmen Saeculare in praise of the new era inaugurated by Augustus. History
and politics take possession of poetry.

∾o∾

At the end of the Hermes chapter, we looked briefly at the way both the
Hebrew and the Christian Bible present the image of the eagle and doves.
Now, as we continue to fly in circles, it is time to return to this theme. The
books of Exodus and Deuteronomy, we will remember, use the eagle as icon
of God and of his love for Israel, while in Isaiah and Psalm 102 it is a symbol
of rebirth: those who hope in the Lord will rediscover strength and youth
and don the wings of an eagle. In contrast to this, God swoops down like
an eagle on the enemies of his chosen people, as in the oracle of Edom in
Jeremiah. Conversely, in similarly perfect *contrappasso*, those same enemies
will descend on Israel when it transgresses the laws of the Lord: thus Hosea
prophesizes the Assyrian invasion, Jeremiah the arrival of the army from the
north, and Habakkuk the terrifying Chaldean horsemen.[63]

The Hebrew Bible, however, does not neglect the epic aspect of the great
winged creature. In the second Book of Kings, David laments the deaths of
Saul and Jonathan, with whom his relationship was, to put it mildly, complex:
son, rival, and more than just a brotherly friend. In an elegy whose only
equivalent in antiquity is Achilles' lament for Patroclus, he says that they were
caring and beautiful in life, and that even in death they will not be separated:
"they were swifter than eagles, they were stronger than lions."[64] David is the
singer and player—the poet *par excellence*—of the biblical tradition. Just as
unique, and equally surprising in the context, is the use of the image in the
Book of Job. When Job bemoans his poor life, he cries out that his days have
flown, without ever seeing good, swifter than a post, like a reed ship "as the
eagle that hasteth to the prey."[65]

In both cases the text is exquisitely and powerfully *poetic*. It is superbly
dramatic in the words of David which pour out his regret and recall his
devotion and love for Saul and Jonathan, and wonderfully lyrical in the words
of Job. The latter's conception of life as a swiftly passing reed ship suggests
speed and lightness. The Vulgate adds that the ship is "laden with fruit,"[66]

and thus enables the reader to focus on that speed, since the vessel's cargo goes rotten quickly. It therefore offers two similes, direct and indirect, of the rapid and transitory nature of the time conceded to humankind. To imagine an existence that passes like an eagle in flight towards its prey implies yet another challenge for the reader, for besides the first and fairly obvious simile of the bird's speed, we are told of its goal. And it is devastating for any human being to see this end—death—as quarry, for it makes us feel like victims of a "predatory" death feeding off life itself. Behind the line's self-pity, there is a sense of inevitability: following its instinct and the laws of nature, the eagle cannot avoid swooping down on its food. Finally, what is perhaps a death wish also emerges from the image, which would be in keeping with the kind of feelings often expressed by Job. Probably not by coincidence, in the Book our disturbing questions about the eagle are answered by God himself with one final, definitive interrogative which permits no appeal. The Voice from the whirlwind heard by the desolate man of Uz asks: "Doth the eagle mount up at thy command, and make her nest on high? She dwelleth and abideth on the rock, upon the crag of the rock, and the strong place. From thence she seeketh the prey, and her eyes behold afar off. Her young ones also suck up blood: and where the slain are, there is she."[67]

The eagle, like the sea, the stars, the wild ass, Behemoth and Leviathan, is part of the unfathomable mystery of Creation with which Yahweh answers Job's insistent, desperate questions about the injustice of his fate. This mystery is reiterated also in Proverbs, according to which the path of the eagle in the air is among the three most difficult things to understand.[68] But the image of the bird of prey ready to swoop down on its ultimate quarry, the dead animal's carcass, is taken up in the Christian Gospels with quite different intent. When Jesus of Nazareth preaches to his disciples about the day on which the Son of man will return and reveal himself,[69] taking some with him and leaving others to their fate, he says that, just as lightning from the east shines also in the west, so shall be the *parousia:* "wheresoever the carcase is, there will the eagles be gathered together." Thus will come the Day of Judgment, terrible for sinners: like eagles on carrion. Preaching reaches the depths of terror.

Yet it is for Jesus that birds conjure up the sweetest and most delicate images of all. In the long passage of Matthew's Gospel that begins with the Beatitudes, he advises his disciples not to concern themselves with what to eat or wear, for life is greater than food and the body greater than clothing: "Behold the fowls of the air: for they sow not, neither do they reap, nor gather into barns; yet your heavenly Father feedeth them. Are ye not much better than they?" And further on, in a passage recalled by Hamlet: "Are not two sparrows sold for a farthing? And one of them shall not fall on the ground without your Father. But the very hairs of your head are all numbered. Fear ye not therefore, ye are of more value than many sparrows."[70]

This is simultaneously *sophia* and *poietike*: of what is humble and human, but most of all of the divine leaning towards the world. With the eagle that carries Israel on its wings, the Hebrew Bible celebrates Yahweh's love, caring, and grace towards his people. The Christian Gospels take up these themes, extending them to all birds, even those that, like sparrows, sell for next to nothing: to all human beings. In the Gospels, paternal *care, attention,* and *concern* are shown towards humanity that the gods of Olympus never dreamed of. Only through passages like these can we begin to understand the meaning of "providence," which is manifested, incomprehensibly, both in the sparrow's fall—in its departing from this world, its dying—and in its feeding without cultivating the earth or "planning ahead."

The caring embodied by Jesus—extended in perfect parallelism to clothing: "Consider the lilies of the field, how they grow; they toil not, neither do they spin. And yet I say unto you, That even Solomon in all his glory was not arrayed like one of these"—brings God and humankind together in nature, which human beings are both part of and superior to (because worth more than the sparrows). Perhaps the reply to Job lies in this reminder of what constitutes the *constant* work of God, his continuous Creation, not primordial but daily, ordinary, "natural": for Yahweh has not only made the sublime, inaccessible eagles, but, as Father, "knows that ye have need of all these things."

∾o∾

The Bible, however, composed and stratified over time, is intrinsically polysemic. To return to our theme, the eagle also represents the transitory nature of earthly belongings and the pride that will be punished by God. In Proverbs, for example, we are warned against aiming high at unattainable riches, "for riches certainly make themselves wings; they fly away as an eagle toward heaven." In the vision of the prophet Obadiah, the Lord speaks to Edom, ordering him not to exalt himself like an eagle and set his nest among the stars, or he will bring him down.[71]

And finally, we come to the prophetic visions, where the eagle is decidedly preeminent. The Book of Ezekiel opens with a famous, dazzling example in which the prophet contemplates divine Majesty, which appears first as a whirlwind from the north, a great cloud and a large blinding flame which gives out an amber-colored glow. The shapes of four human figures gradually emerge, bright as burnished bronze, incandescent like burning coals, shining like torches: each of them has four faces and four wings, each face human in appearance but also like that of a lion, ox, and eagle. The creatures are in the lower part of the fiery cloud, as if holding it up, joined together at the wing tips. Underneath each of these creatures, a great wheel filled with eyes follows their movements; above and held aloft by them, a block of crystal or ice, and above that, a throne of sapphire which seats a brightly flaming human figure framed by a rainbowlike radiance: the Glory of God.[72]

I do not intend to dwell on the exegesis of this extraordinary passage, here simplified by omitting, for example, the terrible roar produced by the wheels and wings—comparable to that of the ocean, the voice of the Almighty and the tumult of an army—as well as the "spirit" that moves within them and many other spectacular images. I simply wish to point out its terrible splendor and its composite and highly baroque nature, made up of figures resembling those of the Babylonians and Assyrians. Above all, for reasons that will soon become clear, I wish to indicate the presence of the *hayyot*— the living creatures—and their faces of human being, lion, bull, and eagle. A midrash on Exodus should provide sufficient justification: "Four types of proud beings were created in the world: the proudest of all, man; among birds, the eagle; among tamed animals, the ox; among wild beasts, the lion: and all are placed beneath the chariot of the Saint."[73]

The four faces reappear, in the Book of Ezekiel, in the description of the cherubs, while the eagle is at the center of the double "parable" in which it flies up, majestic and swift, tears the tops off the Lebanese cedars and carries them to the land of Canaan, where it plants the seeds: they grow into a vine which turns its roots towards another eagle so that it may receive water for nourishment.[74] The prophecy announces the Babylonian invasion and the aid Israel will receive from Egypt. In other words, the eagle now has the meaning of imperial symbol, as it will for Rome. As such it is also used by Daniel in the famous prophecy of the four animals—the eagle-winged lioness, the bear, the leopard, and the horned beast—which traditionally represent the Babylonian, Persian, Macedonian, and Roman empires.[75] In the Vulgate, the fourth Book of Ezra takes up Daniel's vision explicitly, concentrating it on the eagle and the lion and giving it a political-messianic interpretation with the bird standing for the "fourth kingdom" of twelve kings and the feline for "the anointed one" set aside by the Almighty for the end against the godlessness of pagan realms.[76]

The four creatures—lion, ox, man, and eagle—reappear at the end of the Christian Bible, in the Apocalypse, Revelation, traditionally attributed to John the apostle and evangelist. In the vision of the Throne of God in the fourth chapter, clearly inspired by Ezekiel, the four "living creatures," full of eyes in front and behind, stand around the throne and on each side. They are not so much—as has been maintained—symbols of the four constellations of the Zodiac marking the four corners of the world (Leo, Taurus, Aquarius, Scorpio), but rather of a power that dominates the entire universe and manifests itself in the strongest and most noble beings in creation.[77]

But Revelation too is polysemic: after the opening of the seventh seal in chapter 8, the fourth of the seven angels blows his trumpet and a third of the sun, moon, and stars falls into darkness, and when this occurs, he who is contemplating the vision hears the voice of an eagle in flight cry out from the sky: "Woe, woe, woe, to the inhabiters of the earth by reason of the other voices of the trumpet of the three angels, which are yet to sound!"[78] Following Exodus and Deuteronomy, the eagle here may represent Yahweh. However, this is not a God who takes care of his people, but one who threatens them. As elsewhere in the Bible, the eagle appears to be the instrument he uses to punish his children—thus, the standard of the Roman army invading Israel. Finally, too, the woman clothed with the sun, crowned with twelve stars, and with the moon under her feet, aided by the wings of a great eagle, flies over the desert and escapes the dragon that seeks to devour her newborn child "who was to rule all nations with a rod of iron" and who is carried off to heaven "up unto God, and to his throne."[79] While the woman here stands for "community," or perhaps "Church," it is the caring Lord of Exodus and Deuteronomy who gives her eagle's wings so that she may survive her enemies' attacks.

Without wishing to become entangled in the vast and inextricable density of apocalyptic symbolism which has confounded interpreters for two thousand years, I would like to stress the fact that the Bible uses the "sign" of the eagle and its flight in a far more complex way than classical literature does. The only two points they have in common are the bird "of God" (Zeus or Yahweh), and imperial power, that of Rome in particular.

◦◦◦

Flying from antiquity to the Middle Ages, the eagle bears symbols and legends: *psykhopompos*, leader of souls, in the apotheosis of the Roman emperors, ideal go-between for heaven and earth, it could not be struck by lightning and could contemplate the sun without being blinded; in old age, it would fly straight towards the sun and then, as reported by Aristotle in the

Historia animalium,[80] dive three times into water and emerge rejuvenated. The Christians are unhesitating: the eagle is the symbol of the Ascension and the Resurrection, and the four animals of Ezekiel and Revelation are simply the mysterious prefiguration of the four evangelists. In figurative art, as in the Fathers and in the *Physiologus,* these meanings are constant: the eagle represents triumph over the forces of evil (for example, over the serpent it snatches up in its beak and wrestles with), and accompanies the great symbols of Christ, the cross and the lamb. In his *Disputatio puerorum,* commenting on Psalm 102, Alcuin likens the eagle's *renovatio* to Christ's ascension and resurrection. In his *Bestiary,* Philip of Thaon claims that the great winged creature stands for "the son of Mary:" later on in the same work it represents the angel that carries souls to God. In European sepulchral art (for example on the sarcophagus of doña Sancha in Jaca, Spain) the eagle, together with the angels, accompanies the soul of the deceased. But it is mostly linked, through the *renovatio* consecrated by the ancient legends and by Psalm 102, to the three great themes of baptism, ascension, and resurrection: from Ambrose to Maximus of Turin, from Augustine to Gregory the Great and Honorius of Autun, and, of course, in an almost infinite variety of figurative art, such interpretations recur with astonishing frequency.[81]

In short, the eagle soars higher and higher: to consider it a symbol of baptism, ascension, and resurrection means to place it at the very center of Christianity, at the mysterious and ineluctable heart of the new religion: "but if there be no resurrection of the dead," writes Paul to the Corinthians, "then is Christ not risen. And if Christ be not risen, then is our preaching vain, and your faith is also vain."[82] The eagle is the symbol of the new Christian *sublime.* It is no coincidence that it will soon become the symbol of John the Evangelist. When Jerome in his *Commentaries* on Matthew and Ezekiel, and Augustine in *De consensu Evangelistarum,* identify the four animals of Ezekiel's vision and Revelation as the four evangelists, they are in no doubt (unlike, for example, their predecessor Irenaeus). Matthew is the man, because his Gospel begins with the description of a man: "The book of the generation of Jesus Christ, the son of David, the son of Abraham." Mark is the lion because his voice echoes the roaring of a lion in the desert: *Vox clamantis in deserto.* Luke is the ox, because his Gospel begins with the sacrifice of Zacharias the priest. But John is the eagle because, writes Jerome, "taking on the feathers of an eagle and flying up fast to the loftiest things, he talks about the Word of God"; because, *ad excelsum evolans,* it opens: "In the beginning was the Word, and the Word was with God, and the Word was God." "John," claims Augustine, "flies like an eagle above the mists of human infirmity and sees the light of immutable truth with the extremely sharp and steady eyes of the heart."[83]

Augustine, theorizer of the Christian sublime—the style of Scripture may be *sermo humilis*, but its subject matter is lofty—exalts the fourth Gospel as its supreme example. He goes as far as saying of John's Gospel that its author was not a man, because he was already on the way to becoming an angel: in fact all saints are angels in that they announce God. John, who says *In principio erat Verbum*, comes from the mount that announces the peace and justice of the Lord. Augustine continues fervently, saying that this mount transcends all earthly peaks, transcends all the fields of air, transcends all the heights of stars, and transcends all the choirs and hosts of angels. For if it did not transcend all these things that were created, it could not reach Him who created them. John has done just this: this is why he can say "In the beginning was the Word . . . All things were made by him; and without him was not any thing made that was made." John has transcended the creatures and risen up to the Creator: he is a true eagle.[84]

John is the only one to recount the resurrection of Lazarus, mention the episode of the adulteress, make Pilate ask "What is truth?" tell of Mary Magdalene and the Gardener and of doubting Thomas. As Origen observed,[85] John is the only one who has Jesus say, "I am the way, the truth and the life," "the light of the world," "the resurrection," "the door," "Before Abraham was, I am," thus showing Christ's divinity in an "absolute" manner. He is "firstling" of the Gospels; he is, as Dante will say, "Christ's Eagle":[86] the Christian Pindar. Jerome reports from Eusebius's *Church History* that when John's brothers asked him to write, he called for communal fasting and prayer first; then, "filled with revelation, he burst forth (*eructavit*) into his Prologue, reaching heaven: In the beginning was the Word."[87] As poet, prophet and mystic, the fourth evangelist begins, according to Augustine, "inspired" by God:[88] like Etna, he erupts. A few centuries later, writing in a reinvented Latin as only an Irishman could, John Scotus Eriugena sees the John of the Prologue as a spiritual bird, flying swiftly, with the eyes of one who can behold God, transcending every visible and invisible creature, penetrating every object of intellection, and "deified, achieving his entry into God who deifies him." From the very start of his *Homily*, Eriugena sings the Prologue's praises with unusual fervor: "The voice of the spiritual Eagle," he writes, "resounds upon the Church's ears. Turned outwards, may the senses grasp its fleeting sound, may the inner soul penetrate its unchanging meaning." It is the voice, he continues, of the "bird of heights," which flies not only above the physical element of the air to the very limits of the known universe in its totality, but which succeeds in transcending every "theory," beyond all things which are and are not, "with the swift wings of the most inaccessible theology, with the expressions of the most shining contemplation, and the loftiest."[89]

Comparable only to the opening of Genesis, which is rewritten within it, John's Prologue was to dominate the peaks of Western literature for a long time, like the flight of an eagle: to it, as to the supreme example of thought and language, Goethe's Faust will return.[90]

∽o∾

As tradition has it, John the evangelist is also Jesus' "beloved" disciple and apostle, the one who rests his head on his master's breast, and of whom Jesus says to his mother from the cross, "Woman, behold thy son."[91] Since John is a sublime and inspired *writer*, we should, says Origen, make ourselves like him if we are to understand the Gospel. John rests in the Word and in its mysteries just as the Son rests in his father's bosom: thus, to understand his writings, we must rest on—or, as Origen puts it, *anapesein*, lie down and simultaneously fly up and bend into—Jesus' breast until we become "like Jesus himself." In other words, to read and understand John the eagle, we must become eagles, leaving earth and human beings behind, *anapesein*: return. For a Christian, it is not enough to *read*, he must live, fly, transcend.[92] The advice is true for all real reading.

When Gregory the Great in his *Homilies on Ezekiel*[93] reaches the vision of divine Majesty described above, he comes across a verse describing how, the moment a voice beyond the firmament descends upon their heads, the four beasts must lower their wings. He maintains that the voice mentioned by Ezekiel in his vision is the "sound of intellect," but that what our senses perceive is at times the voice of the flesh, at times that of the soul, at times that of the firmament, and at times a voice from above the firmament. So we must "transcend" the voice of the flesh and of the soul and seek that of the firmament: in it we will find the infinite multitude of angels in the presence of the Lord, the happiness (*festivitas*) that they find in the vision of God, "faultless joy," the ardor of love which does not harm but delights, both the satiety and desire of contemplating God, beatitude: the endless contemplation of eternity, which makes them eternal, their union with light, which turns them into light, their steady gaze toward the immutable, which makes them immutable.

Nevertheless, all these thoughts about angels still are a voice within the firmament. But the soul must go beyond this, "transcend all that has been created," fix with the eyes of faith on the sole light of the Creator, as John did and as Dante was to do: like the eagle that gazes at the sun. "Let us then put before the mind's eye," writes Gregory, "the being that holds, fills, embraces, exceeds and sustains all."[94] When the spirit is caught up in such being and considers its power, the voice comes from above the firmament, because it is able to conceive an idea of He who transcends the intuition of the angels with His incomprehensibility. Here the flying ends: Ezekiel's creatures lower their wings, men may no longer transcend but must "tremble with great fear" and "humble" their own virtues. Abraham lowered his wings when, speaking with the Lord, he acknowledged that he was dust and ashes: Moses did the same, in front of the burning bush; as did Isaiah, when the burning coals of the altar touched his mouth; and Jeremiah, who exclaimed, "Lord God! Behold, I cannot speak for I am a child"; and Daniel, who fell ill after his vision; and Job, who recognized his own insipience after hearing the Voice from the whirlwind.[95]

Gregory depicts the wondrous sequence of *contemplation* using the image of flight: first transcending, and then folding wings in recognition of finiteness and ignorance. This is precisely the *occulti iudicii profunda cogitare*, to think of the depths of secret wisdom. Likewise, advocate of the biblical sublime, Augustine outlines a theology of beauty. In book XI of his *Confessions*, when confronting the beginning of the Scriptures in Genesis and John, Augustine confesses to God his burning desire to meditate upon his law, admitting both his knowledge and ignorance of it, the first signs of divine light and the remaining darkness. His chaste delight shall therefore be Scripture: full of unfathomable mysteries, but not without purpose, for God did not wish for so many pages of "dark secrets" to be written in vain. Thus, Augustine prays the Lord to reveal these enigmas himself. Moses, who wrote them, has passed on and cannot be asked. Augustine will listen and understand how, in the beginning, God created heaven and earth, because Truth itself will tell him. Heaven and earth cry out that they were made because they have changed since their beginning. They cry out too that they did not make themselves. Therefore the Lord made them: *tu ergo, Domine, fecisti ea, qui pulcher es: pulchra sunt enim; qui bonus es: bona sunt enim; qui es: sunt enim:* "It was you, Lord, who made these things: You are beautiful, thus they are beautiful; You are good, thus they are good; you are, thus they are." But they are not as beautiful, nor as good, nor as truly real as their Creator. The truth of Moses and of the Scriptures can only be known thanks to divine Truth. Beauty and goodness are only one aspect of being: but the startling beauty of heaven and earth is not as *complete* as that of their Creator, because their being is not as complete: *quid enim est, nisi quia tu es?*: "does anything exist but because you exist?" This is why God *spoke* and heaven and earth were created *in* his Word.[96]

Augustine is struggling with the irreducible absoluteness of Scripture, behind which he feels the steadfast and elusive hand of the beauty, goodness, and being of God. This feeling is not very different from that expressed in Pindar's "Hymn to Zeus," or in Plato's *Timaeus*, in that it simply expresses the common human perception of the immense force which lies behind the visible universe and which appears to move it. Indeed, in this book of the *Confessions*, Augustine achieves the two flights for contemplation indicated by Gregory: he listens to the voice of the firmament and that from above the firmament. And *he writes of them:* with both knowledge and ignorance, with the exaltation of one who has understood, and the frustration of one who cannot understand fully, transcending and folding his wings at the same time. He does not have Pindar's miraculous measure, but the tremendous lack of measure of the Bible: not the eagle that sleeps on Zeus' scepter, enchanted by the golden lyre, but the eagle that, at Someone's command, rises up and makes its nest on mountain peaks, lives among rocks and dwells among crags and inaccessible cliffs, seeks out its prey with eyes that see from afar: and wherever there is carrion, is immediately upon it.

⁀〇⁀

Dante meets "Christ's Eagle," John, in the eighth heaven of Paradise. The light emanating from the apostle's spirit is powerful enough to blind the pilgrim, like someone staring at a solar eclipse. In *Paradiso* XXV, Beatrice reverently refers to this eagle as "he who lay upon the breast of Christ our Pelican," and was "asked from on the Cross to serve in the great task." In *Paradiso* XXVI, John begins questioning Dante on charity (in the preceding cantos he had been questioned by Peter on faith and by James on hope). Dante responds by saying that charity is driven first of all by the same Good that satisfies the blessed in heaven, Alpha and Omega of all the "scripture" that Love makes him read; moreover, in him charity is satisfied by "philosophic arguments" and by the authority of divine revelation which descends from heaven through Scripture: by Aristotle, who maintains in the *Metaphysics* that the heavens, moved by the Intelligences, are turned by the unmoved first cause; by the voice of God, who says to Moses in Exodus, "I shall show you all goodness;" and by John's Gospel itself.[97]

After recognizing, as Origen would have it, the most beloved disciple, he who rests his head on the breast of "our Pelican," Dante celebrates, along with Augustine, the sublime nature of John's Gospel: *l'alto preconio*

che grida l'arcano / di qui là giù sovra ogne altro bando, the supreme announcement which proclaims, louder than the other Gospels—in particular in the
Prologue—the heavenly mysteries "of this place" down there on Earth. A few
lines on, John is called "Christ's Eagle." Dante has fully grasped the lesson
and purpose of the Fathers. John is truly an eagle, and the man of the *Comedy*
knows how to lie down and fly up and bend into his Gospel.

But Dante is the only medieval writer capable of drawing together an
entire tradition of images with a range of meanings as vast as that of the
Bible, and of making daring innovations at the same time. The first time we
meet the eagle in the *Comedy*, the great winged creature is not an icon of
John the Evangelist, but of the poet Homer. Ancient and pagan, and thus
confined to Limbo along with Virgil, Horace, Ovid, and Lucan, just like their
mythological predecessors Orpheus and Linus, he is nevertheless the *sire*, the
"lord" who, brandishing the sword of epic poetry, precedes Horace, Ovid and
Lucan: he is the *sovereign* poet. And more, for he is "the lord of song incomparable, / who like an eagle soars above the rest" (*quel segnor de l'*altissimo
canto / che sovra li altri com' aquila vola).[98] Homer, whom Dante never read
and knew only through his fame. Not Virgil, who is nonetheless described as
"estimable poet" (altissimo *poeta*), also in *Inferno* IV. Homer: of whom Virgil
says to Statius "that Greek to whom / the Muses gave their gifts in greatest
measure."[99] Reassured by Aristotle,[100] Dante recognizes, with sound intuition, Homer's superiority and his mastery of the *bella scola* that is "his." The
altissimo canto, the most noble song—the "tragic" style, according to Dante—
belongs to both Homer and Virgil. But the flight of the eagle, supreme poetry,
the truly winged word, belongs exclusively to Homer: he reigns over what
Keats, six centuries on, was to call the "wide expanse" of poetry, as though it
were his personal realm, "his demesne."[101] In the *De vulgari eloquentia*, Dante
advises writers of verse without art or science against attempting the loftiest
style: "if they are geese (*asteres*), let them not try to imitate the eagle that
soars towards the stars (*astripetam*)."[102] Much more so than Virgil, Homer
is a shadow for Dante, yet at the beginning of the "comedy" he is eagle: the
primordial, unknown yet irresistible model of poetry.

౼౿

From Homer to John: the flight of sublime writing and "re-turning" dominates the *Comedy*, changing it. Dante, however, cannot forget the other
meanings of the eagle brought to him by tradition. He uses them on four
occasions in his poem, with the genius we expect of him. In *Purgatorio* IX, the
pilgrim falls asleep in the valley of the Princes of ante-Purgatory:[103] and as he

sleeps the next morning—when Dawn is already breaking "along the eastern balcony" and the swallow "begins her melancholy songs," and when, "free to wander farther from the flesh / and less held fast by cares, our intellect's / envisionings become almost divine"—he dreams of a golden-plumed eagle hovering in the sky and swooping with wide open wings towards the summit of Mount Ida where he stands, like Ganymede carried off by Jove to Olympus in the form of an eagle. After circling several times, the bird darts "terrible as lightning" and carries Dante off to the sphere of fire, when man and bird burn together. Woken by the "imagined conflagration," Dante the character learns from Virgil that he is in Purgatory proper, led there by the same Lucia who had saved him from the dark wood.

A dawn ("she who shares the bed of old Tithonus") whose forehead gleams with gems; a swallow recalling the sad fate that turned Philomela into such a bird; Ganymede "snatched up for the high consistory" by the bird of Jove. The golden-plumed eagle is shaped by these mythological images, linked in the Christian world to penitence, redemption, and spiritual rebirth—to the entrance into Purgatory. Dante fully recalls the passages from Exodus and Deuteronomy we considered earlier, where the eagle is the image of Yahweh's love for his people: his Eagle, prefiguring Lucia, most certainly indicates the divine grace that raises man to God by acting within his conscience or within the *res pubblica*, in the individual or the community.

But it is Dante who gives the plumes their gold, who makes the bird hover in the sky with wide open wings and then dart like lightning: and for the first time since Pindar we see once more the golden brilliance, the lightning, the myths, and a poetic force—a flight—in full tension. Dante the writer is aware of this too, and points out the efforts he must make in order to exalt his subject:

> Reader, you can see clearly how I lift
> my matter; do not wonder, therefore, if
> I have to call on more art to sustain it.
> [Lettor, tu vedi ben com'io innalzo
> la mia matera, e però con più arte
> non ti maravigliar s'io la rincalzo.[104]

∽◦∾

Incidentally, it may be of interest to readers, if not to literary history, to note that Dante was soon to become exemplary in this. A couple of generations

after him, the father of English literature, Geoffrey Chaucer, used the trope
in his *House of Fame*, bestriding *Purgatorio* IX and *Paradiso* I and presenting
a golden eagle so dazzling that it seems as if "the heven had ywonne /
Al newe of gold another sonne." It descends like lightning, snatches up
the main character and carries him off to the House of Fame. In Dantean
fashion, Chaucer invokes Venus, the Muses, and his own art, while the
dreamer likens himself, echoing *Inferno* II,[105] to Enoch, Elijah, Romulus, and
Ganymede. The flight in the eagle's talons is rendered part-comic on account
of Geoffrey's terror and the bird's pedantry, but it takes an extremely serious
turn when the eagle turns master and shows his frightened disciple all the
heavens, explaining to him the nature of language, and taking him to the
two extraordinary buildings of Fame and Rumor, where he discovers the
primordial mechanisms of oral narrative.[106]

∽◦∾

Meanwhile, Dante's poetry shifts in dimension, its new loftiness marked
by its passing—via the eagle, one might say—from Aurora, Philomela, and
Ganymede to the sacred texts of Exodus and Deuteronomy. The great leap
is complete by the end of *Purgatorio*. Cantos XXIX to XXXIII present, in
the Garden of Eden at the summit of Purgatory, an allegorical procession
that precedes and follows the appearance of Beatrice and the disappearance of Virgil. Amongst other things, it includes seven candlesticks giving off a golden light, seven rainbow-hued lists, twenty-four Elders, four
winged animals, and a griffin-drawn chariot. Dante has now reached the
level of the radiant biblical visions of Ezekiel and Revelation. In canto
XXIX of *Purgatorio*,[107] he refers to them explicitly with reference to the
four animals, and is fully aware of their *poetic* value when he invokes the
Muses:

> O Virgins, sacrosanct, if I have ever,
> for your sake, suffered vigils, cold, and hunger,
> great need makes me entreat my recompense.

> Now Helicon pour its fountains for me,
> Urania must help me with her choir
> to put in verses things hard to conceive.
> [O sacrosante Vergini, se fami,
> freddi o vigilie mai per voi soffersi,
> cagion mi sprona ch'io mercé vi chiami.

Or convien che Elicona per me versi,
e Uranìe m'aiuti col suo coro
forti cose a pensar mettere in versi.][108]

Forti cose: for Dante does not limit himself to transcribing Ezekiel and John, but rewrites them, correcting one against the other, going so far as to maintain that the second agrees *with him,*[109] and making the procession astonishingly dramatic beyond its symbolic meaning. While this procession has full ritual import, the first part, crowning the appearance of Beatrice, has a slow, solemn rhythm similar to that dominating the story of salvation in the Old and New Testaments represented in it. The pace quickens considerably and the lacerations become violent, as happens in Revelation, when, in canto XXXII, Dante deals with the events of the world and the Church after the Incarnation. It is precisely at this point, after the griffin has tied the chariot to the tree, which then reblossoms, that the eagle reappears. The *uccel di Giove,* the bird of Jupiter, as the poet now calls it in Roman fashion, swoops down from the heavens quicker than lightning from a cloud thick with vapor: it descends on the plant, breaking its bark, destroying its leaves and flowers, and with all its strength, damaging the chariot, forcing it off course like a storm-tossed ship. This is a vivid, emphatic, and apocalyptic image of the persecution inflicted on the Church by the Roman Empire. The eagle soon returns, leaving its feathers inside the chariot: and this time it represents the Donation of Constantine, an evil even greater than the persecutions.[110]

We are in the *Heilsgeschichte,* the sacred history of salvation. Dante rewrites it with the passion of a prophet, with the sense of sharing, suffering, and exultation of one who has given long and deep thought to it,[111] in preparation for an unprecedented *tour de force*: the evocation by Justinian in *Paradiso* VI, of the whole course of the domination of Rome, "from that hour when Pallas died that it might gain a kingdom," when Aeneas landed in Italy, to the Holy Roman Empire.[112] With the supreme gaze of an eagle and the speed unique to its flight, Dante condenses into fewer than one hundred lines the two-thousand-year story of the *uccel di Dio* (the "bird of God," as he now terms it), which he believes is Providence's chosen instrument. From Lavinia to Belisarius, from Alba to the rape of the Sabine women, from the Seven Kings of Rome to Scipio, from Caesar to Augustus, Tiberius, Titus, Constantine, and right up to Justinian himself and to Charlemagne: the "sacred standard" marches relentlessly on: it sets out, leaps, turns, strikes, stirs, shakes itself, swoops, races, takes revenge for original sin by condemning Christ to the cross, and avenges this vendetta with the destruction of Jerusalem, the city whose authorities, in Dante's belief, passed the sentence.

It is *poetry of history*: a complete, if fundamentalist, vision of Western vi-
cissitudes. Dante, who comes centuries before political correctness, pays
no attention to the doubts the West has entertained about itself, nor to its
errors or faults. He concentrates, rather, on the incomparable continuity and
extension into space and time: he aims at the ultimate telos of the underlying
ideology: not power as such, but what it should be used for, justice on earth.
It is the poetry of a "sign," of an idea: the idea that Rome has embodied in the
imagination both of Europe and of its offspring throughout the continents.[113]

꙼꙳

The portrayal of the Roman eagle in *Paradiso* VI is truly original. When the
same image returns in *Paradiso* XVIII–XX, its biblical inspiration is evident.
The entire sequence seems to be dictated by the Wisdom of Solomon, from
the first line of which—*Diligite iustitiam qui iudicatis terram*, "love righteousness, you rulers of the earth"—the eagle itself takes form, and to which
the representation of the spirits that shape it in the guise of "sparks" is indebted.[114] A further sapiential passage suggests the grand image with which
the eagle opens its first speech on divine justice.[115] Yet another sapiential
text, this time from Job, via Paul, provides the source for the question with
which the eagle removes Dante's doubts in that same speech: "Now who
are you to sit upon on the bench, / to judge events a thousand miles away,
/ when your own vision spans so brief a space?"[116] A direct quotation from
Matthew's Gospel supplies the beginning of the second speech: "*Regnum
celorum* suffers violence."[117] Yet here too, the visionary texts are not far away:
when Dante sees and hears the eagle's beak speak, he is echoing Revelation,
while the murmuring of a river to which the bird's voice is likened derives
from Revelation and, ultimately, from Ezekiel.[118]

Nonetheless, Dante has abandoned even the biblical mimesis of the final
cantos of *Purgatorio*. The setting he invents, starting from the Scriptures, is
totally new, conceived in a single block of three hundred and eighty lines,
from the middle of canto XVIII to the end of canto XX of *Paradiso*. The plot
is simple: now in the sixth heaven, the pilgrim witnesses the extraordinary
coming to life of a talking eagle, which explains to him the mysteries at the
heart of divine justice.

This plot, however, unravels through movements, interruptions, and
pauses; a complex sequence of twelve in all, each accompanied by words,
songs, and flickers of light. When Cacciaguida stops speaking in the red
heaven of Mars and joins in the song of the other spirits who have fought
for the faith, showing "his artistry" as he sings "among the singers in that

sphere,"[119] Beatrice and Dante rise—in the first phase of the scene—into the silvery heaven of Jupiter. Here Dante sees the light of the "righteous and pious" sparkle with love and write out human language in the sky.[120] Indeed, the spirits flutter around and flock together, birdlike, to form the shapes of the capital letters *D*, *I*, and *L*. Gradually, in gold against a silver background, they form the entire first verse of the Wisdom of Solomon, *Diligite iustitiam qui iudicatis terram*. Then more lights land on top of the final *M* of *TERRAM*, forming first a heraldic lily and then the head, neck, and finally whole body of an eagle.

After a ferocious invective by Dante against Pope John XXII (making up the second movement, which closes canto XVIII), the eagle rears up—in the third stage—with outspread wings before the pilgrim and each of the spirits within it appears like a ruby reflecting the sun and giving off a blinding light. As though it were one sole being, "one sole warmth" which is felt "from many embers," the eagle begins to speak, presenting itself as both a "just and merciful" standard. At this (fourth) stage Dante asks it to explain to him, once and for all, the capital question about divine justice burning inside him on account of the "great fast" which has kept him hungry for so long.[121] So in its first words—the fifth section of the episode—the eagle formulates the question Dante has been wanting to ask for years: "A man is born along / the shoreline of the Indus River," where no one speaks to him of Christ; this man is good, without sin, righteous in the eyes of human reason, but he dies unbaptized and without faith. Church doctrine denies him salvation. So "where is this justice that would condemn him? Where is his sin if he does not believe?"[122] The eagle replies that divine justice is unfathomable and everything that assents to the will of God is just. Then, flapping its wings and circling around Dante, it returns to the topic in the seventh stage, reaffirming the traditional doctrine that states that no one who does not believe in Christ will ever go to Paradise. But he also adds, with unusual emphasis, that on Judgment Day, many who have never known him will be closer to him than many who call themselves Christians:

> But there are many who now cry "Christ, Christ!"
> who at the Final Judgment shall be far
> less close to Him than one who knows not Christ;
>
> the Ethiopian will shame such Christians
> when the two companies are separated,
> the one forever rich, the other poor.

[Ma vedi: molti gridan "Cristo, Cristo!,"
che saranno in giudicio assai men *prope*
a lui, che tal che non conosce Cristo;

e tai Cristian dannerà l'Etïòpe,
quando si partiranno i due collegi,
l'uno in etterno ricco e l'altro inòpe.][123]

Dante immediately proceeds to list a series of evil rulers of the day, includ-
ing Emperor Albert of Hapsburg, Philip the Fair of France, "the Scot and
Englishman" driven to insanity by their thirst for arrogance, and the kings
of Spain, Bohemia, Naples, Sicily, Portugal, Norway, "Rascia" (Yugoslavia),
Hungary, Navarre, and Cyprus:[124] in other words, practically the whole of
Europe.

Paradiso XX begins—we are now at the eighth movement—with the angelic song of the righteous spirits. In the ninth, the eagle begins to speak
once more, revealing six supreme lights that sparkle in its eyes, not only
those of Christians but also of Jews and pagans; David, "the singer of the
Holy Spirit," and Trajan; Hezekiah and Constantine; William of Hauteville
and Trojan Ripheus. In his surprise and confusion Dante cannot hold back
his question (tenth movement): "Can such these things be?" (*Che cose son
queste?*). And the eagle begins (eleventh) a second explanation: the Kingdom
of Heaven lets itself suffer violence from the love and hope of man, and the
will of God is conquered by them. Of the two pagan spirits pointed at before,
Trajan was saved because, despite being condemned to Hell, he had fostered
hope, and that hope was comforted by the prayers of Gregory the Great,
which brought him back to life, making him believe and, "kindled to such
fire of true love," he went to Paradise (a widely believed legend in medieval
times).[125] Ripheus, through divine grace, placed all his love in justice, so that
"through grace on grace," God himself revealed the coming Redemption to
him, and he found faith. Dante bases his account on just two lines of the
Aeneid, elevating it to sublime invention and counterpoint, for the almost
unknown Ripheus, classical equivalent of the man "born along the shoreline
of the Indus River," is defined in that poem as more "loving of justice" than
all the other Trojans, but Virgil has him left by the gods to die on Troy's fatal
night.[126]

The eagle then celebrates predestination and exhorts men to refrain from
judging others, for even the righteous saints, although they see God, do
not yet know "all the elect." In the twelfth and final scene, which closes

canto XX, the two lights just mentioned—"like eyes that wink in concord"—
harmoniously accompany the discourse of the "divine image," the eagle, with
the flickering of their flames, just as a good player accompanies an able singer
on the strings of his lyre, and in perfect balance.[127]

✌◦✍

This complex sequence gushes forth from the single problematic area of
divine justice, which Dante personally feels acutely, especially in relation to
the salvation of non-Christians and predestination. The sequence, however,
is compact even on the plane of poetic imagination, like a magnificent, airy
fresco, or a symphony, in which seven series of background images play
the main theme and its variations continuously for three hundred and eighty
lines. The most prominent, used throughout to highlight the most significant
moments, is of course that of birds, and it is dominated by the great speaking
eagle. In the final part of the conversation with Cacciaguida, Dante is already
observing the movements of the lights of Charlemagne and Roland "like a
falconer who tracks his falcon's flight." As soon as he reaches the heaven of
Jupiter, the spirits of the righteous arrange themselves in letters of gold on
a silver background "just as birds that rise from riverbanks, / as if rejoicing
after feeding there, / will form a round flock or another shape." In canto
XIX, when the pilgrim asks the eagle, which has meanwhile changed shape,
to solve the problem tormenting him, the "sign" becomes "like a falcon set
free from its hood, / which moves its head and flaps its wings, displaying / its
eagerness and proud appearance." At the end of its first speech, the eagle and
Dante become like the stork and her young, the former circling round the
nest after feeding her little one, the latter gazing at her contentedly. Finally,
after pointing out Trojan Ripheus, the eagle appears to Dante like a lark "at
large in the air, / a lark that sings at first and then falls still, / content with
final sweetness that fulfills."[128] The simile comes at the center of the canto
and closes the series, confirming yet again that Dante uses the icon of the
birds to indicate indescribable joy, intimate satisfaction, the contentedness
with which the spirits of the righteous are replete: "Blessed are those who
hunger and thirst after justice, for they shall be filled." Gospel, theology, and
poetry take each other by the hand in tranquil beauty.

Similarly, in the image of the sparks, inspired by the Wisdom of Solomon,
biblical text and everyday experience move together in two wonderful moments: when the thousand lights descend on top of the M of IUSTITIAM to
form the head and neck of the eagle ("Then, as innumerable sparks rise up

/ when one strikes burning logs"), and when the eagle itself, despite being made out of many spirits, utters a single sound: "Thus one sole warmth is felt from many embers, / even as from a multitude of loves / one voice alone rose from the Eagle's image."[129] The fire flares up out of poetic invention or glows inside it like embers: and the heat fires its words as much as it enflames the love of the righteous.

The fire dyad is matched by a water triad: sea, river, and spring. Twice inspired by Scripture,[130] the poetry at first penetrates and sinks down into a fathomless expanse of water; then it murmurs, descending from rock to rock, as if anticipating Petrarch's clear, fresh, limpid waters; finally, alone and without any biblical help, it surges back to the inaccessible spring and the impenetrable "primal wave" (the *prima onda*). This is truly divine justice, a sea of absolute transcendence, whose ultimate depths cannot be seen by the human eye up on its surface:

> Therefore the vision that your world receives
> can penetrate into the Eternal Justice
> no more than eye can penetrate the sea;

> for though, near shore, sight reaches the sea floor,
> you cannot reach it in the open sea;
> yet it is there, but hidden by the deep.
> [Però ne la giustizia sempiterna
> la vista che riceve il vostro mondo,
> com'occhio per lo mare, entro s'interna;

> che, ben che da la proda veggia il fondo,
> in pelago nol vede; e nondimeno
> èli, ma cela lui l'esser profondo.][131]

The eagle falls silent after pointing to the evil kings of today, while the shining lights begin singing "labile" songs that escape the poet's memory; the singing stops, and Dante hears a murmur coming from the bird's neck, as though it were hollow. It is like the voice of a river:

> I seemed to hear the murmur of a torrent
> that, limpid, falls from rock to rock, whose flow
> shows the abundance of its mountain source.
> [udir mi parve un mormorar di fiume

che scende chiaro giù di pietra in pietra,
mostrando l'ubertà del suo cacume.][132]

Finally, Trojan Ripheus entrusts all his love to justice, thanks to the grace coming directly from God, the spring whose pristine waters no creature has ever set eyes on:

The other, through the grace that surges from
a well so deep that no created one
has ever thrust his eye to its first source,

below, set all his love on righteousness.
[L'altra, per grazia che da sì profonda
fontana stilla, che mai creatura

non pinse l'occhio infino a la prima onda,

tutto suo amor pose a drittura.][133]

The aesthetics of the primeval elements illuminates and refines all the immaterial poetry of *Paradiso,* and there is little point in mentioning here the thousand variations of light that in the third cantica form the objective correlative of the theme of God, the beatitude of the saints, the love and the Spirit that rule the Kingdom. A poetics of auroral radiance reigns supreme in *Paradiso:* clear, warm, and joyful. It is a *claritas* that returns things to a state of innocence, watching over them as at the dawn of the world—a *radiance* (as Stephen Dedalus will call it six hundred years later in Joyce's *Portrait of an Artist*) that reveals their essence.[134]

So while the opening of the sequence in canto XVIII had in the "torch of Jove" a "sparkling" of love that drew *our own human language* in the heavens with flights of birds and flourishes of letters, canto XIX opens with a double image of sunlight burning in a ruby glow, and then reflected in the eyes of the protagonist:

The handsome image those united souls,
happy within their blessedness, were shaping,
appeared before me now with open wings.

Each soul seemed like a ruby—one in which
a ray of sun burned so, that in my eyes,

it was the total sun that seemed reflected.
[Parea dinanzi a me con l'ali aperte
la bella image che nel dolce *frui*
liete facevan l'anime conserte;

parea ciascuna rubinetto in cui
raggio di sole ardesse sì acceso,
che ne' miei occhi rifrangesse lui.][135]

In the solemn *incipit* of canto XX, the poet leads us once again to the sun—
the natural icon for God—and again with the double image of direct and
refracted light. Here the star that illuminates the entire universe sets at
the close of day, while the sky becomes visible in the darkness thanks to
the infinite lights of the stars—which, according to Ptolemaic astronomy,
continue to reflect the light of the sun:

When he who graces all the world with light
has sunk so far below our hemisphere
that on all sides the day is spent, the sky,

which had been lit before by him alone,
immediately shows itself again
with many lights reflecting one same source,

and I remembered this celestial course
when, in the blessed beak, the emblem of
the world and of guardians fell silent;

for then all of those living lights grew more
resplendent, but the songs that they began
were labile—they escape my memory.
[Quando colui che tutto 'l mondo alluma
de l'emisperio nostro sì discende,
che 'l giorno d'ogne parte si consuma,

lo ciel, che sol di lui prima s'accende,
subitamente si rifà parvente
per molte luci, in che una risplende;

e questo atto del ciel mi venne a mente,
come 'l segno del mondo e de' suoi duci
nel benedetto rostro fu tacente;

però che tutte quelle vive luci,
vie più lucendo, cominciaron canti
da mia memoria labili e caduci.][136]

The simile runs on, calmly and astonishingly, from the one to the many, sight to hearing, day to night, from the sun that gives light to the whole world to the eagle, "emblem of the world," from silence to song.

∾o∾

Throughout this episode in *Paradiso* XVIII–XX, Dante focuses repeatedly on the theme of music and art anticipated in the final modulation of Cacciaguida, most skilful among the singers of heaven (*tra i cantor del cielo artista*). In this section, he establishes an order of *poietai*, from the supreme painter and architect of the universe down to David, "singer of the Holy Spirit," then to the "good singer" at the close of canto XX, returning to his own, unique voice; the voice of Dante Alighieri *poietes* of *Paradiso*.

At the highest rank of this order is He who paints heaven, with no guide directing his hand to follow any model. He himself is the guide, and we recognize that the *virtù* that gives shape to all embryonic creatures derives from him. With Platonic perception, Dante sees the archetypes of all existing forms within the divine mind. Yet, when he reminds us of the "shaping force" (the *virtù ch'è forma*), the formative principle, by which He creates all beings, Dante does not forget the *tode ti*, Aristotle's concept of the universal-particular: *per li nidi*—"from nest to nest"—has the general sense of "place where the living being forms from seed and grows," but it is also specific, in that it applies to *this* celestial eagle: painted in the heavens by God and the model for all eagles of the terrestrial world. In a word, we are contemplating the Idea of the Eagle as if it were something we could touch. Moreover, we cannot avoid thinking that while God paints without a guide, this celestial eagle was created and drawn by none other than the poet Dante. It follows, therefore, that the poet is claiming for himself the divine ability to paint:

He who paints there has no one as His guide:
He guides Himself; in Him we recognize
the shaping force that flows from nest to nest.

[Quei che dipinge lì non ha chi 'l guidi;
ma esso guida, e da lui si rammenta
quella virtù ch'è forma per li nidi.][137]

In canto XIX, however, there is an absolute image of the supreme architect drawing the outer limits of the cosmos with his compass and placing in it many manifest and secret things, without, however, investing them with all of his own *valore*—the power of the Father Creator—so that his *verbo*, the "Word" (the Idea and the Son) remains "in infinite excess" in relation to the world he has created. In just two terzinas, the Creation (and the structure of the universe, in which things visible and invisible are separate and ordered) is recalled in all its theological and philosophical complexity through the immense biblical image of the turn of the compass. This constitutes an immediately identifiable introduction that shocks and pulls the reader inside "difficult" poetry. Dante rewrites[138] the beginning of Genesis and the prologue to John, following in the footsteps of the book of Job:

> Then it began: "The One who turned His compass
> to mark the world's confines, and in them set
> so many things concealed and things revealed,
>
> could not imprint His Power into all
> the universe without His Word remaining
> in infinite excess of such a vessel . . ."
> [Poi cominciò: "Colui che volse il sesto
> a lo stremo del mondo, e dentro ad esso
> distinse tanto occulto e manifesto,
>
> non poté suo valor sì fare impresso
> in tutto l'universo, che 'l suo verbo
> non rimanesse in infinito eccesso . . ."][139]

On the human side of the *poiein*, cantos XVIII to XXV of *Paradiso* have no loftier creator than David, "singer of the Holy Spirit" and "sovereign singer of the Sovereign Lord," and according to tradition, author of the Psalms. Dante recognizes David's inspiration as coming directly from God (*cantor de lo Spirito Santo*, meaning that David sang of the Spirit, but also that his song was guided by the Spirit). He also sees David's poetry as a particular poetic genre, *theody*, declaring it—in a moving moment of "re-turning"—a fundamental experience in his own life as a man in that it was the first to instil hope in him.[140] *Tëodia:* God's ode, a song in his honor, the monotheistic equivalent of the Greek ode in honor of the winners of the races, of the songs in honor of the gods; the supreme lyric model of what *Paradiso* sets out to achieve on the narrative level.

Dante draws daringly close to this in the sequence of the eagle, as clearly shown in two passages from *Paradiso* XVIII and XIX. Here, the *poet* shows an earnest, strained self-awareness of both his efforts and his success. The former comes just before the terzina dedicated to the celestial painter: Dante invokes the Muse to shed her light on the human painter, so that he may draw the letters and the words formed by the spirits of the righteous as *he conceived them.* The author is undoubtedly God, but the writer is Dante, and the Muse awards glory and long life to *human* genius, and man, in concert with the Muse, lends luster to the cities and the kingdoms of the world:

> O godly Pegasea, you who give
> to genius glory and long life, as it,
> through you, gives these to kingdoms and to cities,
>
> give me your light that I may emphasize
> these signs as I inscribed them in my mind:
> your power—may it appear in these brief lines!
> [O diva Pegasëa che li 'ngegni
> fai glorïosi e rendili longevi,
> ed essi teco le cittadi e ' regni,
>
> illustrami di te, sì ch'io rilevi
> le lor figure com'io l'ho concette:
> paia tua possa in questi versi brevi!][141]

Furthermore, Dante is well aware that the "power" of the Muse unfolds fully in these cantos, for at the beginning of canto XIX he proudly proclaims that what he is about to relate about the eagle has never been sung by any *voice,* nor *written* by any hand, nor *conceived* by any imagination:

> And what I now must tell has never been
> reported by a voice, inscribed by ink,
> never conceived by the imagination.
> [E quel che mi convien ritrar testeso,
> non portò voce mai, né scrisse incostro,
> né fu per fantasia già mai compreso.][142]

Thus, here and now Dante's poetry brings something completely new. No models exist for this imagination, which celebrates divine justice and faces delicate issues such as predestination and the salvation of pagans by rein-venting the eagle of Ezekiel and John. He gives this eagle shape and an articulate voice, unity and plurality of movements and arabesques, a golden color against a silver background: fire, water, sun, birds: *poetry of justice*, in which Dante's re-turning becomes a gentle murmuring, now purified and happy, of contemplation.

∽ઝ๑৺

Perhaps, at this point, we should ask what idea Dante has in mind for this kind of poetry. Before recalling the theody of David and the "sublime announcement" of John, Dante calls his poem "sacred": "to which both heaven and earth have set their hand" (*al quale ha posto mano e cielo e terra*).[143] Thus we might compare Dante's conception of paradisal poetry, by approximation, to the supreme song of the Holy Spirit and of the "Supreme Lord" in the Psalter, and to the proclamation of the "secret" which Christ's Eagle, John, makes in his Prologue, Gospel, and Revelation.

I suggest, however, that we search for this idea in the eagle itself, which Dante evokes and depicts so frequently in his poem, since he was presumably familiar with the patristic and biblical tradition mentioned above. At the beginning of *Paradiso*, when he announces "the glory of the One who moves all things," the poet quotes with precision the well-known passage from Paul describing being "caught up" to the third heaven:[144]

I was within the heaven that receives
more of His light; and I saw things that he
who from that height descends, forgets or
cannot speak.
[Nel ciel che più de la sua luce prende
fu' io, e vidi cose che ridire
né sa né può chi di là sù discende.][145]

Precisely because of this being "caught up," his preaching of Jesus Christ crucified, and his proclamation of the good news to the whole world, Paul was known as the "eagle." One significant example of this comes in a passage from the *Moralia in Job*, in which Gregory the Great comments on the verses from the book of Job discussed above, synthesizing the whole tradition: *Paradiso* XXVIII indicates that Dante must have read this passage carefully.[146] If Paul is an eagle, then so too is Dante, despite his protestations to Virgil in *Inferno* II, "I am not Aeneas; I am not Paul." Moreover, Dante indirectly identifies with Paul in canto I of *Paradiso* when he asks Apollo-Word to make him the "vessel" of his poetic virtue,[147] and indeed flies beyond the apostle, since he states that "nevertheless" (*veramente*)—despite what he has said about being unable to tell again what he has seen—the subject of his poem, from now on, will be what has remained in his memory "of the holy kingdom."[148]

The suggestion is minimal. But Dante's poetic imagination seems Pindaric by nature. Soon after, still in the first canto of *Paradiso*, Beatrice turns her gaze toward the sun. Dante the poet seizes the opportunity to liken her to the eagle: "no eagle / has ever stared so steadily at it" (*aquila sì non li s'affisse unquanco*). With one leap Dante attains the dimension and language of mysticism, in which the sun represents God, and the eagle the soul of man contemplating Him. However, Beatrice is not alone in becoming an eagle, for by reflection, the gaze of Dante the character also fixes on the sun:

> And as a second ray will issue from
> the first and reascend, much like a pilgrim
> who seeks his home again, so on her action,
>
> fed by my eyes to my imagination,
> my action drew, and on the sun I set
> my sight more than we usually do.
> [E sì come secondo raggio suole
> uscir del primo e risalire in suso,
> pur come pelegrin che tornar vuole,
>
> così de l'atto suo, per li occhi infuso
> ne l'imagine mia, il mio si fece,
> e fissi li occhi al sole oltre nostr'uso.][149]

In short, Dante becomes an eagle ("one of the noble young of this lofty eagle")[150] and the whole of *Paradiso* turns out to be a flight toward that sun: a flight with the appropriate wings and destined to come as close as possible, with those wings, to the "first love," and to enter, eaglelike, "into His effulgence." To such an extent Dante Alighieri the poet, who even has wings—Italian *ali*—in his family name, will fix his "look on the Light Eternal," until his sight is all consumed, namely, until he attains the visionary blindness of the prophet and the mystic:[151] and, it may be added, of Homer, "that lord of loftiest song who flies like an eagle above the rest."

Could it be that in using the image of the eagle Dante wishes to present himself in *Paradiso* as the new Homer? As the lord and master of a new supreme song that comprehends, because the poet relives them in life and in writing, the theody of David, the "sublime announcement" of John, and the preaching of Paul? I cannot state this with absolute certainty. What is certain, however, is that while the eagle is contiguous to the Muses and Apollo in *Paradiso* I, in *Paradiso* XVIII–XX the poet associates the golden eagle deliberately and intimately with the Muse, song, and the lyre. When the bird of divine justice speaks once again in *Paradiso* XX, Dante hears not only the murmuring of a river but also the sound of a lyre and of pipes:

> Even as sound takes shape at the lute's neck,
> and even as the wind that penetrates
> the blow-hole of the bagpipe, so—with no
>
> delay—that murmur of the Eagle rose
> straight up, directly through its neck as if
> its neck were hollow.
> [E come suono al collo de la cetra
> prende sua forma, e sì com'al pertugio
> de la sampogna vento che penètra,
>
> così, rimosso d'aspettare indugio,
> quel mormorar de l'aguglia salissi
> su per lo collo, come fosse bugio.][152]

Later, the canto comes to a close with the lyre alone, concluding the epiphany of the eagle in perfect harmony:

> And as a lutanist accompanies—
> expert—with trembling strings, the expert singer,
> by which the song acquires sweeter savor,
>
> so, while the Eagle spoke—I can remember—
> I saw the pair of blessed lights together,
> like eyes that wink in concord, move their flames
>
> in ways that were at one with what he said.
> [E come a buon cantor buon citarista

fa seguitar lo guizzo de la corda,
in che più di piacer lo canto acquista,

sì, mentre ch'e' parlò, sì mi ricorda
ch'io vidi le due luci benedette,
pur come batter d'occhi si concorda,

con le parole mover le fiammette.][153]

The eagle, gold, Apollo, the Muses, the *lyre*; how much time has passed since we leafed through Pindar's first *Pythian* at the start of this chapter? Almost two thousand years, and Dante never read a single line of the Theban poet whose name, despite Horace, he seems not even to have known. Yet in the end, unaware of its own primal source, and singing of a contest somewhat different from that of Delphi—a struggle[154] with the inarticulate, with ultimate transcendence, with the rise towards it, and hence with man's bending back into his own small, frail nature—Dante's poetry leads us back there, to that golden enchantment of flight and of the lyre.

Musée des Beaux Arts 6

The sun is sinking on the horizon. Only two-thirds of it is visible above the water, but a burst of gold surrounds it, sending a glow across the landscape. The turquoise sea dissolves into the far-off, possibly snow-capped mountains, one of them extremely high, conical, and, at this distance, darkly brown, like the mountain which appeared to Ulysses moments before his shipwreck and death in canto XXVI of Dante's *Inferno*. In the foreground, an immense gulf of water opens up towards the viewer, bordered on both sides by high, light-colored mountains.

The tall, almost-vertical range to the left drops into the sea around a small inlet similar to those of the Riviera or the Amalfi Coast, sheltering a turreted seaport; a ship is sailing in to port. To the right, beneath the mountain range, a city appears. The landscape and colors are most definitely Mediterranean. The sky rises away from the sun, clouding and darkening over the mountains around the gulf. Two islands are also visible, the one on the right flat, with an irregular coastline, golden on the side facing the sun, white in the middle, and already in shadow on the other side; the other, smaller island on the left, rocky and topped by what seem to be the ruins of a castle perched above the water, with a clump of trees and scrub behind it, to the left, on a low, sandy shore. The light here is also distributed according to the lay of the land in the sun. The wide bay is broken up by cliffs and rocks, singly or in clumps, like the *Faraglioni* on Capri.

To the left, three birds with outstretched wings circle the mountains, sea, and city: they look like birds of prey, too big for gulls or king-fishers. One hovers between earth and water, the second flies almost vertically upward, while the third, the biggest, has almost reached the flat top of the mountain in front of it.

The turquoise gulf opens from left to right, where a wooded isthmus splits it into two channels. Just off the coast, to the right, a fine triple-masted Dutch cog of the sixteenth century heads for the open sea, its fore and aft sails already unfurled. The sailors are visible in the rigging, about to unfurl the remaining sails. The bay actually contains three ships, perhaps caravels: the one entering from the left is followed on the diagonal toward the bottom right by another, and, in the expanse of water in the immediate foreground, by the large sailing ship that is the first to catch the observer's attention. On a closer look, the whole sea is bustling and busy: one vessel, which seems to be a rowboat, plies the left shore; four more sailboats circle the central ship in a loose rhomboid formation.

The stately, triple-masted ship is pulling out from a channel where the water's surface—only now do we notice—is broken by two legs, the feet waving frantically in the air: feathers and plumage fall softly all around, drifting in the breeze, their whiteness merging here and there with the foam of the waves. Someone has obviously fallen into the sea and is drowning.

Not far from him, on a rock, sits a stocky fisherman, wearing a white flannel smock, a red kerchief around his neck, and a dark cap, casting his line. His bait in a bucket to his left and his head bent over the water, he pays no attention whatsoever to the tragedy taking place nearby.

We are now with him on the dry land that frames the lower half of the picture: we see it from behind the foreground. The side that faces the sea looks jagged and rocky. Leafy boughs are to the left, a clump of bushes almost in the center, and to the right, lower down the slope, the occasional branch bending toward the sea. On one of these sits a bird, brown with white underside—at first glance, it seems to be a plump partridge. Behind the central clump of bushes a tongue of land juts out: a light-colored hillside on which sheep graze, some of them perilously close to the edge. All are white except two, which stand out, blackly, to right and left. In their midst stands the shepherd, in brownish breeches and grayish shirt, a pannier on his back. He leans on a stick, his dog at his side, brown, with white paws and head; his head is raised, turned away from the sailing ship, fisherman, and drowning legs; he peers into the sky, though toward what we have no idea: even if we follow the direction of his gaze, there is nothing to be seen.

The immediate foreground is dominated by a field, which a huge farmer is plowing. He wears dark hose, a red shirt, dark cap, and dun-colored tunic, pleated behind from the waist and open at the front. His face is bent over the furrows left in the earth by the plow. His left hand holds a whip over the broad rump of a plow horse. The solid wooden plow has obviously been at work for some time, for the field stretches toward us in soft and tidy folds.

A dagger-shaped knife, pouch, and belt lie on a stone to the left, right in front of us. Also to the left, among the bushes beneath the tall, elegant trees, between the vegetation and the tilled field, lies a small, round, light-colored object. Careful scrutiny reveals it to be a bald human head: it lies inert upon the soil, facing upward, dead.

◦◦◦

Painted between 1555 and 1560, and attributed to Pieter Bruegel the Elder, *The Fall of Icarus* has hung since 1912 in the Musées Royaux des Beaux Arts in Brussels. I have described it in such detail because everything about it seems of equal importance, from the objects and figures to the light that washes over it, the sea that both amplifies and compresses it, the sky above and the earth that appears to underpin the whole canvas. It is not a large painting, and little is known of its history:[1] even the authorship is uncertain, although it is commonly held to be Bruegel's, and the preparatory sketch is certainly his. There also exists what would appear to be a copy in the Van Buuren Museum in Brussels. This is slightly smaller, most probably not painted by Bruegel, and differing in at least two details: no setting sun illuminates it, while high in the sky, meeting the shepherd's insistent gaze, is the bearded face of a man, light-skinned and naked, with wide wings attached to his arms: Daedalus.

What happened between the first and second painting? Did Bruegel, whose conception and general design are apparent in both paintings, have second thoughts? The second painting is clearly inferior in quality, yet it eliminates the setting sun (which indeed initially seems incongruous, since it is presumably the *midday* sun that melts the wax of Icarus's wings),[2] and adds Daedalus, who thus becomes coprotagonist alongside his son. The "copy" thus seems to rationalize the original, as it were, bringing it into line with tradition. It is, however, less attractive and inspired than the first, which possesses a rationality and balance of its own, albeit with a number of disquieting details.

Bruegel painted a number of seascapes. There are two, for example, one *With Boats and a Burning City*, the other *With Christ and the Apostles at the Sea of Tiberias*, which are so similar to *The Fall of Icarus* as to raise the doubt, expressed by the German poet Wolf Biermann, that what we are looking at is not the sea at all, but a lake.[3] A *Seascape* in Vienna's Kunsthistorisches

. . .

Figure 1. Pieter Breugel the Elder. *Landscape with the Fall of Icarus.*
Musées Royaux d'Art et d'Histoire, Brussels, Belgium.
Photograph: © Bridgeman Giraudon / Art Resource, New York.

Museum, complete with dark storm clouds and rain, undoubtedly depicts
the ocean. *The Fall of Icarus* is different. Ships of this size could move over
no lake smaller than the Caspian, while the watery horizon does not end in
closure but opens up towards the far-off mountains and beyond, into infinite
space. Bruegel was well acquainted with the geographical discoveries of his
time and with his compatriots' busy trade through a good half of the known
globe. Moreover, as mentioned above, this sea and landscape are decidedly
Mediterranean, and Bruegel had lived for some time in Italy. There is also,
of course, the Bruegel of *Children's Games, The Return of the Flock, The Land
of Plenty, Peasant Wedding,* and *Country Dances,* not to mention the Bruegel
who created the haunting landscapes of *Hunters in the Snow* and *Stormy Day.*
This is the Bruegel who places the plowman center stage on the shore in
the *Fall of Icarus,* with the shepherd and fisherman beside him: the Bruegel
of the humble, ordinary life of Flemish peasants. It is equally the Bruegel
of *The Blind,* of the *Fall of the Rebel Angels,* and, above all, of the *Triumph of
Death,* which terrifies visitors at Capodimonte, at the Musée des Beaux Arts

Figure 2. Pieter Bruegel the Elder (?). *Landscape with the Fall of Icarus.*
Collection: Museum David and Alice van Buuren, Brussels, Belgium.

in Brussels, and at the Prado in Madrid.[4] Is this the painter who tosses the bare head of the dead man into the bushes in the *Fall of Icarus?*

Let us take one thing at a time. One immediately obvious quality is the painting's exceptional equilibrium. There are mountains on all four sides, with a noteworthy left-right balance, as in the two parallel towns, and the two islands on the diagonal. A small bay and port are embedded in the larger gulf that dominates the scene, subdivided into two inlets. Three ships cross the sea in an almost straight line from bottom right to top left, on a diagonal that crosses that of the islands. A rhomboid crown of boats surrounds the second ship.

All is in order, it seems, in the natural and human world. The cosmos looks equally at peace, represented by the four elements of the fire of the sun, the air of the sky, the seawater, and earth. For all this, of course, the sun is necessary. Even now, at sunset, it emanates a miraculous, almost unearthly light: still "trailing clouds of glory," but also of imminent darkness and mystery. But it still gives off enough heat to melt wax.

Icarus has fallen and is no more than a pair of legs and a cloud of feathers planing down to the water. The element of air belongs not to man but to the three birds that fly ever higher. Daedalus's absence is meaningful, therefore, underlining the message that humans cross the threshold of the heavens at their peril. In any case, the fall of Icarus seems a matter of no importance whatsoever: the sailors on the mast do not care about him, the fisherman and the shepherd ignore him: the farmer, busy plowing away, does not know of his existence. The myth is deconstructed and destroyed. But the shepherd looks upward.

Humanity's seafaring activities—trade, fishing, and perhaps exploration, encoded in the distant, defamiliarized mountains—are balanced with land-based ones: fishing, sheep-farming, and plowing. Lord of the land is the plowman in the center, a figure from the northern European medieval and Renaissance imaginary:[5] the first Adam who, eyes lowered under the burden of his sin, works the land with the sweat of his brow, and King Ulysses who plows the fields of his native land to escape the Trojan War. An aspect of regality is apparent in his anomalously ceremonial dress code, the long and elegant skirt pleats, corresponding to the soft and ordered furrows of earth left by his plow, and the brush strokes with which the artist paints both. But beside him, on the stone, lie the dagger, pouch, and belt; further off, in the bushes, lies the head of the dead, blind man. True, a German proverb quoted by several commentators has it that "no plow stops for a dying man;"[6] but *this* plow, which has already passed close to the bare head, will never come into contact with it, for it lies on nonarable land in the middle of a thicket.

No plow stops for a dying man: not even for an Icarus falling from the sky. This is perfectly in line with traditional wisdom, which condemns Ulysses for his wanderings—of which Icarus's flight is a miniature figuration—and modern hubris generally, that of Leonardo, perhaps: a tradition that continued into the Renaissance, voiced by Erasmus of Rotterdam, for example.[7] It might equally be a figure of the Adam who tills the land, and the Adam who, like Icarus, falls from heaven: one and the same figure, since the first man to aspire to forbidden knowledge is the memory, "the most intimate twin," of his earthly cousin.[8] And with the Fall of Adam, death enters the world: the head in the bushes.

It is possible that the shepherd with upturned head, the only figure to maintain a firmly Ovidian posture in the general subversion of the myth, is looking for Hermes, the god of commerce and messenger of the gods who flies through the ether and, as we saw in chapter 3, skims the waves of the sea. De Bosis, with his *Icaro*, would agree.[9] The shepherd holds a stick that might well be a humble, human version of Hermes' rod: its tip certainly forms the exact center of the painting's geometry. The picture thus becomes a labyrinth of earth, sea, and sky, the work of the supreme artist, Daedalus: Pieter Bruegel.

The plowman might also be Cain, of course, a "tiller of the ground," who in Genesis is reprimanded by God for his "fallen face": "If thou doest well, shalt thou not be accepted? And if thou doest not well, sin lieth at the door." The shepherd, the only one to look upward, would then be Abel, a "keeper of sheep." The knife, pouch, and belt would thus stand for menace and man-to-man violence, and the head in the bushes would become the symbol of the very first murder. If the sun were rising, the whole scene would evoke humanity's beginnings, between the Fall and the murder: a moving away from God. A setting sun, on the other hand, offers an eschatological prolepsis: the moment before the end of the world and the coming of the Son of Man: on an ordinary day, at an unexpected moment, when "two shall be in the field," and "the one shall be taken, and the other left."[10]

The picture thus is considerably more complicated than would seem at first glance, and its symbolism and readings multidirectional. A number of elements remain enigmatic: the setting sun and the unreal light; the object of the shepherd's gaze and the totally empty sky; the significance of the dagger, pouch, and belt; the bare, blind, dead head; the significance of the partridge. Then, more in general: why produce such an ordered and beguiling world as a backdrop to Icarus's most insignificant fall?

Only the partridge finds an answer, and then only by raising a further question. When, in chapter 2, I gave Ovid's version of the myth, I deliberately omitted its coda: while a weeping Daedalus buries his son, a *garrula perdix*—a partridge species that makes a grouselike sound—spots him, flaps its wings, and emits a joyful trill. It is the bird into which Athena had turned Daedalus's nephew, Perdix, who, as clever if not cleverer than his uncle, had invented the saw and compass. The envious Daedalus had thrown him from the Acropolis, a place sacred to Pallas, afterward putting it out that the boy had fallen. Athena, however, who protects talent, transformed the falling Perdix into a partridge; the bird has preserved all its old cleverness in its wings and claws, but, recalling its far-off fall, always flies cautiously close to the ground and lays its eggs in hedges or brush.[11] The partridge is thus Daedalus's nemesis and the perfect counter-icon of his son. Icarus falls and dies by imitating the birds and flying too high, forgetful of the "middle way"; Perdix falls and becomes a bird, through divine wisdom, maintaining his intelligence and keeping a low profile.

In chapter 4 we heard Alcman claiming he had invented words and melody by observing and patterning the singing call of the partridge. Bruegel cannot possibly have known *The Marvels* by Antigonus of Carystus, in which the fragment appears;[12] but he was well aware, from Ovid, that Perdix was equal to Daedalus in ingenuity and had invented the compass. The partridge in his painting might, then, be an enigmatic meta-stroke, representing the artist— the painter drawing the horizon of his painting with an ideal compass, establishing coordinates, diagonals, and center, or, perhaps, the poet Ovid, who had already seen, sung, and narrated the entire business.

Turning to other matters, we find a major puzzle in the shepherd's upward gaze. He is looking in the wrong direction, gazing into thin air, whereas Icarus has fallen on the right. The sky in that point contains neither birds, nor flying men, nor gods. But, since the time of Abraham and the *Iliad*, shepherds have always been stargazers, not least those of the Nativity, up to Leopardi's wandering shepherd in his "Pastore errante dell'Asia." The perception of the invisible and marveling at the universe appear to belong to shepherds by archetypal right. Bruegel's shepherd is the only one in the painting to have heard something rustling up there, and his scrutinizing gaze in some way deconstructs the stolid fisherman and plowman, whose eyes are fixed on the ground. In rejecting the traditional rhetoric of human flight, they also seem to be rejecting all transcendence or cosmic wonder. True, in so doing they keep to the *facere quod in se est*, the "doing what is in oneself" that represents the highest ethic of the medieval and Protestant *moderns*; but the bent head of the farmer, particularly, evinces a surprising obstinacy: plow and furrow and nothing more. And "no man having put his hand to the plow, and looking back, is fit for the kingdom of God," writes Luke in his Gospel.[13]

The plowman's concentration is so intense that it suggests he is thinking about something within himself. This may be the dagger, pouch, and belt left on the stone although there is no way of knowing whether he has even seen them, let alone whether they belong to him. But the dagger is definitely menacing. Some past or present Peasants' Revolt?[14] A threat to the harmony of the known world? The plowman may be quite oblivious to such concerns, but a mind fed on detective stories might just harbor the suspicion that it was he who killed the man whose head lies in the bushes, making off with the pouch and *unbuckled* belt.

The knife is equally threatening and enigmatic, as is that bare, blind head. It drags death into a picture that otherwise, in the figure of Icarus, ignores it. It ensures that we are unable to forget death but also unable to respond, other than through German folk wisdom. The plow plows on, but the man dies and is left dumped in the woods like some disused object: some dagger, pouch, or unbuckled belt, or a handful of feathers and plumage.[15] Folk "wisdom" indeed! Surely the reverse is true: as the Bruegel of the *Triumph* well knew, it is death that stops for no plow, for it possesses a scythe more potent than any plowshare!

Directly above the lifeless head buried amid the dark foliage, a light shines between the branches of the trees, oddly, given such thick vegetation. It must be the last rays of the sun, striking the side of the mountain, which can be seen beyond the branches. The sun, too, is dying, dropping like Icarus into the sea, sending out this mysterious light: the lightness of being here, still, but already elsewhere—the mystery and splendor of departure.

∽o∾

How long does it take for literature to notice such an astonishing painting? In this case, almost four centuries, and if the interval is significant in itself, so too is the moment of awakening poignant. Humanity now does, indeed, fly: across land and oceans, conducting battles from the air. The absolute irrelevance of the fall of Icarus declared in Bruegel's painting emerges just as the mythical fall loses any point. But literature has its own times and seasons, helped on its way by the technical reproduction of the work of art:[16] it slowly contemplates the painting, interrogates it, chews over the details, reconstructs it, translates it into knowledge, ethics, metaphysics, aesthetics, history, and politics. And the old image falls, at the point of contact with the new moment—with the *kairos*—in a different mix: it coagulates into words.

The first writer to treat Bruegel's poem was the Dutchman Albert Verwey, who in 1930 wondering whether the Icarus of the Musée des Beaux Arts really fell at all, describes the adamantine indifference of the natural and human world as encapsulated in the shepherd's skyward gaze.[17] But it was only in 1938 that W. H. Auden gave utterance to what quickly became a topos in his poem *Musée des Beaux Arts*. Auden inserts the painting into the cosmic canvas of human suffering: the Old Masters—of literature and of the visual arts—"were never wrong," always understanding its "human position": how it takes place while the world goes on "eating or opening a window or just walking dully along"; "How, when the aged are reverently, passionately waiting / For the miraculous birth, there always must be / Children who did not specially want it to happen, skating / On a pond at the edge of the wood." The Old Masters never forget that "the dreadful martyrdom" will "run its course / Anyhow in a corner," some nontranscendental spot where "dogs go on with their doggy life and the torturer's horse / Scratches its innocent behind on a tree." Nativities and Crucifixions are always set in scenes of daily life, where bystanders, if not directly involved, simply get on with their humdrum tasks: history, including the story of human suffering, takes place in a corner where the mass of humanity is unaware, or indifferent, or even unwilling for it to happen. This is precisely what happens in the case of Icarus, the first man to fly, with his father, and who then falls: a mythical "disaster" that is the catastrophe of humankind:

> In Brueghel's *Icarus*, for instance: how everything turns away
> Quite leisurely from the disaster; the ploughman may
> Have heard the splash, the forsaken cry,
> But for him it was not an important failure; the sun shone
> As it had to on the white legs disappearing into the green
> Water; and the expensive delicate ship that must have seen
> Something amazing, a boy falling out of the sky,
> Had somewhere to get to and sailed calmly on.[18]

All seems well, and the sun continues to shine as, indeed, "it had to." And if the plowman has heard the shout and splash, it represents no great loss for his personal world. The ship inevitably saw the catastrophe but is not about to allow the occurrence, however "amazing," to divert it from its course. It has a job to do, and "expensive" interests to represent. The "something amazing" is less Icarus's flight in itself than the fact of "a boy falling out of the sky," materializing from nowhere; the fall of an angel, a god descending to earth, and the fall of every human being from Adam onward: in a word, suffering. The rest of the world receives it—when it does not, simply, ignore it—not with amazement but "leisurely": ironic poetic wisdom refracted through the visual arts.

It was this aspect of indifference, the painting's most foregrounded aspect, which appealed to the twentieth century. The writer Raïssa Maritain, for example, in her "La chute d'Icare d'après Brueghel" (1939), has Icarus fall from the zenith like a swooping seagull, the simile we saw Homer used for Hermes: but, with time brought forward to midday, to make sure he falls at the sun's highest point, it is a moment in which "everything rests in the sun," and nothing disturbs the *beauty* of the universe: *rien ne trouble la beauté du monde*.[19] For the New Zealand writer Allan Curnow (1943), too, the sunny coast, quiet farming, and sailing are "like a crystal brimming with fine weather," and when Icarus precipitates a fiery ball, everything holds together "true to earth's ancient compact against caring": that same sun that burns his skin is warming the plowman's back; the same wind that buffets him is guiding the ship through the busy archipelago, where no one takes pity on him or even notices the tragedy. The landscape immediately reassembles into itself. Among the "headlong" pilots, Curnow comments, "no revenge

/ Was wild enough for that indifference." Icarus immediately becomes the emblem of all those fighting the Second World War from the air: when the flames marking each "prouder plunge" die down, a "mere" breeze whisks the stain cleanly away.[20]

But this brief excursus into history is quickly superseded by the ancient, metaphysical issues: on the one hand the ordinary world, the "sheepish present," bumbling, docile, herd-like, the "illimitable juiciness of things," and the yellows, greens, and browns that the sheep see and "are what they see"; on the other the "worst," which has already happened, the Fall of Icarus, the angel, "lost to man, forever failed," hurtling down because the sun, the star that orders the cosmos, has melted his wings while—such mockery— setting, only to rise the following day. The English poet Michael Hamburger wrote in 1951 of the dramatic contrast between the destiny of things and that of fallen angels and men: Icarus, too far from his "half-brothers"—the plowman, the fisherman, and the sailor: all men whose behavior is almost animal-like—"is left to drown."[21] Some inflexible Moira, some inscrutable god, shifts things onto a negative axis, "the worst." The same force moves the sun in mockery of "superior" beings, while their lesser brothers continue calmly about their business. William Carlos Williams, in 1962, perceives the indifference as lying in a pathetically fallacious landscape, and his reading is equally metaphysical, à la Auden and Hamburger and aesthetic à la Maritain. It is spring when Icarus falls, and the "whole pageantry / of the year" is preening and buoyant: the edge of the sea is concentrated on itself, while, sweating in the sun that is melting the wax of his wings, "unsignificantly," far from the shore, there is indeed a thud and splash: Icarus drowning.[22]

It is above all the writers of continental Europe, however, who have worried at Bruegel's painting and its existential enigmas. In 1942–43 Erich Arendt, for example, announced, pace the Gospels, that "the blind shall not see": the world offers no miracles, and so the painting tells no lies, hence Bruegel's depiction of the fall of Icarus as unseen. A lifetime is contained in the farmer's plowing; the harmony that the painting celebrates lies in the woods and fields and sun and the daily round of men and women, and happiness is to be judged by the gold of the grain. But this same happiness disappears if we add the sweat of the brow: the earth, Arendt concludes, is turning while humanity eats.[23] The Polish writer Ernest Bryll goes beyond this fierce antimaterialist irony, concentrating on Daedalus: everyone writes of Icarus, he points out, but Daedalus too has reached his goal. True, the farmer never moves from the furrows and never raises his eyes, but Bruegel knows that it is the doing that matters, and not the open-mouthed gazing at those who fly. Daedalus might even have gone back to save his son.[24]

These observations remain on the first, ethical level at which the painting operates, that of *facere quod in se est*. In 1947, however, Stephan Hermlin noticed the body in the bushes,[25] and a series of German writers in the following decades dwell on the tragic details. In Marie Luise Kaschnitz's memory, for example, sunset becomes sunrise, changing the sense of the scene considerably. The painting should have shown the eternal, self-evident wisdom of proverbs, enshrining not "Truth," but only experience. No plow stops for the sake of a dying man: the show must go on, regardless of the grieving of the bereaved. Fair enough. But what the writer cannot tolerate is the fact that Bruegel's sun is smiling: "actually smiling: the splendor of the morning is in every corner—a victory of life which goes well beyond the wisdom of the proverbs," reiterating the secondary importance of Icarus's death. Life and death develop in parallel, Kaschnitz deduces: death for the single individual, life for the masses. But finally, death for all, universal extinction, the end of all things:

> Life goes on, then, not simply for the common man, but even for Icarus: fields are plowed, sheep are grazed, fish are caught. It makes no difference who dies, it is still the individual against the multitude, which has the will to live, and will live. The difference lies in annihilation: the total extinction which now, today, is there before our eyes with ungraspable imperturbability. Icarus is long gone: but so are the farmer, the shepherd, and the fisherman, the city and the ship: only the sun remains, and rises just the same: a situation which reflects neither the splendor of the legend nor the simple wisdom of rationalist proverbs.[26]

Is the idea of looming catastrophe—Apocalypse soon, if not now—a reasoned response to Bruegel's *Fall of Icarus*? It would certainly have seemed so in 1963, when this passage was published and the Cuban Missile Crisis had taken the world to the edge of disaster. Soon forgotten? Ulrich Berkes offered two prose passages on the painting, in 1976 and 1980.[27] The first is ostensibly a celebration of the morning sun, a D'Annunzio-like yearning for the sky and reaching for dizzying heights. The ephebe, he writes, has become an angel. Then his luck changes and he falls into the sea, unnoticed by the farmer, the fisherman, and the shepherd. He had aimed too high but obtained an unprecedented, privileged view of the world. In the second passage, however, Berkes's slant changes: why, he asks, does it have to be Icarus? Couldn't it be the son of the plowman? There he is, having a last, late afternoon swim, before returning home with horse and plow, to eat and then sleep, and perhaps dream of a ship sailing to distant shores.

This, of course, turns our Old Master perspective inside out and offers a revisitation: an escape from reality into the world of dreams. But death is always lurking in the background and emerges, legs kicking in the water and bare head visible in the bushes, in Gisbert Kranz's "Bruegel" from 1981. Daedalus? The "body" of the proverb? No: the only certainty is:

> Only this, surely:
> whether someone plows
> or flies—
> death,
> albeit unseen,
> is always there
> [Sicher nur dies:
> Ob einer pflügt
> oder fliegt—
> der Tod,
> auch ungesehen,
> ist immer dabei.][28]

✃∞✃

In Curnow's "The Fall of Icarus," we saw the present, the historical reality of the Second World War, interacting with myth. The poetry-history encounter now becomes unavoidable once more, and Bruegel's painting suddenly touches a raw nerve. In his *Short Stories* from 1945, Polish writer Jaroslaw Iwaskiewicz mentions the painting hanging in the Musée des Beaux Arts. Every time it appears before his eyes, he writes, he recalls a particular event. One fine June evening of 1942 or 1943, in German-occupied Warsaw, the narrator is standing at a tram stop; the trams are bursting at the seams, people hanging from every bar of metal. When a less-crowded vehicle comes by, he has lost the wish to go anywhere, preferring to stroll around the city, among his fellow-citizens. Suddenly, from the right, behind the red side of the tram, a boy appears, fifteen or sixteen years of age, immersed in the book he's reading, with another volume sticking out of his pocket. He is too engrossed to notice the crowd pushing and shoving him, and, never lifting his eyes from the page, suddenly finds himself on the tram line. At that moment, a car arrives at top speed; it brakes, its tires screeching on the asphalt; swerving, it comes to a halt. It is the Gestapo. The boy attempts to walk on, but two soldiers jump out from the back seat: one yells something at him, the other orders him into the car. The boy tries to explain himself, pointing at the book, and "in the last moment of his lost life" puts up a resistance. They ask for his papers, snatch them from his hands, then push him violently into the car, get in behind him, and shut the car door. The car drives off at speed towards the Gestapo headquarters.

The boy has disappeared in a flash, but the busy crowd sees nothing: the women continue debating the most comfortable tram to take, two men light a cigarette, the Mickiewicz monument stays where it is, the flowers give off their scent, and the birches wave in the breeze. "The disappearance of one man meant nothing to anyone. I was the only witness to the fact that Icarus had drowned." The protagonist remains at the tram stop, brooding over the event, wondering whether "Michael," as he has dubbed the boy, will ever return, and imagines his parents waiting at home for him. But in vain: the ways of occupying forces leave little room for hope. The boy had fallen into their clutches so foolishly. "The absurd cruelty of the abduction shook me to the core, and still today makes me tremble." Today, the narrator meditates:

> Those who fell in battle, those who knew why they were dying, possibly found consolation in the fact there was some sense in their death. But how many of them would have wanted to be like my Icarus, falling into the sea of oblivion for the absurdity of such a cruel cause?[29]

"Only a poet or painter saw that death and handed it down to posterity," writes Iwaszkiewicz of Bruegel's *Fall of Icarus*. In his version, the narrator has chained the myth to history, the painting to the present, chance to unflinching causality, the love of reading to Nazi brutality.

There can, perhaps, be no better comment on much of what this book is trying to say. History and literature, of course, recognize no bounds to their imagination. Stephan Hermlin, author of the 1947 poem "Landschaft mit dem Sturz des Ikarus" mentioned above, and of the "Ballade vom Gefährten Ikarus," from 1944, dedicated to the memory of his brother Alfred,[30] experienced firsthand the full force of twentieth-century German history. Born in Chemnitz in 1915 to a German Jewish industrialist father and an English mother, in 1931 he joined the Communist Youth Party and after Hitler's rise to power fought in undercover operations. In 1936 he emigrated to Egypt, then Palestine, then England. He fought in Spain with the Republicans, and during the Second World War, in France with the Resistance; in the same period he began publishing his poetry. In 1947 he settled in East Berlin, joining the Socialist Unity Party of the German Democratic Republic and becoming secretary of the Poetry Section of the Academy of Arts, and vice-president of PEN. It was Hermlin who discovered the poetess Sarah Kirsch and the poet and song-writer Wolf Biermann, publicly protesting in his name when he was stripped of his East German citizenship. He died in 1997, after the fall of the Berlin Wall.

Abendlicht is a poetic autobiography on his childhood and youth.[31] It begins with a scene on the English Channel, where it opens into the North Sea. From the air, Hermlin looks out to sea: the wing of a Spitfire juts out of the water, holding a dead man, his brother Alfred. Beside him, his colors; in his hands, the page of a calendar with the date June 22. It seems like a nightmare. Several chapters later, however, we learn that Alfred, some years younger than Stephan, had always wanted to be a pilot, and when war broke out, had managed to join the British Royal Air Force, despite being a native German. All Stephan can learn is that he died in action in the early months of 1943. His only personal effects are a letter, written but never sent. In it Alfred recounts that he had entered the war hoping that it would be the last, but had had a dream in which he found himself in some infinite space, among the fallen of all the nations, and realized he had died in vain.

Alfred Hermlin's is an "Icarian" fate, not unlike that of Valente de Bosis in the First World War, his last letter uncannily mirroring his brother's Lauro de Bosis's own *Storia della mia morte*. Much later, however, Stephan Hermlin dreams he is in the Alps, at sunset. As his plane descends, wooded hills open up before him, then a wide bay; far off, on the coast, a town; in the shadow, a farmer at his plow, and a shepherd with a stick; in the water, sailing ships, and the foot of someone drowning; on the horizon, a rayless setting sun. His dream is Bruegel's painting, relived in Hermlin's psyche: center-canvas, again his brother's death: "always, always, always."

But war produces infinite Icaruses, and the Battle of Britain, over the Channel and English countryside, repainted the *Fall of Icarus* thousands of times. It is also true that the war in the skies above Germany, with the bombing of entire cities, in some part determined the drift of postwar literature. This is the thesis propounded by writer W. G. Sebald, who became famous for *The Rings of Saturn* and *Austerlitz*. In his *Luftkrieg und Literatur*, Sebald maintains that German literature shrank from that war, barely speaking of it and thereby inflicting a wound which has still not healed: it repressed the "grey" reality which destroyed half of Germany, abnegating its responsibility towards historic and poetic truth.[32]

It is only recently that Icarus, celebrated earlier by Georg Heym and Gottfried Benn, and Bruegel, rediscovered by many after the war, has fully reemerged within the German psyche. The two poets discovered by Hermlin, Sarah Kirsch, and Wolf Biermann, return to the figure of the myth. For

Kirsch, in 1992, his flight prefigures her own across the Wall,[33] while Biermann, who in 1975 published a celebrated "Ballade vom preussischen Ikarus"[34] and in 1987 translated Auden's poem, concentrates on the Bruegel painting itself. No one in the picture observes the tragedy: one might take this, Biermann writes, as "culpable negligence," as it were; this is not the truth, however, for there is also a looking away which is blameless, and it is this that Bruegel sets out to show. The way in which "people we knew more closely" looked away from Auschwitz is another matter. But, argues Biermann, a "moral" reading of the painting is also possible. For the West, this would be that, unlike the plowmen, fishermen, and sailors, people who in the painting mind only their own business, we should try for a wider vision. For the East (what was then Eastern Europe and the Soviet Union), the moral would read: act like Bruegel's farmer, the fisherman, the shepherd in the picture: do your own work, cultivate your field, and never mind the grand flights of those who are out to improve the world, or the escapades of the famous, who only end up ruining the world.[35]

One set of ethics for the capitalist and materialistic West, and another for the ideologized communist East, therefore, in the Europe before the fall of the Berlin Wall: medieval moralizing, but with two versions: *facere quod in se est* depends on the context in which the *doing* takes place. While the prescription remains absolute, its enactment varies according to the political, historical, and cultural situation of the individual. Bruegel teaches both.

When Biermann returned to the painting in 1992,[36] the world had changed. East and West no longer existed, and the first Gulf War had broken out. Biermann now contemplates the painting with different questions in mind. He notices the dagger and the dead man in the bushes. Above all, he asks how the sun can stay below the horizon. The wax of Icarus's wings must have melted at midday: at the chilly altitude at which he was flying, only the midday sun could have had such an effect on the wax. But Icarus can't have been dropping for hours and hours, down to the sunset: the Earth's gravity would have intervened. By the Newtonian laws of gravitation, Icarus must have fallen at considerable speed. But even if we are reluctant to interrogate the Dutchman Bruegel, or Zeus's daughter, Athena, the goddess of wisdom, represented by the partridge, in terms of physics, why the son of Daedalus took so long to fall to his death remains a good question. The answer may be moral: the punishment, says the painter with his brush strokes, must be harsh. Punishment, revenge, and expiation: if the ethical flaw disturbs us, innocent Icarus has to be considered a proof of the goddess's overbearing power. Athena sacrifices a man so that Daedalus, killer of Perdix, can see with his own eyes the pain of his son's fall and death: the goddess's bullying arrogance (*Rechthaberei*) becomes the myth's highest justice (*Gerechtigkeit*).

A fascinating reading, in which poetry, *poietike*, plays with mythological and painterly data and whirls them in a totally Greek, utterly German turbine of logic, physics, ethics, and law, offering also an explanation of the sun and sunset, and the presence of the partridge. Biermann, however, does not stop here, but moves immediately on to the other *Fall of Icarus* attributed to Bruegel, in which Daedalus also appears, high in the air, still flying, but with his eyes fixed on his dying son, an attitude, he writes, "which I know well." It is the "Angelus Novus" by Paul Klee, which Walter Benjamin has described as the angel of universal history. "A whirlwind from Paradise urges it on in frightening progression. The Angel freezes, its face turned back towards the permanent catastrophe of our history."[37]

The analogies are indeed appealing, and urge us constantly towards new apocalyptic fantasies, like those which Berenger, Ionesco's "pedestrian of the air," describes to an astonished public after his flight to the "other" world.[38] But Daedalus is not flying down from heaven, and though no whirlwind is driving him on, he never turns back to save his son. The New Angel is transported by some superior and irresistible force. Daedalus, however, is a mere man, part animal, part angel: his is the tremendous freedom to decide. It is free will, rather than the storm of original sin, that drives him on. "Icarus' father flies over the sea to some safe shore. Coming from the hell of a Crete prison, he flies towards the saving hell of solitude."

Thus, when we learn from myth to spare the life of "the misanthropists grown guilty of, and refined in, revenge," we will have found some detachment: "we will not even need to stain ourselves with the blood of our torturers." Two friends of Biermann's, both German, are now imprisoned, alone, in an inhospitable Moscow, behind the Chilean Embassy, each the other's punishment. His "malicious heart" laughs at the idea. They must survive, of course: but this is the liar, the killer, the thief within us, as it was within Daedalus. Each of us is Daedalus the killer. The dagger and the dead head of the painting are a warning to *us*.

Through Bruegel's painting we have entered Klee's, his "Angelus Novus": from myth to interpretation, from philosophy to history. Yet history is not enough: the painting has to enter the imagination, the *poietike* of every individual. Each human being possesses it, because we all, like the many professional writers we have examined, can reflect upon Bruegel's painting and rewrite it.[39] According to Aristotle, history deals with the particular, and poetry with the universal. History recounts things as they have taken place, in sequence and, sometimes, according to cause and effect. Poetry, poetic mimesis, recounts them as they *could* be, viewed within the perspective of probability and necessity, grasping from without, in imitation, what is essentially within, human praxis. Poetry is then par excellence the "work of man," and thus necessarily measures itself in terms of the ethical project which aims at reconciling the individual good with the good of all.[40] This is what Biermann aims at with his moralizations before and after 1989. It is also the message entrusted by the Old Master, "never wrong" despite all his enigmas, to the *Fall of Icarus* in the Musée des Beaux Arts.

Night Flights 7

On December 17, 1903, the Wright brothers managed to raise a machine heavier than air a few yards above the ground. It was the first airplane in human history. In just one hundred years this machine has revolutionized and shrunk our world with a speed unprecedented in the evolution of humanity. Sailing, mythologically initiated by Jason and Ulysses, took thousands of years to develop the compass, measure longitude, and invent steamboats. For almost as long a time, the horse held out against the invention of the automobile. But in one short century, aviation moved from the first tentative experiment of the Wright brothers and their immediate successors to the planes that fought two world wars and countless minor, though equally bloody, conflicts; machines that fly faster than sound; jets that transport hundreds of passengers; rockets that launch satellites and inhabit space stations, shuttle people to the Moon, or travel for years toward other planets,[1] not least the space probe *Ulysses*, which in 1990 set off, as Dante puts it, *di retro al sol, nel mondo sanza gente*, "to the unpeopled world behind the sun."[2]

The old dream of flight had finally come true, enabling Apollinaire to write, in *Alcool*, a collection of poems published in 1913, that "made bird-like, this century rises into the air like Jesus . . . / The angels circle the handsome, circling figure / Icarus Enoch Elijah Apollonius of Tyana / Hover around the first aeroplane."[3] Eighty years later, the writer and pilot Daniele Del Giudice, pronounced decisively: "No, myths have nothing to do with it. Flight was inextricable from myth as long as it was not humanly feasible. After the invention of the aircraft, there remains only one thing in the world with which flight is really

167

connected, and that is childhood."[4] In this chapter I am concerned with the reality that turns into literature, flights that *are* writing: night flights, shadows that lift from the ground.

In fact, as we saw in the first two chapters, a borderland continued to exist for some time between myth and technology: Chagall, Matisse, and Picasso painted Icarus, while Breton, Brecht, Savinio, Gide, and Ayrton wrote about him; in 1968, Raymond Queneau based his burlesque, para-Pirandellian novel *Le vol d'Icare* on him, while in 1988 Christoph Ransmayr made him one of the protagonists of his *Last World*.[5] There was also a "heroic age" of flying, which in many respects continued up to the end of the 1930s and the Second World War, celebrating the near-mythical names of Blériot, Latham, Chávez, Baracca, the Red Baron, Lindbergh, De Pinedo, Balbo, and a host of others, down to the Battle of Britain.

The passion that gripped the Western imaginary was perhaps even stronger than the earlier myth of the sea and sailing.[6] William Faulkner, who began his writing career by publishing tales of pilots, and a novel, *Soldier's Pay*, about the homecoming of a First World War pilot, owned and flew his own plane. Ludwig Wittgenstein designed airplane engines in Berlin and Manchester before coming across the works of Russell, Frege, and Whitehead, which turned his interest toward logic and philosophy. Bertrand Russell at first thought him "mad," dubbing him "my German engineer." He recounts that Wittgenstein, wavering between philosophy and flying, went to see him in Cambridge at the end of his first term there, between 1911 and 1912, asking if Russell considered him a "complete idiot." "My dear fellow," Russell apparently replied, "I've no idea. But why do you ask?" "Because if I'm a complete idiot," Wittgenstein replied, "I'll become a pilot, otherwise I'll be a philosopher."[7]

While nowadays we may agree with Del Giudice that "pilots do not have feathered wings, they are not angels, much less heroes; they are child-adults, latent children," and no one knows "whether there is some special relationship between childhood and death,"[8] the history and literature of aviation most certainly presuppose both, especially death, or at least the likelihood of disaster. The "Airport" films could not have worked *without* potentially fatal error or engine failure, playing as they did on viewers' terror of what is after all such an unnatural activity, namely, flying. Such stories need disasters: an ordinary plane trundling between two points on the globe will only hit the headlines if it hits the ground.

The "poetry of aviation" begins, not incidentally, with a poem by Yeats written in 1918 and published the following year in *The Wild Swans at Coole*, "An Irish Airman Foresees his Death." The "airman" in question is Robert

Gregory, who died on the Italian front on January 23, 1918, and to whom Yeats dedicated the longer "In Memory of Major Robert Gregory." The Irish Gregory is nonetheless in the *British* Royal Air Force, fighting against the Austrians and Germans, defending the Italians and the British, which is why Yeats has him admit that "Those that I fight I do not hate, / those that I guard I do not love." The only homeland he cares for is Kiltartan Cross, Coole, in County Galway in the west of Ireland, where the lot of his "countrymen" will be in no way changed by this flight:

> I know that I shall meet my fate
> Somewhere among the clouds above;
> Those that I fight I do not hate,
> Those that I guard I do not love;
> My country is Kiltartan Cross,
> My countrymen Kiltartan's poor,
> No likely end could bring them loss
> Or leave them happier than before.
> Nor law, nor duty bade me fight,
> Nor public man, nor cheering crowds,
> A lonely impulse of delight
> Drove to this tumult in the clouds;
> I balanced all, brought all to mind,
> The years to come seemed waste of breath,
> A waste of breath the years behind
> In balance with this life, this death.[9]

About to leave for his last mission, in the poem Gregory predicts his own death, a Lauro de Bosis *avant la lettre*, but feels perfect equanimity at the idea: neither resignation nor indifference, but the wisdom of readiness that Hamlet feels at the end of his short life, an acceptance of that threshold between life and death that is the supreme moment of human wisdom. We hear Gregory's voice moving from the present and presumed future to the past, as if in an epitaph: as if, after his flight, he were already dead and looking back on what has happened. The "lonely impulse of delight" that urged him to fight is grander and purer than Icarus's *cupido caeli*, driving him to this particular air battle, at this crucial moment of his personal destiny, as confidently stated in the first line of the poem.

In the "fate" foreseen, he encounters the *limen*, the threshold, in a final, total reckoning. With life as mere survival now pointless, the pilot finds himself "in balance" with *this* life, and *this* death. Gregory's insight now seems to come from some other dimension: from the *readiness* and *balance* he has reached. Prescience, knowledge, awareness, and wisdom: but, as emphasized by the repeated deictics and possessives, the stress is on the *tode-ti*, the "this," the personal, the "my-now." Only here can the universal be perceived: as the inescapable journey from the "death" of the title toward the "fate" of the first line, to the "end" of the seventh, and again the "death" of the last.

Flight's peculiar quality is precisely this: death no longer appears as remote possibility but as "likely" end, quickly becoming "inevitable" at the least turbulence or air pocket. It presents death as we expect to be confronted with it in old age, or terminal illness, or, as in Gregory's case, in war. In flight we are all potential Ivan Ilychs and Robert Gregorys: our fellow passengers in the next seat become our closest friends, we take stock of our lives. When the cabin pressure drops, when a sudden gust of wind hits the propeller, or a billowing storm has us lurching in our seats, we become what we should always be: *morituri hinc et nunc*, people who are going to die here and now. The Irish poetess Eiléan Ní Chuilleanáin puts it with startling poignancy in her poem "Death and Engines," which begins with a vision of the iced-over rear of a burnt-out plane in a Paris airport, and moves to another flight where the metallic cold of the wings becomes "contagious" and the passengers find themselves in a corner "where / time and life like a knife and fork / cross." They will find themselves alone, she concludes, addressing them directly, "Accelerating down a blind / Alley, too late to stop / And know how light your death is; / You will be scattered like wreckage, / The pieces every one a different shape / Will spin and lodge in the hearts / Of all who love you."[10]

Nowadays, airline companies do their utmost to provide travelers with conditions as similar as possible to those on the ground, in a vision that is essentially vertical. The consciousness of today's passengers has dwelled upon ecstatic impulses of delight at the sight of seas, islands, deserts, rocks, glaciers, shining cities strewn like untidy galaxies, gleaming skies over white oceans of cloud, dark nights dotted by stars. It varies according to individual scope for astonishment. The passengers' happiness, based on the pilot's knowledge and our vast array of technological tools, lies in ignorance; their wisdom derives from abdication and resignation, or even boredom; their essence consists of becoming—and sensing themselves as—mere objects.

Morituri hinc et nunc: but in 1931, when Faulkner published *These 13*, he saw "all the old pilots, dead on the eleventh of November 1918," at the end of the First World War. They were alive in the faded sepia photographs of the time: lean and mean in their leather flying suits, which made them seem not quite human, "like some dim and threatful apotheosis of the race seen for an instant in the glare of a thunderclap and then forever gone." Now, however, they are all dead: in this "saxophone age of flying" they seem out of place, these men who had learned to respect "that whose respect in turn their hardness had commanded before there were welded center sections and parachutes and ships that would not spin." Dead, all of them, because they had then returned to normal life, and had fattened and grown complacent behind desks, and with wives and children in suburban houses, the mortgage almost paid, they who in war had lived and drunk as if there were no tomorrow.[11]

"All the Dead Pilots" is an epitaph, like Yeats's for Robert Gregory, or Simonides' for those who fell at Thermopylae. The death Faulkner writes of is that of the heroic age of flying, the "apotheosis of the race," the return to the normal that everyone craves, not least the pilot and passengers as they happily touch down: the "waste land" of modernity, senseless and empty, described only a short time previously by T. S. Eliot,[12] but also the "instant between dark and dark," the pilots' discovery that "being dead was not as quiet as they had heard it would be." It is the death of an era and of a generation, the sense of history, but also recognition of what will always exist: the fact of dying.

◌◦◌

As a "novelist of aviation," Faulkner is a failure; with the exception of the later novel *Pylon*,[13] his narratives are never about the flight itself, but what comes before or after. With the partial exception of the Futurists, this is common to the literature of the period, and lasted a surprisingly long time— as if writing could not grasp the opportunities that real flight had to offer. Daniele Del Giudice is right in pointing out that

> an airplane is not like a ship, where the moral laws of the mainland are transferred to a more restricted autonomous domain and tested to breaking point, an airplane retains nothing of land and home: in a ship people sleep, relax, plot, enjoy lengthy hours of idleness, endure stifling delays in ports; in an airplane there is no space for humdrum existence, and the only valid rules are the operational rules of the air. Mistakes are committed, but these are almost invariably of a technical, and scarcely ever of a moral, nature. The human spirit needs time and space to uncover its inner darkness, to display its ignominy and depravity, and on a plane there is too little of both time and space; in other words, while airborne, human beings are temporarily deprived of their own evil, reduced to bewildered silence in the face of procedural

routine. In flight, even those who make every effort to bring out the worst in themselves find themselves implacably condemned to a certain nobility of spirit.[14]

All very true, at least until September 11, 2001, when terrorist groups hijacked four planes flying over the United States, flying two of them into the towers of the World Trade Center in New York City, and one into a wing of the Pentagon in Washington, D.C.; the fourth, possibly aimed at the White House or the Capitol, crashed in Pennsylvania apparently as a result of passengers' attempts to disarm the hijackers. I shall be returning to this in my next chapter. For the moment I would just like to point out that, although aviation has had to face a disaster of such magnitude in its short lifetime (less than a century), produced by a religion and ideology warped in reaction to centuries of Western dominion, and manifesting here a hatred and evil that touch on the absolute, to my knowledge no writer has yet tried to engage imaginatively with the tragedy as it unfolded in midair.[15] Even before 9/11, however, literature had basically ignored the new world of flight, while sailing, from the *Odyssey* onward, had always caught its fancy. The first to realize its cognitive, cultural, and social implications was, as Del Giudice points out, the architect Le Corbusier.[16]

The single, great exception from the first half of the twentieth century is Antoine de Saint-Exupéry. His whole life, death, and writing are bound up with flight, which in his hands becomes existential, dramatic, literary, ethical, political, and metaphysical. In his novel *Courrier Sud*, which appeared in 1928, narration itself seems transformed, and right from the first page, with its two beginnings, separated in time and space, and two spaces: Toulouse and the Sahara.

> "By radio. Six ten. From Toulouse for stopovers: France–South America mail delivery departs Toulouse five forty-five stop."
> A sky as pure as water bathed the stars and revealed them. Then there was night. The Sahara spread out, dune after dune beneath the moon.[17]

This is a startling *incipit*, exhibiting wireless telegraphy—a modern means of communication between the far corners of the earth—and the ancient sight of the desert under the stars and bathed by moonlight, in which the night reigns unchallenged. An extreme voice and vision, bursting into the narrative as the voice of God and the long journey of Exodus once did, but now on a totally human plane.

Courrier Sud is based on the author's personal experience on the Toulouse-

Dakar mail route for the Latécoère Company and is one of the first works of literature organized around the accelerated time and potentially ubiquitous space of aviation. The protagonist, Jacques Bernis, recounts his memories of near-mortal combat with the elements, his sense of oneness with the world as his plane is caught in a near-fatal whirlwind, and his recollections of transcendent dawns and sunsets. Bernis's co-narrator, however—his copilot, as it were—draws on different, specular, experience, despite their shared childhood and youth. After an emergency landing, Bernis writes to him that in Paris he had found the "sense of things," namely, the Geneviève both had been in love with since their childhood. She had married someone else, experienced the tragic death of her only child, and had turned to Bernis for comfort. The adolescent dream of love proves impossible: on the drive out of Paris to fulfill their dream, they stop at the first hotel they find, only to realize that there is something "sick" in their relationship. Geneviève refuses to make love with Jacques. He returns to Paris and, like Joseph K. in Prague Cathedral, overhears a sermon in Notre Dame that he finds full of words but empty of faith: a "perfectly desperate cry." He attempts more bodily satisfactions, but the experience with a prostitute is equally empty.

Geneviève returns to Paris but dies soon after; Bernis returns to his courier work between France, Spain, and Africa, still on the run from himself, his childhood, and his home. In a mission beyond Casablanca and some small French fortress, the "sad archangel," the man-plane, disappears in the desert. The account of his last exploit is shattered as if by the light of a prism: radio communications, flashbacks, sensations, imaginings, a heart-warming encounter with a sergeant in the fortress, flight paths, air loops, winds, altitudes, sand. Then silence. Bernis has been claimed by destiny and nothingness.

It is the narrator himself who sets out to find his vanished friend, showing us the latter's desperate obsession, need, and love for life, which, however, he had never understood, never knowing what Bernis really needed, never grasping the mystery that he intuitively sensed behind all things. As the narrator one day confesses, "It seemed to me that with an effort, I would understand, finally know the secret and make it my own. And here I am, leaving, troubled by the presence of a friend which I have never been able to bring to light."[18] Having observed the world *from above*, Bernis has not understood it. His airplane experience has led him to bitter detachment, a resentment toward everything he is unable to grasp. His flight does not discover life, and the moment of fellow-feeling toward the sergeant has been too short. His search for what is human, his childhood, and love has produced neither ecstasy nor empathy, merely an unfathomable solitude, and absence of all that was real, concrete, and at hand. He has sensed the *philia* linking humanity and things, without succeeding in bringing it to light.

The book ends as it began, at night, with the voiceless voice coolly communicating the bare facts of his location: "From Saint-Louis of Senegal to Toulouse: France-America found east Timeris stop. Enemy action in vicinity stop. Pilot killed airplane destroyed mail intact stop. Continuing to Dakar."[19] Courier to the South: all the rest—the harrowing death of a child, nostalgia for lost childhood, love, and the desperation of a man and woman—count for nothing. They are simply a parenthesis within the scheme of things: individual destiny has not found its *kairos*, has experienced neither readiness nor balance: it merely chanced to happen.

∽∘∾

Saint-Exupéry, however, had learned a number of things from *Courrier Sud* and his Latécoère experience, from practicality and philosophy to ethics and literature. For the sake of clarity and convenience, I shall simply list them. First of all: flying is no game, "but something else, something inexplicable, a kind of warfare."[20] Second: the fear of crashing into the ground is not "hateful" but part of "a new, indefinable intelligence." It may happen to the pilot, in these circumstances, to feel at one with the fields and the sun, and "all the fullness" of the day's sparkling tranquility "built solidly like a house" in which he feels totally at home.[21] Third: he should never let the clouds close beneath him, but should dive through them at the right moment, through the last hole, "even if it means flying at an altitude of fifty meters." "Navigating by the compass in a sea of clouds over Spain is all very well, it is very dashing," he had been told, "but you want to remember that below the sea of clouds lies eternity."[22] Fourth: ideas are not tennis balls or daily currency—"you can't play at thinking," as Pirandello does in his plays.[23] Fifth: if anything, the model should be Ibsen, who tried to create "not a new lottery game, but nourishment," and whose works "are played out on the human plane" of the inner life.[24] Sixth: staging a metaphysical problem, and creating "a Russian salad of the various meanings of the word 'truth'" is a trick: not simply a literary question but a "moral problem."[25] Seven: "only perpetual discipline can educate the appropriateness of thinking, the most precious thing we possess."[26] Eight: however hard the inner life is to express, it is the only thing of any importance to him, since what he writes is the "scrupulous and pondered result" of what he thinks and sees. Ninth: only by finding himself in the quietness of his room or of some *bistrot* can he look himself in the eye and "avoid all literary formulae and tricks" in his attempt at self-expression.[27] Tenth and last: learning to write means above all learning to see: not taking an object and trying to embellish it, but deciding how to describe an impression. "If the objects are created from a reaction they produce in you, they have been properly, profoundly described."[28]

The similarity between points one and four hardly needs underlining: flying is not a game; you can't play at thinking. The same goes for points five and eight, Ibsen and the inner life, and Saint-Exupéry's own stand on the subject. The "new intelligence" born of fear, and the practical advice to avoid flying by the compass above the clouds, based on aviation *praxis* (second and third) are reflected in the concern for rigor of thought and educating the eye (seven and ten). While the first three concern flight praxis, the last seven outline an ethics of thinking and writing. Flying produces a new awareness: in writing, a new way of seeing. There can be no tricks in metaphysics, and there should be none in literature (sixth and ninth). Above all, flight leads to an in-depth understanding of things, enabling us to rediscover their fresh and essential dimension, making us feel at home within them.

In *Figaro littéraire* of May 27, 1939, Saint-Exupéry states that as far as he is concerned, flying and writing are one and the same thing.[29] There is no difference between praxis and poetics, ethics and metaphysics: what counts is action. Flight inculcates discipline, rigor, and precision; it leads to recognition of self and the world; it teaches us to "search for the man,"[30] to observe him, love him, and cultivate him as a gardener would. This is the self-image offered by Saint-Exupéry's next protagonist, Rivière, in *Night Flight*, who sees his work like a gardener's on a lawn: "the simple weight of his hand pushes the primitive forest back into the earth, which eternally prepares it."[31] Saint-Exupéry himself ponders the gardener's position on a night train from Russia to Poland among a group of Polish miners sent back to their home country, when he catches sight of a lovely child asleep between its parents, and imagines he is Mozart as a child: "When by mutation a new rose is born in a garden, all the gardeners rejoice. They isolate the rose, tend it, foster it. But there is no gardener for men. This little Mozart will be shaped like the rest by the common stamping machine. This little Mozart will live shoddy nights in the stench of night dives. This little Mozart is condemned."[32] The gardener supreme will be the Little Prince, perhaps born on this same train, who will appear to the pilot in his broken-down plane in the desert.[33] From this point on, Saint-Exupéry's literary work was itself one long act of "cultivation."

For a considerable time this meant digging with a heavy spade, through night and war: a painful weeding out of actions and a gradual pruning of the page. The results are evident in *Night Flight*, his second novel, after moving to

South America to work for Aéropostale. It is a swift, lean, and steely nerved novel that has pared down the minor excesses of *Courrier Sud*. It is centered on the night flights of air couriers connecting Patagonia, Chile, and Paraguay with Buenos Aires, and Buenos Aires with Europe (via Dakar in Africa): in other words, an almost abstract, rectilinear geography drawn by radio links and flight paths, in parallel to the human, "thing-centered," and internal geography that the pilots fly over or imagine, above or below the clouds—a story that will become history through the destinies and souls of the human beings that people it.

The central figure is Rivière, founder and staunch defender of the dangerous but time-saving night flights. Rivière runs the airport at Buenos Aires, which includes all the pilots on the ground or in the air, the wireless operators, mechanics, and company inspectors. Other protagonists include the pilots themselves, particularly Fabien, the Patagonia courier, Pellerin, the Chile courier, and Fabien's young wife. Overseeing them all is the night, the backdrop, unity of time and action, and the novel's basic theme, as Saint-Exupéry himself stated, "in its most intimate meaning."[34] The novel opens as night falls, with a passage as enthralling in its lyricism as one of the Alcman fragments quoted in my fourth chapter:

> Already, beneath him, through the golden evening, the shadowed hills had dug their furrows, and the plains grew luminous with long-enduring light. For in these lands the ground gives off this golden glow persistently, just as, even when winter goes, the whiteness of the snow persists.
>
> Fabien, the pilot bringing the Patagonia air mail from the far south to Buenos Aires, could mark night coming on by certain signs that called to mind the waters of a harbor—a calm expanse beneath, faintly rippled by the lazy clouds—and he seemed to be entering a vast anchorage, an immensity of blessedness . . .
>
> But night was rising like a tawny smoke and already the valleys were brimming over with it. No longer were they distinguishable from the plains. The villages were lighting up, constellations that greeted each other across the dusk. And, at a touch of his finger, his flying lights flashed back a greeting to them. The earth grew spangled with light signals as each house lit its star, searching the vastness of the night as a lighthouse sweeps the sea. Now every place that sheltered human life was sparkling.[35]

Fabien discovers that men can be revealed by darkness. Caught up in the hurricane, he perceives his own destiny and searches desperately for dawn.

Pellerin, the Chile courier, also journeys by night: crossing the Andes, he discovers in their perfect peace the anger of stone and snow, as if the peaks and crests had sharpened into blades against him, the white powder a floating veil ready to shroud him, the mountains suddenly ricocheting round the airplane in a "miracle" that nonetheless spells disaster; having crossed paths with the phantom, however, he lands safely in Buenos Aires. The courier for Europe is already waiting, ready to depart. The flight for Asunción lands later, descending through the night from Paraguay "as though from a marvelous garden of flowers," skirting the cyclone.

Taking place amid all this is the narrative action of *Night Flight*: the devastating hurricane which Fabien experiences, Rivière's struggle with himself, his men, and Fabien's wife. The plot has a plane's rhythms and speed: an hour's reading with no respite, a continual alternating of sky and earth, and the growing solitude of Fabien and Rivière: Fabien, slowly sucked into the hurricane with his wireless operator; Rivière, exhausted and ill, surrounded by people with leanings toward weakness and happiness, beset by doubt and temptation.

While it is night itself that takes hold of Fabien—playing its hand of the unforeseen, always possible, and ultimately inevitable, destiny—Rivière represents the will that makes that destiny more probable. Asking pilots to make night flights in the 1930s meant exposing them to risks nonexistent nowadays. How *right* is it, the narrative seems to ask, to give such orders, subordinating all human love and compassion to duty, and sacrificing people's lives to progress or economic and political expediency? This is the sort of night Rivière is struggling with, seemingly mistaking a Kantian hypothetical imperative, which considers an action as good with regard to its possible aim, for a categorical imperative, ordering an action which is good in itself, and for itself objectively necessary. Rivière's aim is to replace a *problematically* practical principle, regarding ability, technical imperatives, or rules (in this case, those of aviation and the postal service), with an *apodictically* practical principle, namely, the laws of morality *tout court*.

Central to this is his torment and failure to respond, in word or action, to Madame Fabien, who first phones then comes to his office for news of her husband, whom Rivière knows to be already dead. Two short, painful scenes are narrated with a steel stylus. At the end of the first scene, Saint-Exupéry is explicit:

> He had reached a point where not the problem of a small personal grief but the very will to act was in itself an issue. Not so much Fabien's wife as another

theory of life confronted Rivière now. Hearing that timid voice, he could but pity its infinite distress—and know it for an enemy! For action and *individual happiness* have no truck with each other; they are eternally *at war*.[36]

Madame Fabien represents the hypothetical imperative that considers the action good insofar as its aim is *real*: the assertively practical principle of prudence, the telos of which is happiness. Rivière fully recognizes the logic of this, but sets against it his own version of the truth, at the same time deeming it "inhuman and unutterable." His concept is centered on duty and the construction of something lasting, even if this means sacrificing the individual: like a temple of the Incas to the Sun God, erected high on a mountain at the cost of human lives by a chief who, while perhaps feeling little pity for men's suffering, felt compassion for their death: "not for his personal death, but pity for his race, doomed to be blotted out beneath a sea of sand."[37] Rivière is driven neither by individual glory, the heroic ideal dominating the Western imaginary from ancient Greece onward, nor by the Nietzschean and D'Annunzian idea of a Superman, but simply by his sense of the frailty of *homo sapiens*.

In his famous preface to the first edition of *Vol de nuit* in 1931, André Gide wrote that its paradoxical truth lay in demonstrating how "human happiness lies not in freedom, but in his acceptance of duty."[38] Rivière, Saint-Exupéry's Prometheus, declares, *je n'aime pas l'homme, j'aime ce qui le dévore*: it's not man I love, but what devours him. Here, Gide concluded, lay the source of all heroism. He was forgetting, however, that happiness is the goal of all human action, and virtuous and pleasant *life* and *activity* for the virtuous man: and that, above all, "in practice we must start from *the good of each*, if *universal* good is to become *the good of each*."[39]

Saint-Exupéry, on the other hand, is quite clear on this score, and constructs his novel as if it were a Greek tragedy, a conflict between action and individual happiness; he constantly presents Rivière contemplating the night, the fundamental questions always on his lips. For his part Rivière has no idea whether he is being fair or unfair; he knows that if he is strict, accidents diminish, and senses that it is not the individual who is responsible, but some dark force that cannot be overcome "without getting at everyone." When events take over, this reveals itself as the same force that rips up virgin forests, welling up around the great works of men like the lianas, the woody vines that suffocate the temples in the jungle. Rivière cannot tell whether what he does is good or not; he is aware of not knowing the exact value of human life, justice, or pain: "No, I cannot say if I am doing right or what precise value should be set on a human life, or suffering, or justice. How should I know the value of a man's joys? Or of a trembling hand? Of kindness, or pity?"[40]

In spite of this not knowing, Rivière is still able to choose, and since he can do nothing for Fabien, decides to continue with the night flights, ordering the European courier to depart as if nothing had happened. It is a choice conforming to the hypothetical imperative, a good action with regard to a possible aim, matured through inner struggle and dictated by a higher goal: "to endure, to create, to barter this vile body."[41] Rivière aspires to immortality, transferring onto the level of action the behavior Aristotle reserved for contemplation, the supreme earthly happiness: "as far as man can, he should behave as if immortal (*athanatizein*) and do his utmost to live according to the noblest attributes within him."[42]

Rivière "wins," but his is a heavy victory, as the last line of the novel declares: "Rivière the Great, Rivière the Conqueror, bearing his heavy load of victory." The narrator warns of this as he concludes: "Victory, defeat—the words were meaningless. Life lies behind these symbols and life is ever bringing new symbols into being. One nation is weakened by a victory, another finds new forces in defeat. Rivière's defeat conveyed perhaps a lesson which would speed the coming of final victory. The work in progress was all that mattered."[43]

✧

Saint-Exupéry has succeeded in turning ethics and aeronautics into tragic poetry. Cinema, in the person of Clarence Brown, understood the combination well: he directed a heroic American film, *Night Flight*, in 1933 (starring John and Lionel Barrymore, Clark Gable, Robert Montgomery, and Myrna Loy), which turned Saint-Exupéry into a household name. Martin Heidegger understood it even better, proclaiming the author "the greatest existentialist of the century."[44] Most clear-sighted of all was Luigi Dallapiccola, who between 1937 and 1939 converted *Vol de nuit* into a one-hour, six-scene musical *Atto*, premièred in 1940 at the Florence music festival Maggio Musicale Fiorentino.

Dallapiccola caught perfectly both the technique and the message of the novel. To solve the theatrical problem of the unity of place, he used the wireless operator (the tenor) as narrator—the "historian of Greek tragedy," as he himself put it—pronouncing Fabien's thought processes during the storm. To lend urgency, Rivière's bass-baritone voice, Pellerin's tenor, Inspector

Robineau's bass, the soprano of the Inner Voice who proclaims "Love, joy in the world, love joy!" and the voices of the wireless operator and other employees are all superimposed in the first three scenes. In the fourth, the exchange between Madame Fabien and Rivière is presented as a fragmented dialogue between bass-baritone and soprano, ending with the desperate, suspended notes of the woman's voice, "Signor Rivière! M'ascoltate! Signor Rivière! Fate, dite qualche cosa!" (Signor Rivière, listen to me! Do, say something!), and her last, piercing sob: "Signor Rivière . . . eravamo sposi . . . da sei settimane . . . appena" (Signor Rivière . . . we had been married . . . only . . . six weeks).[45]

This is the central scene of the *Atto*. Having talked the idea through with Saint-Exupéry and received his full approval, Dallapiccola admitted quite openly that their ethical concepts diverged: "Unaware of it at the time, and for the first time in my life, in *Volo di notte* I made my choice: preferring the sufferer to the victor."[46] Significantly, for the scene between Rivière and Madame Fabien he uses the music composed for the third of the *Tre Laudi* (*Madonna Sancta Maria / Recevi chi vol tornare*, "Holy Madonna, receive those who wish to return"), and for Pellerin's landing the theme of the second, *Ciascun s'allegri* ("Let all rejoice"), which there symbolizes "joy at the birth of Christ." Dallapiccola has taken on board the basic conflict underlying Saint-Exupéry's work and absorbed it into what he defines as the basic idea behind all of his own work: "man's struggle against something which is greater than himself" (here, Rivière's struggle concerning night flights and Fabien's struggle with the elements).[47] He alludes to a resolution of this conflict within a Christian perspective, thereby almost prefiguring Saint-Exupéry's own Christianity.

But Dallapiccola has done more than this. In one intensely dramatic *Atto* he has underlined that technological conquests do no damage to poetry.[48] Above all, he has given voice to light, retrieving the other pole of the original *Vol de nuit*, framing the whole *Atto* with the opening theme of the first *Lauda*, "Altissima luce," which accompanies the fall of the plane and Fabien's death,[49] while the "Stella marina" of the *Lauda* is heard again in the fifth scene of *Volo di notte* when the tenor voice of the wireless operator, after the soprano's drawn-out sob, sings Fabien's: *Scorgo le stelle*—I glimpse the stars.[50]

For we must not forget that the "shoreless" night that engulfs Fabien in the hurricane then dissolves into blinding light. With fuel for one hour and forty minutes, the pilot will at some point have to descend into the black density. And this is exactly what happens: sucked into the darkness, buffeted by waves of rebellious matter, unable to distinguish sky from land, plunged into a leveling, undistinguishing shadow, "an original shadow, similar to the one from which worlds emerged," Fabien turns to the gyroscopic horizon, reads the five-hundred-meter altitude and the level of the hills, decides to chance a landing, launches the only flare he has on board—and discovers that the sea lies below him. He is lost. His numb hands gripping the wheel, "he might keep up the struggle, chance his luck; no destiny attacks us from the outside. But within him, man bears his fate and there comes a moment when he knows himself vulnerable; and then, as in a vertigo, blunder upon blunder lures him."[51]

These words, cited also in chapter 2, mark the novel's point of no return: the moment when error becomes vertigo. Stars are shining above Fabien's head, through a break in the storm: "like a fatal lure within a deep abyss." He knows full well that this is a trap, but his thirst for light is such that he decides to increase the altitude. He spirals upward through the clouds of shadow, and finds himself dazed by blinding light: moon, stars, and clouds reflect each other in a "milky stream of light," a radiant galaxy. Total calm surrounds him, the hurricane now silent, offering to the stars above "a face of crystal snow." Fabien believes he has discovered an unknown part of the heavens, "in an unknown and secret corner of the sky . . . as in a harbour of the Happy Isles," some strange limbo that makes his clothing, hands, and the plane wings glow. "Too beautiful," he exclaims, as he wanders "amid the far-flung treasures of the stars," in a world in which he and his companion are the only live beings. "Like plunderers of fabled cities they seemed, immured in treasure vaults whence there is no escape. Amongst these frozen jewels they were wandering, rich beyond all dreams, but doomed." With half an hour's fuel left, Fabien speaks for the last time: he moves over the splendor of the sea of clouds, but below, as all pilots know, as he himself knows, is eternity. For half an hour he grips the wheel and carries out his last desperate delivery: "from one star to the other, he trafficked this useless wealth, soon to be his no more."[52]

On his flight from Paraguay, Pellerin had encountered a veiled and unknown face, which seemed to grow out of live rock: the *unheimliches*, the uncanny phantom that embodies our fear of solitude. Fabien, on the other hand, flies into the splendor of the stars, in an ocean of light, toward the "Happy Isles" and a "strange limbo." His ascent is sensed as a blessing—a common experience among pilots, apparently—transforming into pure light clothing, hands, and wings that are no longer simply the plane's, but "his wings."

Does the text allow the possibility that Fabien is on the point of *trasumanar*, as Dante would put it:[53] "transhumanising" into an angel, and that this is Paradise or an Elysium? Fabien and his wireless operator smile as they

wander through the stars and the river of light. But the pilot knows that
he is mad, that they are doomed. In comparing the men to thieves who are
infinitely rich but trapped in a cave of treasure, the narratorial comment is
clear. "Too beautiful," Fabien exclaims for the last time, now full of "lust for
light." This excess of beauty is the last, mysterious, blinding passage linking
life and the final blackness of death: a transcendental announcement that
is both ecstasy and, again in Dante's word,[54] "oltraggio," an outrage, excess,
and disproportion, over the top.

Two pages later, as Rivière, safe on the ground, muses over Fabien's last
communication—simply, "half an hour"—reality inevitably breaks through,
expressed by Saint-Exupéry in a delicate, hesitant lyricism. Rivière's hopes
have gone, and he imagines the bodies being found in the plump furrows
of soft grass that springs up after a hurricane: two sleeping children. The
enigmatic relation between the pilot's "milky stream of light," with his radiant
wings, and the image in Rivière's mind is the same as that between the
sunlight and the dead head in Bruegel's *Fall of Icarus*.

Rivière thinks of Fabien's wife and of Fabien's hand on the controls, "a
hand that brought miracles to pass." Fabien is still drifting "in the vast
splendour of a sea of clouds"; beneath him lies eternity. It is unclear whether
these and the following words, which take up the theme of the treasure like
a musical leitmotiv, are part of Rivière's meditation, narratorial comment, or
the continuation and conclusion of Fabien's own story. All three seem linked
within a composite human consciousness. At the beginning of the following
paragraph, Rivière's thought process seems to dominate for a second, while
he thinks some radio station is still connected with the pilot. Then the music
joins all three, and that of the reader: "The only link between him and the
world was a wave of music, a minor modulation. Not a lament, no cry, yet
purest of sounds that ever spoke despair."[55] It was this modulation in a minor
key that Dallapiccola was to recreate shortly afterward. Night flights—real
ones, taking place not in prose but in the air—were becoming tragedy, poetry,
and music, just as the falls of Icarus had been for millennia.

✄∘✄

Where could Saint-Exupéry go after a novel as perfect as *Vol de nuit*? His
work for Aéropostale and civil aviation had come to an end. Time to turn
to earth and the people encountered during his flights round the world,
to translate his pilot's knowledge into a form to be shared with others.
His following book, *Terre des hommes*, a version of which was published in

America in 1938 as *Wind, Sand and Stars*, was a reworking of a series of articles and correspondence around a common theme. Its starting points, naturally, are Saint-Exupéry's airplanes and aviation companions, Mermoz and Guillaumet. The latter is compared to an elderly gardener, who muses on his deathbed upon digging and turning over the earth: digging, he insists, makes a man free. And besides, who will prune his trees after he is gone? He is leaving behind an uncultivated garden, an uncultivated planet, the narrator comments: "bound by ties of love" to all the gardens and trees on earth, he is "a generous man, a prodigal man, a nobleman," courageous like Guillaumet, "battling against death in the name of his Creation."[56]

It is with this Creation that *Terre des homes* deals. The airplane has changed the world but cannot be considered an end in itself: it is simply a tool, like the plow. All manmade machines are tools in his service, something that humanity tends to overlook. The speed of invention in the modern age outruns the user. For the soldier conquering colonies, victory is an end in itself; but the real aim is the human community to be established there. We have built factories, railways, and oil rigs, and done so with the consciousness of soldiers. The colonization stage comes next: "we must . . . make this house habitable which is still without character." First we build, then we inhabit: and we have yet to humanize the industrial revolution, technology and machines. Meanwhile, it is evolving, perfecting and simplifying itself. Engineers, planners, and designers work for generations to turn the first machine into a natural, organic, aesthetic object; to give a hull or fuselage "the elementary purity of the curve of a human breast or shoulder," and balance a wing to the point where it passes unnoticed and seems "a form flawless in its perfection, completely disengaged from its matrix, a sort of spontaneous whole, its parts mysteriously fused together and resembling in their unity a poem."[57] We have only to look at the wings of a plane of the 1930s and compare them to a Concorde or spaceship to follow Saint-Exupéry's thinking.

When the engine fulfils its function, that of turning, it becomes like a human heart: its beating is taken for granted. A machine becomes simply that: a tool for rediscovering our nature, as is the concern of the gardener, the sailor, or the poet. Cultivating, crossing seas, writing poetry: earth, water, and writing. To this the pilot adds air, but the operation is the same: to create. A hydroplane is about to take off; the pilot feels the pull of the water, then the lift of speed and power, and feels, in this weight of matter, the development of "a maturity that is about to make flight possible"; laying his hands on the panel, he receives into the palm of his hand the full power of the engine, "a gift." At the right, "ripe" moment—the *kairos*—"in a gesture gentler than the culling of a flower," like God on the second day of Creation, the pilot "severs the ship from the water and establishes it in the air."[58]

Writing such as this, simultaneously concrete and meditative, contains something of the Gospel parables; it unites poetry with philosophy, technology with nature: matter, form, potency, act, perfection, ripeness, and gift; earth, water, and air. This is the language of *Wind, Sand and Stars*: a *sermo humilis* and highly refined discourse where, according to the Eliot of the *Four Quartets*, "every word is at home, / Taking its place to support the others, / The word neither diffident nor ostentatious, / An easy commerce of the old and new, / The common word without vulgarity, / The formal word precise but not pedantic."[59]

For Saint-Exupéry, this is a language that reveals the universal, a language able to "grasp the essential reality of mankind." Truth is that which "clarifies," simplifying the world, not "that which is demonstrable," not that which creates chaos. Beyond ideology and fanaticism, "truth is the language that expresses universality." Newton did not "discover" a previously unknown law: what he did was to carry out a *creative* act, establishing a human language that could simultaneously describe an apple falling in a field and the sunrise.[60] The lands, deserts, cities, and men that Saint-Exupéry was able to "discover" by means of the airplane are all individual: expanses beyond the horizons of Patagonia, the rocky peaks of the Andes, the bare, starry Sahara, Spain during the Civil War, postrevolutionary Russia, Polish children like little Mozarts: all worldly details, and of a single human earth. Saint-Exupéry has founded a language upon it, able to describe both the fire from the wing of the crashed plane in the desert and an old, dead Provençal peasant woman. He alternates narration with meditation, an awareness of difference with that of brotherhood: he concentrates on the human. Although tormented by the idea of a doomed Mozart, he still ended *Wind, Sand and Stars* with another reference to Genesis, the Creation he has modeled himself on: "Only the Spirit, if it breathes upon the clay, can create Man."[61] The whole of Saint-Exupéry's work can perhaps be interpreted in the light of the Nicodemus episode in the Gospel, when Jesus, rewriting Genesis, states:

> Except a man be born again from above, he cannot see the kingdom of God. . . . Except a man be born of water and of the Spirit, he cannot enter into the kingdom of God. That which is born of the flesh is flesh; and that which is born of the Spirit is spirit. Marvel not that I said unto thee, Ye must be born again from above. The wind bloweth where it listeth, and thou hearest the sound thereof, but cannot tell whence it cometh; so is every one that is born of the Spirit.[62]

Saint-Exupéry sees and dreams of a kingdom of God on earth and his observing is an attempt to be born again of the Spirit.

᠁ᢀᡃ

Saint-Exupéry never wanted to be a Joseph Conrad. In a chapter entitled "The Elements" in *Wind, Sand and Stars*, he maintains that in *Typhoon* Conrad only touches on the external terrors of the hurricane, concentrating on the human and social drama on board when the storm breaks. The pilot, on the other hand, Saint-Exupéry insists, is powerless to transmit his experience; while it is being lived through, the tension and drama are all concentrated on the instrument panel and on trying to force through the hurricane into survival. In his account of a Patagonia flight and the cyclone he flew into, he personalizes the Conrad of *Typhoon*. What he is forced to take on single-handed is the Peak of Salamanca, as threatening as the Peak of Tupungato for Pellerin in *Night Flight*: an indescribable struggle with an alien world, like Jacob's with the angel. He succeeds in communicating the experience not through horror but by presenting a checklist of his technical actions, mistakes, physical sensations, impressions, and a few brief notes on the landscape: "The sea was white and it was green—white with the whiteness of crushed sugar and green in puddles the color of emeralds."[63] He may have come away "with very little booty indeed,"[64] but makes himself perfectly clear in communicating to us the full force of the following: "Hanging on with all the power in my engines, face to the coast, face to that wind where each gap in the teeth of the range sent forth a stream of air like a long reptile, I felt as if I were climbing to the tip of a monstrous whip that was cracking over the sea."[65] The pilot's nerves, the plane, and the natural elements are synchronized and coordinated into a central nervous system: writing.

Saint-Exupéry's dual battle is with expression on the one hand, and the individual on the other. But his worst trial was yet to come: 1940, and the French defeat at the hands, rifles, and tanks of the German army. Saint-Exupéry made it his business to be in the center of things, enlisting in a reconnaissance squad. Demobilized after France's armistice with Hitler, he was soon back in America, where in 1942 he published *Flight to Arras*, in French *Pilote de guerre*. This is a bird's-eye view of war: rows of tanks ready to attack, carcasses of abandoned cars, the exodus of thousands of refugees— all the disarray, disorientation, and defeat of a nation. In the general ruin, creation turns to a more elemental question: how humanity defines itself as such, through love; self-sacrifice; civilization; the sense of belonging to a homeland, a history, and a culture; equality; and freedom. This is not bad rhetoric offered by *Pilote de guerre*, but a disabusing of illusion and an acceptance of things, a painful humanism *in extremis*, with the awareness that true freedom is that of the tree that grows "in the field of energy of its seed."[66] "I believe in the primacy of Man above the individual and of the universal above the particular," Saint-Exupéry writes toward the end of the book, "I shall fight for Man. Against Man's enemies—but against myself as well."[67]

Fighting, then, is his way forward: sending messages to the Americans and appeals to the French, arguing with André Breton and Jacques Maritain, while continuing to write, and returning to active service as soon as possible. This is the period in which he begins work on *Citadelle*,[68] at the same time as publishing the *Lettre à un otage* and *Le Petit Prince*, and getting ready to rejoin his old reconnaissance squad, first in Morocco, in 1943, then Sardinia and then, the following year, Corsica. Things move to a head. The tree grows, and dies.

Citadelle seems written in desert sand. Dominated by the smile and invisible face of God, the book speaks to God with Biblical fire and anger, and in the lyrical-prophetic tones of *Thus Spake Zarathustra*. It culminates in a page not long after the beginning, when the future Berber *cadi*, still a child, witnesses together with his father the punishment of a young woman tied to a post in the hot sun, until her head droops upon her shoulder. His father is aware he will be thought cruel, but his son also perceives his father's kindness when he expresses his wish that all his men should be like the olive branch, which bides its time. Then they will feel within themselves God's breath, "like the swirling gust which tests the tree":

> For, as with the tree, of man too you know nothing if you spread him out across his allotted span and disperse him in his differences. The tree is more than first a seed, then a stem, then a living trunk, and then dead timber. The tree is a slow, enduring force straining to win the sky. So it is with you, my little man. God compasses your birth and growing up; He fills you, turn by turn, with longings and regrets, joys and griefs, angers and forgivings, and then He draws you back unto Himself. Yet none of these transiences is *you*; neither the schoolboy nor the husband, neither the child nor the old man. You are one who fulfils himself. And if you prove yourself a stable branch, well knit to the olive tree, you will taste eternity in all your works and days.[69]

Tree and man: God creates them and calls them back to himself. To know them in depth, there is no need to break them down into their different forms, across different periods: their essence is an entirety within "that which had to be," Aristotle's *to ti en einai: puissance* and fulfillment: *Tu est celui qui s'accomplit*. The precariously balanced branch, *balancée*, must remain firmly attached to the olive tree, to the being human. It swings in the wind, but only a few lines earlier, this *balancement* (which I would like to invite readers to compare to the Yeatsian "balance" of Robert Gregory, with which this chapter began) is the divine "impulse," which comes like a breath of wind—the wind, and the Spirit, of Jesus to Nicodemus—to test the tree. Man must *learn to see himself as a branch*, to taste eternity here on earth: not the eternity waiting for the pilot below the clouds; not death, but eternal life, Dante's *trasumanar*, to be reached only through the awareness of being a separate individual open to the divine breath. The tree is that "potency" that bides its time, then touches heaven.

Saint-Exupéry's is a complex and delicate metaphysical parable, encompassing being and recognition, creation and death, nature and humanity, God and eternity. It comes to the point in the act of waiting: as, indeed, Saint-Exupéry's life was about to come to the point, and his writing, in *Le petit prince*. Fable and parable, it transforms into myth the real and literary flight I have discussed so far: the only myth available to modernity after the fall of Icarus. Here Icarus has already fallen, provisionally: the aviator-narrator protagonist has had to attempt a forced landing in the Sahara after experiencing engine trouble. "What! You dropped down from the sky?" the Little Prince asks him as he glances at his airplane, breaking into delighted laughter at the pilot's reply. As the reader learns later, he himself has come from his far-off planet with a flock of migrating birds. *The Little Prince*, then, contains the basics of all my flights: myth, birds, and technology within history.

But a reading of *The Little Prince* is far too tricky to be left to a literary critic: only children can be competently at home with its gentle melancholy and highly complex simplicity. It was obviously written not just for children, but to make children again out of adults, at least for the space of a reading. Consider, for example, the beginning, where the six-year-old narrator is drawing a boa constrictor digesting an elephant, which the adults (who "always need to have things explained") interpret as a hat. The return to childhood is a paradigmatic choice dictated not just by Saint-Exupéry's own psyche and experiences and his chosen genre, but by an ultimately evangelical inspiration: "Whoso shall receive one such little child in my name receiveth me," Christ said to his disciples, following it up with: "Verily I say unto you, Except ye be converted, and become as little children, ye shall not enter into the kingdom of heaven."[70] Saint-Exupéry also turns Saint Paul's words upside down, and, having become a man, decides to understand as a child, think as a child, and put away adult things.[71] He speaks to "carnal men" as if to newborn babies, giving them milk, which is all they can cope with, instead of solid food.[72]

The Little Prince's tiny planet, where he sits and watches the sunset, is threatened by the giant baobab trees, which could take over the whole asteroid. He needs a sheep to graze off them before they get a chance to grow, and when he arrives in the desert, asks the aviator to draw one for him. But on asteroid B-612 a wondrous flower grows, which the Little Prince has never seen before but immediately personifies "a coquettish creature," extremely vain and petulant, who needs careful tending. The Little Prince leaves her side to wander among the stars and learn something of the world, but continues to worry about his flower, and when the pilot draws the sheep, is distraught at the idea that it might graze off the flower as well. The pilot promises to draw a muzzle for the sheep. Then one day, on planet Earth, the Little Prince discovers a garden of five thousand roses, identical to his own flower, who "had told him she was the only one of her kind in all the universe." He is crying in disappointment when the fox appears and explains to him that he cannot play with him because he is "not tamed"; to tame, he explains, means to "establish ties" so that two beings then "need each other" and know and love each other totally. The fox urges him to return to his rose: he will understand now that she is unique in the world because he has watered her, sheltered her under a glass globe, and protected her with a screen; by "taming" her, he has become responsible for her, for always. "It is the time you have wasted for your rose that makes your rose so important," he points out, finally adding his simple, farewell secret: "It is only with the heart that one can see rightly; what is essential is invisible to the eye."

This is not the rose sung by Yeats,[73] but rather the rose Rilke celebrates in the *Sonnets to Orpheus*: enthroned, a calyx with a simple border, for the ancients, but for us "the full, innumerable flower, / the inexhaustible object"; the body composed only of light, and suddenly appearing "as a glory" in the air. We are unable to name the rose, which we only guess at, but which returns in memory, implored "in hours filled with names."[74] The rose does not exist, Saint-Exupéry points out, until we learn to love it, care for it, "tame" it, and make it *ours*. This is the essential point. Once the Prince has learned this, he can return to his own planet: he can fall, bitten by the snake, "as gently as a tree falls"; he can die and simply *seem* dead ("I shall look as if I were dead; and that will not be true"), leaving no trace of his body behind him. The pilot, who has by this time repaired his plane and spent all possible hours star-gazing to discover the laughing star of his Little Prince, now realizes he forgot to add the leather strap to the sheep's muzzle, and "perhaps the sheep has eaten the flower." Has it, then? "Nothing in the universe can be the same if somewhere, we do not know where, a sheep that we never saw has—yes or no?—eaten a rose." Here, then, is "a great mystery." The important point is that children "look *up* at the sky" and ask themselves that question.

And now we have really come to the point: on July 31, 1944, Antoine de Saint-Exupéry flew out toward France on reconnaissance from Borgo, in Corsica, with a fuel distance of six hours. He never returned. Like Lauro de Bosis and the Little Prince, he simply disappeared, leaving no trace of either his body or his plane.[75] Did the sheep eat the flower or not, we are still wondering.

৵০৲

No writer in the late twentieth century has revisited Saint-Exupéry more intensely than Daniele Del Giudice. Like Saint-Exupéry, his passion for flying started in childhood, but the heroic age of aviation is over, and there are no night courier flights for him, nor any war missions. He follows an ethics of responsibility, freedom, and extreme precision in writing, but his trajectory is essentially of awareness. What interests him is what flight has added to the sum of modern knowledge: this he then translates into writing.

In *Atlante occidentale*, published in 1985, flying is what links the two protagonists, the particle physicist Pietro Brahe, who works in the underground laboratory of the European Centre for Nuclear research (CERN) in Geneva, and the older writer Ira Epstein, a potential candidate for the Nobel Prize for literature. They meet in the small airport where both regularly fly, one day when Brahe is forced into an emergency landing after a dangerous maneuver by Epstein. Their subsequent friendship is rooted in a shared eagerness to articulate the new world they are discovering. Twentieth-century physics and writing are obliged to communicate with the public according to a perception of reality and an imaginary that both have left behind them. The West, in this case Europe, still speaks the old language of simile and metaphor; it seems unable to comprehend the dimensions of contemporary science, with its infinitesimal time fractions, its almost imperceptible traces of matter, and its infinitely complex geometry and mathematics; and it seems reluctant to accept a literary vision that oversteps accepted conventions.

Brahe and Epstein are fascinated by each other and united by their respective goals, the one searching for a theory of elementary particles that will explain the entire universe, the other for a form of narrative in which objects, and not people, are the protagonists: their common aim is "transparency," the "long, clear note in harmony with all the others, and with [a] new ambition, [a] fantasy, to see beyond form,"[76] *inventio* in the true sense of the term: the discovery of what was always present in matter, in things. Epstein defines himself as a "visionary of what exists, of what is;" and vision of the kind, he adds, "can be just as disquieting for its precision and concreteness" as the vision of monsters.[77] In his subterranean laboratory, eyes peeled for the emergence of possible new particles, Brahe knows that there exists another kind of time, a time for emotion, which is out of sync with the tempo of his own life, and it seems to him that "without emotion a thing is incomplete, that it won't be fixed in the mind, won't be remembered."[78]

Epstein yearns for fluid forms: notes that are suspended and complete; Brahe wants first and foremost to *see*, and to do that, as the Nobel physicist Wang tells him, "one needs the energy to produce what one wants to see": to see, it is necessary to create. But creation is impossible without feeling. Brahe has to learn to sense the halo round things, because "sometimes I have the impression that when I experience a thing, I remove it from its halo, and that therefore I won't be able to remember it later": Gilda's "long and tender kiss" will represent the apex of his sentimental education.

The inevitable encounter between the protagonists occurs in two stages. The first is crucial and it is not by chance that it takes place in the air, on an agreed trip, above Geneva and the CERN laboratories, which they look down on *from above*. Epstein asks his friend how the experiment is going, and Brahe searches for the right words, images, and analogies. Epstein interrupts him. He has no need of a "how" description:

> The things that will originate from your experiment will be nothings. Why should I imagine them in terms of the things that already are, and that are disappearing? Why would you have me receive them without their names, however arbitrary their names may be? Why set up a dummy, a mirror before me, which impedes my perception of the otherness? . . . Please start again.[79]

Brahe responds, finally "calling everything by its proper name, its proper sign, its proper formula."[80] By naming things *properly*, for the first time, in their ownness, like Adam, he makes them *his* own.

Some time afterward he admits to the writer that what he is trying to see is a kind of geometry: his work consists of symmetry, with which he tries to grasp "something of the fluidity, speed and unfathomableness." This second crucial moment in their relationship takes place in the garden of Epstein's rented lakeside villa. The fireworks organized in Epstein's honor are fading. Brahe asks him to describe what he has just seen. Epstein launches into a minutely detailed, precise, and magnificent verbal account of the firework display they have just watched together. The description is itself a fiery display detailing the fireworks' geometry and symmetry; Conradian "fact," Saint-Exupéry's "action," and Primo Levi's "phenomenon"; all amid bursts of light and enchantment:

> Fires that are flowers with long red stamens jutting from umbrella-shaped blossoms, like the eucalyptus. Flowers with radial petals burning down into a crown of stars that go from blue to purple to white, like the passion-flower. Flowers with elongated calyxes that burst into double and triple crowns of violet, like the granadilla. Flowers with a vast eiderdown of tousled stamens at the centre of golden yellow corollas, like the hypericum . . . Flowers launched into the sky as thick violet corn cockles that in turn effloresce endlessly, like buddleias . . . Whole swaths of light and dark bend according to other geometries, more complex geometries, non-euclidean, including time in their equation, and spheres explode in sequence, enormous, mighty yellow stars give birth to green stars, which give birth to violet, red, the red of receding galaxies, receding to infinity if the universe is unbounded . . . The coda, then. Fireworks so constant that there is not a moment of darkness . . . The fire blazes brighter, the thunder punctuates blue purple orange green white even white, white which you never think of as a colour but as light itself, light and light and light—and darkness.[81]

The two men are now in total synchrony: soon after this, Brahe discovers the particles he has been searching for, and Epstein receives the Nobel Prize. The trajectory is complete. Epstein is taking the train for Hamburg and thinks over the entire story. Brahe arrives at the platform at the last minute, straight from his night of discovery in the laboratory. Addressing each other in the intimate "tu" form for the first time, they declare the story over. Will someone write it, Brahe asks his writer friend. Epstein doubts it, but no matter: "What was important was not to write it, but to have felt it."

Lines of Light is the story of two parallel flights. At first they almost converge, perilously, on the runway, and they continue in the many dialogues that fill the novel. They then come together in the air, when Epstein and Brahe fly together. These are the flights that science and poetry are finally making, in unison, in an attempt to reach the present, the new world. Shades of Leonardo da Vinci: *piglierà il primo volo il grande uccello . . . empiendo l'universo di stupore, empiendo . . . tutte le scritture*: "the great bird shall take its first flight . . . filling the universe with stupor, filling all writings."

∾⌘∾

Del Giudice loves the geography he flies over, and, like the great navigators and discoverers of the past, frequently manages to convert it into literature and poetry. *Lines of Light* reaches for "a different geography, where a man, raising his eyes from the map in his hand, beholds around him a map that covers the surface of the world, but on which he is nevertheless able to put his finger at any point and say, 'I am here.'"[82] Like the first philosophers and poets, and like explorers, Del Giudice is moved by curiosity and wonder:[83] a lover of both knowledge and myth, and thus of narration and *fabula*. This emerges most clearly in *Taccuino australe* and *Le savoir du pilote*. The *Taccuino*, first published in six parts in *Corriere della Sera* in 1990, is the account of a journey to the Antarctic.[84] Each place visited is the cue for a new story, space thus discernible not only by what is seen and familiar to the eye, but also by *mythos*. The *Taccuino* in fact teaches Del Giudice to *see*, as Epstein says to Brahe. On touching down in the world's remotest continent, he realizes how landscape and narration are intimately linked:

> Since I started out on this journey I have been wondering about the relation-
> ship between nature and stories. The Antarctic, as I discovered, is not the land
> as photographed on rare days of good weather, when everything is "beautiful,"
> beautiful corresponding to the photographic imperative of sunlight. If there
> is beauty here it is a complicated mix of greys, opacity and dramatic, unreal
> light. For all its violence, nature here is neither hostile nor friendly: it is simply
> indifferent to the human presence, a thoroughly incidental matter. For us, the
> landscape is always a feeling for landscape: but here, rather than emerging
> from awareness, the landscape alters it, enforcing its own direction. This is
> why stories of the Antarctic are so nervy.[85]

In other words, a different, noncanonical aesthetic criterion is required, through which, with Epstein, we can discover light. We need to dwell on nuances, tunnel into the seemingly uniform whiteness, and become geologists of beauty and narration. As the glaciologist Xie tells Del Giudice, "The stories are not in the bases: the stories are here. This is a memory of crystal which you must learn to read. In your view white is all white, and ice is all ice. Since your soul is sensitive, it will succumb to the beauty of form. Resist. Look for another kind of attention."[86]

Abandoning the beauty of form, of course, is no small matter for someone who grew up in Rome and lives in Venice, or for all those who take Western aesthetics as their code. What Del Giudice is looking for is a *claritas* revealing the *integritas* of things, searing into their stratified mineral essence and making poetry out of the stuff of history. The Antarctic was once part of the primordial block of southern lands called Gondwana. In 1903, Scott with three of his men, "looked in amazement at the fossil of a plant which grew over much of the African savannah" and were astonished by the dry, ice-free Antarctic valley where they found it. The story could begin here, or at the first meeting not of man with penguin but instead penguin with man: a necessary inversion, given the history of the world, which the writer reminds us of twice: first when he reports the effect that Drake's account of the penguins had on Queen Elizabeth I, and when he tells of his own encounter with a penguin, a merry-go-round of contrasting logics.

This discovery of space is also one of time, given that at five hundred kilometers from the South Pole, for example, the distance between one meridian and another is some fifty kilometers, with a different time zone every seventy-five; "flying along the circumference" you adjust your watch every ten minutes, "one hour back or forwards, as you wish: in any case it's almost always day and almost always night, and passing and passing back the date line, you fool yourself that you can race ahead of the world by two calendar days and then sit down and wait for it somewhere."[87] The Antarctic, and most definitely the South Pole, is the one place on the earth where *ogne ubi e ogne quando* materially come "to a point":[88] its "mystery" is constituted by what it shares with the rest of the earth, but which, there, is exceptional; by what only exists there, "hidden under the ice (and the ice itself) or happens in the sky"; by what originates there and "then influences the whole planet."[89] This is what science has always looked for in the *Terra Australis Incognita*. But Del Giudice's prose also communicates the emotion of exile:

> For all its wonders, my impression was of exile: not the people's, which goes without saying, but that of the Antarctic itself; there was the feeling that once all this had been elsewhere, joined to other lands and other climates; that there was a punishment and a sigh that only those crazy and surreal penguins guarded like angels, and I wondered how Dante had realized that this was where Purgatory was, right under the Southern Sky, where he himself placed it.[90]

The Antarctic is for Del Giudice what the Sahara was for Saint-Exupéry: the place of *studium*, concentration and research, where science and story come together within human beings. I suspect that a further, equally extraordinary, narration will soon emerge from this purgatory before which Dante's Ulysses foundered.[91]

✼

I have mentioned *Taccuino australe* because it is clearly an extreme and therefore vital part of its author's training in perception and contains interesting material for the future. More central so far, however, and complementary, are his flying lessons. Del Giudice worked on the Paris lectures of *Le savoir du pilote* at the same time as he wrote his fifth novel, *Staccando l'ombra da terra*, with clear cross-contamination. *Le savoir du pilote* is linear, as might be expected, passing from the world as map, to flight maneuvers and their correspondence in the maneuvers of life, and from there to the language and imagination of the pilot. *Staccando l'ombra da terra* is composed of eight sections sequentially reproducing the "eccentricity" and "oblique vision" (in the technical sense) of flight.[92] A first-person "persona" speaks in all but one of the eight sections, and there are various different narrators: two ex-pilots, an elderly man, an autobiographical "I," and the first-person narrator. All these voices and characters come together in the last section, "Double Takeoff at Dawn," where the traces of Saint-Exupéry's last flight, and his life and works, are revisited by this "I" in the company of his flying instructor, Bruno. Of these eight parts, four are accounts of air disasters, two are virtually essays (one of them "autobiographical"), and two are "confessions" concerning pilot training. The experience of flight in all its forms thus lies behind the whole novel—flight training, plane crashes, personal history, war, getting lost, maneuvers of technique and life, catastrophe, action, and literature.

The key to its structure can perhaps best be extrapolated from "Reaching Dew Point," where the pilot stalls—"the worst that could befall a pilot"—and finds himself lost in the clouds. He manages, however, to regain control, remaining in contact with the Treviso radar, which will eventually save him, and as he urges the plane slowly forward, he recalls the description of a stalled plane he had come across in the most up-to-date flight manuals and physics textbooks, where it was held up as "a remarkable example of chaos theory":

> Certainly you were honored that a stall was considered by contemporary thought as a "critical point phenomenon," and that in the white vapor in-

dicating the separation of the flowing wisps of cloud and the wing top—a photographic reproduction of the uncontrollability of turbulence—some had seen the ancient consubstantiality, the ancient concurrence of order and disorder; Oh yes, there was one part of you which participated enthusiastically in the wonder that a butterfly beating its wing in New York could lead to etc., etc. . . . but you were the one beating the wings, pilot; order and disorder, separated by no more than quantity, by a curve before which and beyond which lay the realm of the one and of the other, chaos containing order containing chaos.[93]

Chaos containing order containing chaos: a deft definition of narrative organization in *Staccando l'ombra da terra*. But it also indicates the small matter of pilot's and writer's vital limit: "chaos containing order containing chaos, like the white, green and yellow curves in your instruments which indicated stalling speeds, the curve of speeds within which your airplane was an airplane, but under and over which it was so no longer."[94] This is the area *Le savoir du pilote* calls the *zona franca* "between being and non-being": "being in the air, and continuing to be in the world"—a smattering of seconds and yards when the pilot dredges his "knowledge of margins" and "science of limits."[95]

But emergency, for a pilot, becomes habit, discipline, and a science of limits. The whole of *Staccando l'ombra da terra* is centered on this brinkmanship and its possible, tragic shortfalls, in flight and in language. The first lesson the trainee pilot learns, in chapter 1, "All Because of the Mistake," is that he is being offered his first solo flight, without Bruno, his instructor, because in the previous one he had realized his mistake of forgetting to open the flap. Similarly, the arresting way "Reaching Dew Point" opens—"One morning, while airborne, you lost your way, as people do in life, without ever being quite aware that they are lost but drifting bit by bit into a zone where their bearings are gone"—is only "resolved" when he decides to report to the Board (which is both air traffic control and a metaphysical entity, the "Ente") to ask for his position and destination ("*destino* in Spanish, the only language in which the geographical goal coincides with the completion of the individual, personal adventure") in the proper technical terminology, using the alphabet of flight, a procedural register, "the most unreal of languages, with the maximum of density in the minimum of words, embodying the maximum of imagination, each word having to designate instantaneously a geography of trajectories, positions, intentions, of starting points and destinations," "words with consequences, requiring a high quotient of intellectual honesty,"[96] described in a level but dramatic way also in *Le savoir du pilote*:[97]

"Treviso radar. India Echo November is no longer in Victor Mike Charlie. Request a Quebec Delta Mike."[98]

Flight is thus the extreme "accident" disclosing the "substance" of life, just as the Antarctic is the continent where the whole earth "comes to a head." Flight is history, from the history of the mind traced in the chapter "And Everything Else?" to the real, mechanical history dominating the novel and culminating in Saint-Exupéry's real and literary flights. Flight is geography, in "And Everything Else?" as in "Flight Maneuvers": geography as the discovery of a relationship with the earth: oblique, peripheral, consequential, off center, and seemingly artificial, but linked to history. A pilot's knowledge entails faith in instruments, an unnatural instinct that must become natural and congenital, a carefully balanced imagination, "a serendipitous flair," and even liturgy, the parasacred litany of the checklist. It is action, responsibility, discipline, rigor: *conduct*, a piloting of plane and moral self.

Flight is life: the story of a child who "was" a tram and became first a plane then, finally, a pilot, while continuing to remain a child; who began to fly when the era of the pilot began its decline and electronics took over; but who still wanted to learn, to "know everything," all a pilot's complex knowledge, "a more mature grasp of the variety of everything else, with its tangle of plots, its impossible choices, its polarities that tear you apart." The "pilot's lore" is as pliable and complex as the natural element it refers to, "the omnipresent, ever-elusive air with its terrifying laws," requiring "foresight" yet "total adaptability to circumstances." Yet in each of these contexts there is "one point around which that lore [has] to harden or solidify in an instant decision, one gesture that [excludes] all others."[99] Lastly, flight is ethics and philosophy: "to know everything, indeed more than everything . . . To know, but not to know too much, and not to be oversure of that knowledge."

So again we come to the critical point of wounds and laceration. Two pilots, one elderly, the other young, who, in the chapter entitled "Between Second 1423 and Second 1797," think back with a "suffering beyond all endurance" to the 374 seconds, the six minutes, approximately, in which the ice crystals forming on the wing blade stall them three times before plunging them down, "no longer an airplane, just fifteen thousand kilos of scrap metal, fibers, plastic and people, almost overturned, tumbling into nothingness, in the thick darkness of a cloudy night, quite helplessly, with no knowledge of what had occurred, or how."[100] This tragic dialogue, its intense and dramatic rhythm dictated by particles of time ("I first noticed something was the matter with the plane at second 165, but at second 1,797 it was no longer an airplane"), culminates in the final smothered whisper of *precipitiamo*— "we're going to crash."

In the chapter entitled "Pauci Sed Semper Immites," we hear the voice of the elderly gentleman who recounts episodes of individual heroism by the Gruppo Buscaglia, an Italian air squad fighting over the Mediterranean in the Second World War on the torpedo bomber *Settantanove*: bombing enemy ships, raids into enemy territory, battles with Spitfires, disappearances increasing, their separation after the armistice, and the reappearance of the ace pilot believed dead. Everything is narrated in what comes across as a voiced interior monologue, issuing technical details, visual angles, actions, and pauses, with a level glance always for the human element: personal and national wounds, and the young pilots' anguished technical and tactical discussions of daytime and night vision ("night and night attack was all we had: darkness saved us from the Spitfires but tied us to the moon,") "while enclosed inside a shell of their deepest emotions and convictions." Del Giudice's well-tempered prose, epic in tone if not in length, veers the novel toward history, against a distorted and artificial horizon, always taking careful verbal bearings and never dropping in speed or power.

History and literature come to a head in the final section of the book, "Double Take-off at Dawn," where the trainee pilot, the narrating "I," and Bruno, his instructor, retrace Saint-Exupéry's final flight path. I shall not examine it here because this would oblige me, on account of its concision and depth, and its skill in deft maneuvering, to erase much of what I wrote in the first part of this chapter. And because the preceding section of *Staccando l'ombra*, "Unreported Inbound Palermo," is a seven-page masterpiece that overshadows much of the rest of the book with the cry of more recent, unresolved suffering, striking readers with the blow of history, exposing "procedural routine" used to camouflage truth and blame, and at the same time constituting a prelude to the future. Here, the voices of *Staccando l'ombra da terra*, the ghosts of pilots young and old, the roar of engines, the notes of old songs, the liturgical threnodies, and the language of the black box culminate, in crescendo, into a tightly controlled howl as Del Giudice tells the story of *Itavia* flight 870 Bologna to Palermo on the evening of June 27, 1980. The footnote appended to the opening line in the American edition states the facts:

> Associated with the name Ustica is one of the most mysterious incidents and one of the greatest scandals in recent Italian history. On the night of June 27, 1980, a DC-9, owned by the airline Itavia, while on a scheduled flight from Bologna to Palermo, exploded in the air and fell into the sea near the island of Ustica, not far from Palermo. All eighty-one of the passengers and crew on board were killed. The truth about what occurred was covered up

by the secret services and the military elite. The victims' relatives petitioned
the government for seven years until the wreckage was salvaged from a depth
of 3,700 meters. Despite much resistance and little help from international
authorities, the Italian magistrate continues to investigate the theory that the
plane was hit by a missile or exploded by a bomb.[101]

Del Giudice's text heads urgently along the direct-speech communications
between the DC-9 and the various control towers en route, juxtaposed with
static revisitations of the wreckage on the seabed, and its ghostly reconstruction in the hangars in the military base of Pratica di Mare, near Rome ("but
in the unmaking and remaking of the event, something is missing and will
be missing forever"): "a history of things: history of metal, metal sinning and
sinned against."[102] For the time being there is no plot and no action, simply
the molecular memory of the wreckage. Objects, as it were, speak: "the left
side door knows what ripped away the external coating (simply designated
"skin" in the inventory), the wrenched-off rivets know if they were detached
by the speed of descent or the force of a strike."[103] Then, the crescendo
of panic in the terrifying dialogue-become-monologue: "Itavia Eight Seven
Zero, Rome here, do you read?":

> "Air Malta, this is Rome," "Rome go ahead, this is Air Malta," "OK, sir, we
> have Itavia Eight Seven Zero unreported inbound Palermo, please, please try
> to call for us Itavia Eight Seven Zero, try to call for us Itavia Eight Seven
> Zero," "Alitalia Eight Seven Zero?," "Itavia, sir, Itavia, Itavia Eight Seven Zero,"
> "Roger . . . Itavia Eight Seven Zero, Itavia Eight Seven Zero this is Air Malta.
> Do you read? Itavia Eight Seven Zero, do you read? . . . do you read?"[104]

The brief parenthesis ends. A blank space. Then the question, addressed
to us, to everyone: *Do you read?* "Are you receiving us?" of course, but also:
"Do you understand?" Are you taking this in? Can you absorb this image of
"utterly incomprehensible anguish?" Our gut reply is to reject such a reading,
such a world.

But the history of flight is made up of unspeakable tragedy. It is not simply
Seamus Heaney's wonderful "Flight Path," leading from the paper boats his
father made, through the poet's own transoceanic flights and homecomings
full of cares ("Skies change, not cares, for those who cross the seas") and
troubles, the Troubles, bringing the urgent request to serve the political cause
of Northern Ireland with the pen ("When, for fuck's sake, are you going to
write / Something for us?"), and the opening up of the last section to the
"starlight that is light years on the go / From far away and takes light years

arriving," pilgrimage, and the final image of the ascending dove.[105] Flight is also the tragedy of the Itavia DC-9 identified by the acronym painted in black on the underside of its left wing: I-TIGI, which in Del Giudice's story, where plane, crew, and passengers become one and the same, is converted into "the Itigis." Flight is manslaughter in the air and in the sea, perhaps by "mistake," of eighty-one people, men, women and children, a quarter of a century ago.

What has happened to "conduct" and knowledge, then? Literature meets flight and history in a scrap heap of twisted wreckage at the bottom of the sea, at the deepest, darkest point. For twenty-five years Italian justice has been trying to extrapolate the truth from the pile-up of reticence, denial, and feigned ignorance and to establish whether "the Itigis" were shot down by friendly fire aiming at an enemy invader of airspace. It has now reached its verdict, its point, and has condemned and absolved. Trials are, of course, just another form of narrative, of literature: *are you reading?* To become poetry they require a concatenation into art, in sequences in which the possible is both surprising and totally inevitable.

In 2000, Daniele Del Giudice and Marco Paolini produced a stage version, with a choir, trained by Giovanna Marini, performing *I TIGI: Canto per Ustica*. The result is a work of an Aeschylean inexorability, unrelenting precision, and enormous power, which needs to be seen, heard, and as the control tower would insist, *read*, before any discussion of it would make sense to readers. Now that the *Canto* has been recorded, it is possible to see and hear *I TIGI* on our television screens.[106] It may be a coincidence that the *Canto* recording was released in October 2001, less than a month after 9/11, which could also be watched on television screens from the comfort of one's home. This is the *point* toward which the next chapter's "mad flight" is headed.

2001: The Mad Flight 8

At the end of chapter 2 I left Ulysses in mid-, "mad flight." He now
returns to complete his trajectory after the dip back into history in
chapter 7. In the fourteenth century, Dante launched his elderly hero
on a journey that, crossing beyond the Pillars that Hercules had planted
at the Straight of Gibraltar *acciò che l'uom più oltre non si metta* (so that
men should not pass beyond), would continue out into the Atlantic and
south to the other side of the world. After five months at sea—what
Dante's hero himself dubbed his *folle volo*, his "mad flight"— guided
chiefly by the light of the moon and stars, Ulysses and his men come
within sight of a "new land," dominated by a high mountain, dim in
the distance, which later in the *Commedia* is revealed as the mountain
of Purgatory. From it, however, there now comes a storm which whirls
the ship into a triple vortex before sinking it, *infin che 'l mar fu sovra
noi richiuso* (until the sea closed again over us).[1] Ulysses had coaxed
his companions beyond Hercules' limit by appealing to their zest for
knowledge: "choose not to deny experience," he had told them, of the
new, "uninhabited world" to the West, behind the sun, *di retro al sol*.
"Take thought of the seed from which you spring," he had urged them,
alluding to Genesis and to Aristotle's *Ethics*: "You were not born to
live as brutes, / but to follow virtue and knowledge." A perfectly noble
undertaking, then, but one of which the Christian God, Dante seems
to believe, took a dim view, and had already condemned while those
who undertook it were still alive: he is the one (whom Ulysses calls the
"other," *altrui*) who wills the storm on them, thereby killing Ulysses
before throwing him into the hell of the fraudulent counsellors. The
tragedy is more acute in being essentially Dante's own and that of the

civilization then emerging in Europe, whose people continued to push beyond the Pillars to East and West, exploring and conquering the earth.

Dante's Ulysses was to remain an icon in Euro-American culture and literature for all those who would not tolerate limits or dictates.[2] At the beginning of the twentieth century he was still used, via Tennyson's version, for Amundsen, the first to find the Northwest Passage, and for the doomed attempts of Scott and Shackleton to reach the South Pole. And we have seen in the first two chapters how his image and story haunted people like Lauro de Bosis, Gabriele D'Annunzio, and Benito Mussolini. Although the figure of Ulysses is inevitably composite—Homer's fascinating protagonist inevitably appearing now and then as fellow-traveler, occasionally overtaking Dante's before drawing back for a while—it was with similarly mad flights that the twentieth century began, on June 16, 1904, and ended, on September 11, 2001.

Eighteen months after Hitler had been appointed chancellor—to begin *in medias res*—German Jews were already uneasy with the Nazi regime. Some feared for their property; most for their jobs. Among the latter was Victor Klemperer, professor of Romance philology at the Polytechnic University of Dresden. Many of his Jewish colleagues had already been forced to hand in their notice or take early retirement, and Klemperer felt the circle tightening. On October 8, 1934, he wrote in his diary, "I feel like Ulysses in Polyphemus's cave: 'I'll save you for last,'" although as his friend Blumenfeld quipped over the phone, "Ulysses never got eaten, and it was Polyphemus who came to a bad end."[3]

Fortunately, in this case, Blumenfeld was right: but how many were to be "devoured" (*gefressen*) before Polyphemus met his own end? Klemperer himself only escaped the death camps at the very last minute and in a totally unexpected manner. But my question in this chapter is rather more limited: what is Ulysses doing on the lips of a German Jew (who, incidentally, simply considered himself a German, *tout court*, and had actually been baptized into the Lutheran church)? Why does Klemperer (like many others, as we shall see) spontaneously reach for Ulysses to draw a parallel with his own situation? Could it have something to do with the nature of European culture and the deep structures of Western history?

To begin to answer my own question, I intend to start my flight from the point in the early twentieth century when Homer's *Odyssey* was most fully reincarnated—precisely where we left off at the end of chapter 2. Back, then, to the modern *Ulysses* par excellence, Joyce's, and to the next-to-last section, "Ithaca."[4] Leopold Bloom, the English-speaking Irish Jew here representing Homer's hero, has finally returned home, at the end of June 16, 1904, and is about to be reunited with his Penelope, the unfaithfully faithful Molly, in their marriage bed. Bloom ponders the prospect of old age with horror, listing the only alternatives, "by decease (change of state), by departure (change of place)." He naturally opts for the latter, "by the line of least resistance." He then sets off on his mental journey, first through the whole of Ireland, and then through the entire planet, stopping off at a number of significant places: Ceylon, Jerusalem, the Straits of Gibraltar, the Parthenon, Wall Street, the Plaza de Toros at La Linea, in Spain, Niagara Falls ("over which no human being had passed with impunity"), the land of the Eskimos, "the forbidden country of Thibet (from which no traveler returns)," "the bay of Naples (to see which was to die)," and the Dead Sea.[5] The journey takes place "at sea, septentrional, by night" following "the polestar," and "on land, meridional," following a "bispherical moon" revealed in its imperfect phases "through the posterior interstice of the imperfectly occluded skirt of a carnose negligent perambulating female, a pillar of the cloud by day."[6] Here Bloom takes on himself the universal "binomial denomination" of being and non-being, Everyman and Noman, traveling on and on:

> Ever he would wander, self-compelled, to the extreme limit of his cometary orbit, beyond the fixed stars and variable suns and telescopic planets, astronomical waifs and strays, to the extreme boundary of space, passing from land to land, among peoples, amid events. Somewhere imperceptibly he would hear and somehow reluctantly, suncompelled, obey the summons of recall. Whence, disappearing from the constellation of the Northern Crown he would somehow reappear reborn above delta in the constellation of Cassiopeia and after incalculable eons of peregrination return an estranged avenger, a wreaker of justice on malefactors, a dark crusader, a sleeper awakened, with financial resources (by supposition) surpassing those of Rothschild or of the silver king.[7]

Shortly afterward, however, Bloom decides that the journey is out of the question: in the first place, it would be irrational as return; and then "undesirable" as departure, given the late hour, the darkness, the dangers, the need for rest, and above all "the proximity of a bed" occupied by his beloved Molly, and "the anticipation of warmth (human) tempered with coolness (linen), obviating desire and rendering desirable: the statue of Narcissus, sound without echo, desired desire."[8]

Note the way this extraordinary twentieth-century Homer-Dante deals with myth: Bloom-Ulysses, feeling his age (like his *Inferno* counterpart) and fearing old age, has no sooner set foot back home than he wants to leave, like Tennyson's Ulysses. Like Dante's, he wants to travel toward the Pillars of Hercules (where his wife Molly was born and where *Ulysses* ends, with a montage-superimposition of Dublin's Howth Head); to visit the places of death (Tibet, Naples, the Dead Sea); to become "Everyman or Noman" ("Noman" is of course the name Ulysses gives himself in answer to Polyphemus in the *Odyssey*), and move beyond, among the stars, to the outmost limits of space, "passing from land to land" like Coleridge's Ancient Mariner, but *among* peoples, *amid* events, finally returning, like Homer's Ulysses, and like "a dark crusader," like the Count of Monte Cristo and Rothschild the millionaire.

A nocturnal journey toward death, beyond boundaries:[9] a journey like that of Dante's Ulysses. But this is also a biblical Exodus ("pillar of the cloud"); a journey through the universe as theorized by Ptolemy, Copernicus, and Einstein, and mystic flight: transformation into comet, ascent beyond the fixed stars, Ascension to the Empyrean, rebirth, and messianic Advent; a journey through history and peoples; a Homeric *nostos* and revenge à la Dumas. In one page Joyce moves backward through what I have elsewhere called the "shadows" of Ulysses, himself projecting new ones, to create his *own* Ulyssean myth, which remains nonetheless a universal symbol, Everyman and Noman.

Bloom's peripatetic dream also contains, naturally, a psychological-touristic-cultural dimension. His first lap, the tour of Ireland, includes all the places any competent tour guide would still include, for their history or natural beauty, adding, for good measure, a touch of contemporary social history in Belfast's docks. Other Ulysses, preannounced by Joyce, are to follow him: Padraic Fallon, Louis MacNeice, Thomas Kinsella, Eiléan Ní Chuilleanáin, and Michael Longley.[10]

Skipping, significantly, over Britain, after Ireland Bloom lands mentally in Ceylon, exotic for its "spicegardens," demotic in supplying the ritual beverage, tea, to the English producers ("Mincing lane, London") and Irish distributors ("Dame street, Dublin"). In La Linea, Spain, just beyond Gibraltar and the danger-demarcation line of the Pillars, the Plaza de Toros attracts Bloom, "where O'Hara of the Camerons had slain the bull"; he is equally drawn by "the land of the Eskimos," both for its remoteness and because its inhabitants are "eaters of soap." In the New World it is not so much New York that attracts him as Wall Street, "which controlled international finance" (a significant claim to capitalist interests), followed by the archetypal topoi of the West: Athens, or more precisely, the Parthenon (whose statues, "nude Grecian divinities," Bloom finds intellectually and sensually stimulating); and Jerusalem, "the holy city" not only for the people of this particular Ulysses, the Jews, but also for the Muslims—"with mosque of Omar and gate of Damascus, goal of aspiration": the eastern access to the holy places of both religions.

A brief summary of his long day's journey into this final night: for the early twentieth century, Leopold Bloom, a Greek, an Irishman, and a Jew (from Central Europe), reincarnates the Ulysses of the past and foreshadows those of the future. He dreams of a journey, some mad flight, through reality, following his own psychological impulses, but ultimately directed culturally and existentially beyond reality, toward his—and our—roots (Ireland, Athens, Jerusalem, Naples, and Gibraltar), moving ontologically toward nothingness (death) and fullness (the stars, regeneration, and return); toward the "entity" of Everyman and the "non-entity" of Noman: toward alienation and absolute beauty:

> What tributes his?
> Honours and gifts of strangers, the friends of Everyman. Nymph immortal, beauty, the bride of Noman.[11]

Leopold Bloom, this oldest and most modern of Ulysses, is a shadow of the human being of the century that has just ended, a representative of human history and culture. I intend now to follow him, in my own mad flight, along the long cone of a shadow that hangs over our imagination and cuts through the gathering shades.

✧

The first of these, a cinematic and sci-fi shade, takes us to 2001. That the *Star Trek* series has deep Dantean and Odyssean roots is too obvious to demonstrate: each episode originally opened with the portentous announcement, "These are the voyages of the starship *Enterprise*, its five-year mission to explore strange new worlds, to seek out life and new civilizations, to boldly go where no man has gone before." What is equally significant, though, is that the greatest classic of the contemporary sci-fi imaginary is entitled *2001: A Space Odyssey.*[12] Now that the whole of the human planet has been explored and reduced, as Leopardi puts it, *in breve carta*,[13] where is there for Ulysses to travel to besides infinite space and time? This is precisely the journey Leopold Bloom dreamt of. Clarke's and Kubrick's hero, David Bowman—David the Jew, and Bowman, the man-with-the-bow, the Greek Ulysses—figurally "fulfils" Bloom's wish. The appearance of the black monolith in the opening scene, to the notes of Strauss's *Also Sprach Zarathustra*, marks the transformation of ape into man. The stone, silent sign of human destiny, then reappears on the moon to edge David Bowman toward the boundaries of the solar system, *di retro al sol, nel mondo sanza gente*: the unpeopled world behind the sun where Dante's Ulysses was seized by the whirlpool, the sea closing over him. The 2001 vortex, however, instead of drowning his successor, launches him on a mad flight beyond Jupiter and into the mysteries of the cosmos. At the end of his voyage into space and time, David Bowman, like Odysseus, returns home: an old and dying man, an aged child, a new man, another step on the evolutionary ladder—perhaps the superman announced by Nietzsche-Strauss at the beginning of the film. The coming of this man was precisely what Zarathustra had prophesied, using two images of eternity hinged to Dante's and Homer's Ulysses, and just predating the images of the flight of Icarus encountered above:

> If I love the sea and all that is sealike, and love it most when it angrily contradicts me:
>
> If that delight in seeking that drives sails toward the undiscovered is in me, if a seafarer's delight is in my delight:
>
> If ever my rejoicing has cried: "The shore has disappeared—now the last fetter falls from me—
>
> the boundless ocean roars around me, far out glitter space and time, well then, come on! old heart!"
>
> Oh how should I not lust for eternity and for the wedding ring of rings—the Ring of Return! [14]

Is this the resurrection promised us a few years ago, in 2001? Or has the great metamorphosis already happened? Perhaps the 2001 Ulysses, battling with the "too human" computer Hal, is already among us, a reincarnation of Christopher Columbus and Neil Armstrong on the threshold between the second and third millennia. When John Glenn, the elderly astronaut, went back up into space, the American poet laureate, Robert Pinsky, appeared on television to recite canto XXVI of the *Inferno*. Why? Is history fulfilling a prophecy made in a poem or film, using the rhetoric of the traditional imaginary? I have no idea. But if this is the case, we should perhaps recall, à propos of *2001: A Space Odyssey*, that Nietzsche's route was the dead end of Western nihilism, a dark foreshadowing of the Nazi-posited *Übermensch*.

∽◦∾

All we know is what has already happened, which is that poetry and history, imaginary and actual events, have already met, once at least, in the culture—

and in the flesh—of the West, in the splendid, appalling twentieth century. It is here that, following Bloom's itinerary, Athens meets Jerusalem, or, more precisely, enters Jerusalem through Central and Eastern Europe. It is no accident, I believe, that so many of the greatest philosophers and writers to return to Ulysses in the early twentieth century—Ernst Bloch, Max Horkheimer, Theodor Adorno, Kafka, Canetti, Fondane, Mandel'shtam—come from the Jewish diaspora of the East; as if Israel's wandering had finally been incarnated in the figure of a Greek, an eternally wandering Gentile.

Ulysses emerges from this philosophical and narrative context as a singularly divided figure: positive or negative, Everyman and Noman, but always carrying on his back a different weight of signification. For Bloch, fascinated by Dante's forked tongue of flame, Ulysses is a Gothic Faust of the seas, a Christopher Columbus in another guise.[15] For Horkheimer and Adorno, Odysseus incarnates Enlightenment dialectics, not just historically but as a cultural category: the bourgeois man of reason.[16] For Canetti, at a personal level, Ulysses is the hero of metamorphosis and unappeasable curiosity.[17]

So far so good, then. But with Kafka—himself a latter-day Ulysses, according to Walter Benjamin[18]—things become more complicated. Ulysses survives the encounter with the Sirens through his cunning and technical know-how, but the essential point is that, in his famous parable, the Sirens are silent.[19] It is this silence—the silence and death of the gods—that Ulysses contemplates, seeing it as "the supreme test the gods are putting us to, with our entire era: the final divine cunning after a long battle with humanity." To survive, we pitch cunning against cunning, pretending to believe in the protection of chains and wax, namely, believing in "what is decidedly divine," without aspiring to reach it, and thus glimpsing "perfect happiness" on earth, "blasphemous" and "unreachable."[20]

Or perhaps, as Benjamin maintains, the Sirens' silence is due to the fact that for Kafka, music and song are "an expression, or at least a token, of salvation" and of "hope." Their silence then becomes a prelude to nothingness: a silencing of being and of poetry that has by now become mere comment. In the same short story by Kafka, language destroys not only *mythos* but also *logos*, logical articulation, battling with itself and prefiguring the end not only of narration but of interpretation too[21]—both of which, as I hardly need to add, were to roundly resurface, starting from Kafka himself, in Brecht and Blanchot.[22]

The grand design projecting Ulysses' shadow of Noman was now complete, and after the Second World War it was quickly fulfilled. I shall again start from Jewish philosophers. The theories of previous thinkers now seem to have become illusion. Emmanuel Levinas goes as far as to claim that the whole itinerary of Western philosophy, metaphysics, and theology "has remained essentially that of Ulysses, whose adventure in the world was simply a return to his island home":—"une complaisance dans le Même, une méconnaissance de l'Autre" (a satisfaction within the Same, a misrecognition of the Other).[23] Levinas sets this circular, "complaisant" myth of *nostos* against that of the nomadic figure moving from *Même* to *Autre*, namely, "the story of Abraham, who leaves his native land forever for a land as yet unknown, even forbidding his servant to take his son back to the departure point":[24] basically, Athens against Jerusalem.

As a nonphilosopher, I dare rashly to state my case. It seems to me that Levinas is leaving Dante completely out of the equation, while at the same time curiously agreeing with him. What I mean is this: Dante's Ulysses leaves Circe's shores with no desire to return, sailing toward a land that is unknown, although not promised. From then on, in the history of Western culture and poetry, he has never stayed still, representing the restlessness of a whole civilization. At the same time, in *Inferno* XXVI, it is Ulysses, with his tongue of flame and his shipwreck, who experiences the searing, sinking encounter with the supreme "Other": a God who would appear quite the opposite of what Levinas calls "the god of the philosophers," the God of the West, "adequate to reason," who will in no way "trouble the autonomy of conscience."[25] Yet, from such diverse imaginings of Ulysses, Dante, and Levinas reach strikingly similar conclusions, the former condemning to shipwreck and hell, along with the cloven flame, the whole of Western civilization, by means of the Supreme "Other," Levinas, with the narcissistic satisfaction of return, setting fire to the whole *logos* the West has so painstakingly elaborated.

How not to read into this singular coincidence a prophecy on the one hand and on the other a reflection—Harold Fisch[26] would say a "remembered future"—of the terrifying event that marked twentieth-century Europe, the Shoah? The Ulysses-Israel link is a long-established one, going back in the imagination as far as ancient Alexandria. Commenting on God's appearance to Abraham among the terebinths at Mamre, Philo of Alexandria cites Ulysses' return to Ithaca as an old beggar, and one of the early church fathers, Clement of Alexandria, draws a parallel between Ulysses' sea wanderings and those of the Jews through the desert.[27]

In the 1930s and 1940s the Romanian-French poet Benjamin Fondane composed a series of poems significantly entitled "Ulysse," "Titanic," and

"Exode" in which he combined existential and historical anguish in the journeys of the *Odyssey*, Dante's Ulysses, the Titanic, and the biblical Exodus.[28] Ulysses dominates Fondane's life, poetry, and aesthetics generally; autobiographically "Hebrewized," he says of himself, "and yet Ulysses"; then, *tout court*, "Jewish, *naturally*." The aesthetics of the "risque poétique" which Fondane called "*d'Ulysse*" is never a mere quest for form, nor simply an existential pursuit of a Baudelairean "gouffre." What is being questioned in the poetry of Ulysses, as the final pages of Fondane's *Baudelaire et l'expérience du gouffre* put it, is "cette chose *extrême*, cet *apeiron*"—"that *extreme* thing, that infinite, which shone once on the face of the Prophet when he returned from the mountain":[29] the reflection, in other words, of that "Other" which killed Dante's Ulysses. Should we ask ourselves whether it was this same Other who killed Fondane at Auschwitz? The Italian Jew Primo Levi, a fellow prisoner in the same death camp, asked himself the same question indirectly, seeing in the *com'altrui piacque* ("as Another willed") of *Inferno* XXVI "something gigantic . . . perhaps the why of our destiny, of our being here."[30] Victor Klemperer's diary entry of October 8, 1934, is, compared to all this, mere rhetoric—or, if you prefer, prophetic utterance. But for Klemperer, too, the comparison between himself and Ulysses in Polyphemus's cave ("I'll save you for last") becomes an obsession, a leitmotiv that speaks painfully of the sense of gradual strangulation as the Nazi circle tightened on Germany's Jews, bringing the terror that the "last" day had come, and no-one would be "saved." He returns to the comparison at least three more times in the *Diaries* between 1942 and 1945.[31] The last time, significantly, is on February 13, 1945, when Klemperer writes that he had learned only the previous day that he was to report for deportation early in the morning on February 16 (it was his turn to be devoured by the Cyclops). The following night, between February 13 and 14, 1945, the Allies bombed Dresden, and Ulysses was able to throw away his yellow star and escape from Polyphemus. The Odyssey proper, throughout Germany, then began for Klemperer and his wife Eva, ending, as all good Odysseys should, with their return home, to Dölzschen, on June 10, 1945.

The shadow of Ulysses once again enters history, but now history fractures myth and penetrates into normality, into all the topoi by which the imagination constructs our daily reality. The trajectory that had an unexpectedly happy ending for the Klemperers was almost always entirely tragic, transforming the Dantesque flame into crematorium fire so stunningly and unbearably as to lead to its ultimate reversal. Paul Celan's poetry is dominated by the theme of return, and he himself, in ironic reversal, calls Ulysses his "monkey." But when he evokes the Shoah and sings his *Psalm*, Ulysses appears as Nobody, and Nobody is actually God, the definitive Other; His creation, equally, is "nothing," flourishing *entgegen*, for his sake *and* despite Him:

> No one moulds us again out of earth and clay,
> no one conjures our dust.
> No one.
> Praised be your name, no one.
> For your sake
> we shall flower.
> Towards
> you.
>
> A nothing
> we were, are, shall
> remain, flowering,
> the nothing-, the
> no one's rose.
> [Niemand knetet uns wieder aus Erde und Lehm,
> niemand bespricht unsern Staub.
> Niemand.
>
> Gelobt seist du, Niemand.
> Dir zulieb wollen
> wir blühn.
> Dir entgegen.
>
> Ein Nichts
> waren wir, sind wir, werden
> wir bleiben, blühend:
> die Nichts-, die
> Niemandsrose.][32]

Should we, then, recognize that Athens and Jerusalem are irremediably separate: that Athens, not to mention Rome, has destroyed Jerusalem more than once, and that history ends in the Old World, at Auschwitz? From the death camp, Primo Levi wrote that Ulysses' "Considerate la vostra semenza" (Take thought of the seed from which you spring) seemed to him "like the voice of

God": "you were not created to live as brutes," but in his image and likeness, *per seguir virtute e canoscenza*—to follow virtue and knowledge.[33] Derrida, glossing Levinas, calls our attention to the copula "is" that joins the two parts of the proposition in the sentence defining Joyce's Ulysses: "Jewgreek is greekjew. Extremes meet."[34] Perhaps the salvation Kafka despairs of finding will come to us from Bloom, this little Hebrew-Celtic and Anglo-Greek Messiah living in an Ogygia—Ireland—strongly linked to Rome.[35]

∽o∾

It is time, now, to resume our flight and start working toward an answer. Since the Second World War, and in the last two decades in particular, the shadow of Ulysses has extended over the whole planet: not just to Russia (which has been quarrying Homer and Dante since at least the nineteenth century) and Japan, where it may have been felt in the seventeenth century, and certainly in the early twentieth, and the United States and Latin America, which have a privileged, longer-standing familiarity with Ulysses, but even to Canada (Canadian literature finding its basic correlative in the *Odyssey*), Australia (in the collective imaginaire a Dantesque, purgatorial penal colony), in Africa, India, the Arab world, and the Caribbean. An itinerary of this kind would be beyond the scope of most books. What I can, I think, state is that the West's conquest of the earth—by European and North American arms, markets, media, languages, and culture—is the prime cause of this Ulyssean multiplication. It universalizes the symbolic value of the myth, Ulysses becoming even more of an Everyman and Noman: a gesture, an oar, a glance, a mad flight, an endless wandering, lending an already polymorphic hero a new face at each incarnation.

The protagonists of the Anglo-Indian Anita Desai's *Journey to Ithaca*, for example,[36] are a young Italian man searching for the fullness of experience and earthly transcendence that the West now believes resides in India; an Arab girl who searches for herself only to become, via Paris, Venice, and America, an Indian guru, the Mother; and the young Italian man's German wife, who follows through all the stages of the Mother's life. This is a trinary odyssey with a single goal, an Ithaca modelled on Cavafy's celebrated lines[37] and identified with India. The novel's triple Ulysses is astonishingly like the neoplatonic Ulysses of Plotinus and Porphyry,[38] the allegorized wanderer who traverses and attempts to throw off matter to reach the fatherland and his father pure and whole: a Ulysses who is a shadow of the mystic and in whose route the Western, Islamic, and Indian cultures seek to combine.

The syncretism of late antiquity is typical of the postmodern shadow of Ulysses. The greatest living Arab poet, the Syrian Adonis, says of himself:

> Wandering in sulphur caves,
> I catch sparks
> and come by mysteries in clouds of incense
> and under the nails of spirits.
>
> I look for Ulysses:
> Perhaps he will raise his days for me
> like a ladder.
> Perhaps he will speak to me
> And will say what the waves don't know.[39]

Even if Ulysses returned, for Adonis he would always be "the story of departure," lying "in a land without promise, / in a land without return."[40] Ulysses (and elsewhere Icarus),[41] is indeed one of the major myths in Adonis's *Songs of Mihyar of Damascus*, but he is constantly accompanied by Gilgamesh and Sindbad, Adonis maintaining that there exists an ancient Mediterranean tradition in which "life is a vast field for human knowledge," and the seeds from which that field grows to fertility—the seeds of progress—are "expressed by the epic of Gilgamesh and by Homer's *Odyssey*." But is Sindbad, Adonis asks, really different from the Sumerian Gilgamesh or from a Greek Ulysses sung in Arabic? Syncretism, the Syrian poet seems to imply, represents for today's Arab world the only salvation: not mere assimilation to the West, but neither the "closed reality" that fundamentalism would wish to impose. Passionately writing in their own language, contemporary Arab poets want to overcome the "division of cultures" by going back to their more open-minded predecessors and by steeping themselves in the wider civilization of the ancient Mediterranean East.[42] The Tunisian Nur ed-Din Sammùd would seem to agree with Adonis, and similarly compares Sindbad to Ulysses imprisoned by Calypso. For the Palestinian Khàlid Abu Khàlid, *The Odyssey* is the history of his life and his people: exile, "blown by the winds," homesickness, a Ulysses reduced to a shade "in the crack of light in a door jamb, / shoulders against time / which sinks in the sand," the breast "struggling / between a place beneath the ruins / and another, down there, in the desert."[43] A son of Ishmael like a son of Israel: a Palestinian—tragic irony—in the identical position of a Jew in the diaspora.

Yet the Lebanese Khalil Hawi, who committed suicide when Israel invaded his country, created another Ulysses who appears as a bitter, apocalyptic concretion of Gilgamesh, Odysseus and Sindbad, Coleridge, and T. S. Eliot: a "sailor" who wanders through the unconscious, sacrifices his soul for knowledge, despairs of science, and sets sail toward the primordial banks of the Ganges where an ancient dervish foresees his death, the flames and ashes to fall on the coasts of the West, the emergence of boiling mud from a scowling earth, a new Athens or Rome.[44]

For "syncretism" we should read not painless absorption, acquiescence in another's models, but—as the Jews were forced to read—anguish, intercultural conflict, and a tearing divide in life and history. The odyssey of the protagonist of Theo Angelopolous's *Ulysses' Gaze* is the search for an old film reel, through the ethnic massacres and total devastation on both sides in the Balkans, in a very recent Europe. As Dante understood once and for all, Ulysses is no statue, but a flame, the tongue of fire that tells of a Greek condemned to death by the God of another culture.

こ٥ぐ

The great Nigerian writer in exile, Wole Soyinka, describes with scorching irony the British conquerors of Africa as self-appointed descendants of Ulysses. He sees Nelson Mandela, on the other hand, as a Ulysses resisting all the Sirens of the mind and of the white world.[45] "Glued to a promontory," he resists the tide that attempts to "flush the black will of his race," while albino eels "search the cortex of his heart," offering him oblivion and deliverance from jail. He is siren-tempted to become "ebony mascot / On the flagship of our space fleet": after all, history is compromise, time simply passes, his tongue has been chained, and he is a poor Nobody. At every temptation, Mandela-Ulysses replies, "No," because he is not a prisoner of the rock but is instead the rock itself. "Precedent on this soil," he has "toiled," in the guise of an ancient demiurge, "as in the great dark whale / Of time, Black Hole of the galaxy," to give the world new worlds. Ulysses, here, is part-Prometheus, part Antaeus, rejecting the false trophies of the Ancient Mariner or Captain Kirk. His rock, his island, this Ithaca he is bound to and that nurtures his strength, is the whole of Africa. "I *am* that rock / In the black hole of the sky," he ends, with biblical certainty. Ulysses, the cunning politician of Greek tragedy and Latin poetry, Dante's fraudulent counselor, has become a victim of politics: a hero of the ideal—Odysseus once more the king and master of his land.

Nonetheless, though this may be the powerfully political, ethical, and historical message of the Nigerian Ulysses, Soyinka the great writer returns to the general pattern of the *Odyssey* in his autobiographical *Isarà*. Without shrinking from political and cultural conflict, this is basically a journey "round" the life and "heroic" times of his father Essay. The figure of the poet fighting for justice—the Ofeyi of *Season of Anomy*[46]—is also present in Soyinka's work. Last, there is the personal, existential identification with Ulysses. In a short poem from *A Shuttle in the Crypt* entitled "Journey," Soyinka writes:

> I never feel I have arrived, though I come
> To journey's end . . .
> . . . .
>   I never feel I have arrived
> Though love and welcome snare me home
> Usurpers hand my cup at every
> Feast a last supper.[47]

Here the shadows of Ulysses—Dante's, Tennyson's, and Homer's—are clear and stark, overlaid with a shade of the Gospels that is, again, also political: a return that for the soul is never the end of the journey. We sense the presence of the Suitors, too, preparing Passion and death; the awareness of "the road not taken," of possessing flesh "nibbled clean, lost / To fretful fish among the rusted hulls": the awareness of being once again reduced to Nobody.

Ulysses is one of Soyinka's four basic archetypes, with the Biblical Joseph, Gulliver, and Hamlet, as he indicates in the section of *A Shuttle in the Crypt* entitled "Four Archetypes." In one of these poems, "Ulysses," the author writes from his Nigerian prison what he himself calls "notes" for the students of his Joyce class.[48] This time the search is decidedly an inner one. "Haunting the music of his mind," he watches a raindrop trickle down his window pane. Stretched "on this painless rack of time," he feels "the heritage of thought, clay and voices" becoming wind and rain, and drums an imaginary beat with his fingers, to retain his self-awareness. The storm extends its wings of ice. Like a sleepwalker he crosses "the weary cycle of the season's womb / Labouring to give birth to her deathless self," searching for a life that painfully tries every so often to create something that outlives death, and thinking through, over and beyond his past experience. In this way he becomes one with the world "in great infinitudes," slipping slowly into a Hades of the mind, of the "archetypal heart / Of all lone wanderers." Revisiting his former life of the intellect, his toying with concepts, his writing and teaching, he finds them a "crystal cover" on the real world. The old illusion is dispersed by the "rake of thunders" of experience: torn-up tobacco leaves, swollen seas, the rubble of buildings, crushed flowers and thorns, "mud consummation." The question inevitably arises: "How golden finally is the recovered fleece? / A question we refuse to ask the Bard."

Neither Homer nor Shakespeare (the traditional bards), nor Joyce (who has now, finally, joined their ranks), is able to respond to the supreme question of poetry and life. Each individual has to ask her- / himself how much importance to attach to the golden fleece of knowledge and verse. Soyinka searches for the answer in the archetypal image of Ulysses as shadow of himself. The "wine-centred waves" return, with the "swine-scented folds," the Straits "between vaginal rocks." Circe, the transformer of Ulysses' men into pigs, had imprisoned the poet in a very concrete jail, though never managing to turn him into an animal. The passage between Scylla and Charybdis, Nigeria and Biafra, was a horror faced and overcome. Each experience tears away its piece of flesh and erodes the skin. Yet to become an expert in the things of the world, human vices and human worth—to become, as Dante's Ulysses says, *del mondo esperto, e de li vizi umani e del valore*— is the noble part of life, the only one to allow "minds grown hoary from the quest" to remain rooted, in work and commitment, like a "boulder solitude amidst the waves": the only solitude that, paradoxically, allows us, on "dark-fallen seas," to maintain "our lighted beings / Suspended as mirages on the world's reality."

Africa is no New World, but a very ancient one—perhaps the first that *homo erectus* trod with legs, and a *sapiens* mind: perhaps the place where for the first time Hercules and Achilles, the heroes of brute force, became Ulysses, the man of intelligence. It is a land heavy with blood, hunger, injustice, exploitation, and genocide. Soyinka's African Ulysses gives some sort of answer to my question: no, history did not end in Auschwitz. It continues as an individual hell for each of us. Our survival strategy is necessarily to take on the shadow of our archetypes, from the Ulysses of Joyce, Dante, and Homer, to "become" them and finally incarnate a new Ulysses which in the *métissage*, the syncretism of conflict, will contain Joseph, Gulliver, Hamlet, Essay, Ofeyi and Nelson Mandela as well.[49]

As George Steiner has pointed out, humanism did not stop the German gauleiters from slaughtering millions of innocents.[50] It has, however, helped the victims—Primo Levi and, inside and beyond the West, Wole Soyinka. And as individuals subject to events beyond our control we are all victims. History is not just, as Paul De Man interprets Benjamin, a "motion," "an errance of language which never reaches its mark," the "illusion of a life which is only after-life."[51] History is real and human: perhaps, as Nietszche would say, "all zu menschliches," too human. What aspect of it, then, at the turn of the millennium, can Ulysses enlighten us on?

∽◦∾

Perhaps an immediate answer to this comes from Europe itself, divided for half a century by a Cold War which was as terrible as the two wars which bloodied the continent in the first half of the twentieth century, imprisoning, in central and eastern Europe, whole peoples behind an Iron Curtain, and whole sections of society in gulags no less horrifying than the Nazi death camps. Suddenly, in 1989, under the pickaxes of its citizens, the Wall dividing the city of Berlin and two worlds fell. People who had been separated for decades surged together. In Milan Kundera's novel *Ignorance* two such people, a man and woman, return home after exile from a Czechoslovakia occupied by Warsaw Pact troops in 1968. They had once loved each other, and now meet again for the second time. Ulysses stalks through the novel from the first pages, where the narrator evokes the *Odyssey*, the epic of homesickness and the Great Return, in which Ulysses chooses "the apotheosis of the known" rather than "ardent exploration of the unknown" and "the *dolce vita* in a foreign place," chooses "the finite (for the return is a reconciliation with the finitude of life)" rather than the "infinite" ("for adventure never intends to finish").[52]

Ulysses returned to Ithaca on a swift Phaecian ship, and was delicately laid down, still sleeping, on the shore. But the return to Prague, for two human beings meshed in the history of the past two decades, and after the two hundred years which have elapsed between the French Revolution and the fall of the Wall, is going to be a very different affair. Ulysses had been homesick, but remembered almost nothing: in people like him and Irena, the protagonist of *Ignorance*, lacking contact with compatriots in exile, amnesia is inevitable. What Ulysses has actually lost, on his return, are the precious years of wandering, and all he wants to do is narrate them, which he does, for four long Books of the *Odyssey*. No one in Ithaca is in any way interested, Kundera maintains, and Penelope must be satisfied with an expurgated and extremely short version immediately after their lovemaking.[53] History levels, flattens, transforms, and forgets, wiping out landscapes which have lasted for thousands of years, and its once barely-perceptible movements have accelerated violently. Would an *Odyssey* be conceivable today? the narrator muses. Perhaps the epic of return has no place in our time. "When Odysseus woke on Ithaca's shore that morning, could he have listened in ecstasy to the music of the Great Return if the olive tree had been felled and he recognized nothing around him?"[54] Mad flight is perhaps more the style of our time. Yet the novel refutes this. Lotus-eaters all, we live in a state of oblivion of which we have no notion. All we remember are tiny, insignificant particles. Still in exile in Paris, by day Irena receives from the "moviemaker of the subconscious" "bits of the home landscape as images of happiness," but by night they become "terrifying returns to that same land."[55] What then, exactly, is return—this *nostos* preceded by its own illness, nostalgia, and what is memory?[56] The two protagonists, after experiencing the whirlpool of history, are now made to turn round and round these questions. An answer is enigmatically given toward the end of the novel when the reader is presented with an *Odyssey* in Danish, and Josef and Irena speak of Ulysses before turning to their own lovemaking of return: what is needed, to survive the upheavals of history and the individual life, is a knowing—or "cunning," as Homer would have it—*ignorance*. At university, Irena "used to be seduced by the dreams of voyages to distant stars." "What pleasure," the narrator comments, "to escape far away into the universe, someplace where life expresses itself differently from here and needs no bodies!" But in this Odyssey of the third millennium this is no more possible than in Leopold Bloom's: "despite all his amazing rockets, man will never progress very far in the universe. The brevity of his life makes the sky a dark lid against which he will forever crack his head, to fall back onto earth, where everything alive eats and can be eaten."[57] No mad flight, then, nothing of the·sort. The novel ends, instead, with the beginning of a normal flight by airplane. Josef is going back "home," as Irena too will do shortly: "The plane took off toward a dark sky, then burrowed into clouds. After a few minutes the sky opened out, peaceful and friendly, strewn with stars. Through the porthole he saw, far off in the sky, a low wooden fence and a brick house with a slender fir tree like a lifted arm before it."[58]

∽○∾

But let us fly further. Another answer might be found in a Latin American writer from Brazil, the "island" which has produced such an extraordinary *métissage* of peoples, cultures, and history since its discovery in the sixteenth century, and where the Portuguese implanted their own imaginaire of Ulixabona-Lisbon, the last city founded by Ulysses before he disappeared into the Atlantic. In 1990, and then again in 1996, one of Brazil's greatest intellectuals, Haroldo de Campos, published a poem entitled *Finismundo: A Última Viagem*,[59] in which his mythopoeic imagination retraces

Ulysses' journey from Tiresias' prophecy in *Odyssey* XI to Dante's *Inferno* XXVI and on to Joyce. Prompted by Dantean hybris, this Ulysses wants, in the first part of the poem, to "trans-pass" (trespass) the "pass,"[60] to attain the "inhospitable, dark, pelaginous chaos to the point where the forbidden geography of Eden is concealed." There he might reach the "extreme isthmus," the "island" through which one gains access to "earthly heaven," to the "transfinite"—"Finismundo," the end of the world. But the mad flight ends in shipwreck, the whirlpool leaving behind, only for an instant, "passing signs," "foundering leaves," "erasures" that are the fragments of poetry.

In the second part, however, an "urban" Ulysses who has "outlived" myth finds himself in a city, facing "minimal traces digitized and soon cancelled in the liquid green-flowing crystal" of a computer screen. No longer a Promethean fire, he is reduced to the "portable Lucifer" of a "fósforo," a match, contemplating the intermittent, almost meaningless signs of "semáforos," of traffic lights, the "bittersweet cry" of the Sirens of the first section now turned into the sirens of ambulances, police cars, fire engines. A "postcard from Eden" is all that is left now of this "penúltima Tule."

Isn't this the parable of all civilizations, and particularly of ours? The "reversed Ithaca," the Earthly Paradise, the "island" of *Finismundo* might well be Brazil, and the "penultimate Thule" the city itself of São Paulo, the contemporary equivalent of Joyce's Dublin. That is where, according to the Dantean epigraph of the poem's second section, Ulysses, now lost, goes to die . . . or to survive. In order to get to this *finis terrae* he journeys through time, space, being, and non-being—or, paraphrasing Oswald de Andrade's famous question about Brazil, to both "tupy" *and* "not tupy."[61] Not to a place, but to an *outopos*, a utopia, the "aventuroso deslugar": in short, to a *locus contradictionis*: both earthly and Paradise, "umbráculo" and "lucarna." The hybris that prompts Ulysses to "trans-pass the pass" leads him to a nice pre-Parmenidean and postmodern cul-de-sac: an enigmatic "*impasse*-to-be."

Behind all de Campos's Joycean exuberance of language, however, this Last Voyage is clearly a journey of and toward poetry, to its end and its new beginning: toward bare wrecks, to the round Ocean that "resounds silently" and the "convulsive song" of the Sirens presented as "ultrasound unperceived by human ear," but also to what he has called *Crisantempo*,[62] a time of crisis, yet the chrysanthemum, the blooming flower in and of time as well, a crystal and chrysalis of poetry.

Is that where salvation lies, then? After publishing *Finismundo* and *Crisantempo*, Haroldo de Campos worked on a translation of the *Iliad*, the West's first poem ever. Of course, in this Beginning there looms a war of Troy, the First War which is also and always the Last, yesterday's and today's. But taking his multi-cultural cue from Hector, Ajax, and Dante in the dark wood, Haroldo de Campos also embarked on his *terza rima* dialogue with Genesis, Dante, Camões, Carlos Drummond de Andrade, Einstein and the whole of modern physics, exploring first things and last, from the Beginning of the world to Paradise.[63]

∽⊶∾

The itinerary of the Brazilian poet bears an uncanny resemblance to that of Derek Walcott, where—as in his fellow Caribbean poets Harris, Brathwaite and Dabydeen[64]—the shadows of Homer and Ulysses are thick indeed. "The sea is History," he sings in *The Star-Apple Kingdom* of 1979, and proceeds to trace through the books of the Bible, Old and New Testaments, the whole tragedy of Afro-Americans from deportation to slavery to emancipation.[65] The sea is history, and the blood-dark sea of oppression.

Then, in 1990, Walcott published *Omeros*.[66] And *Omeros* is indeed about war: mixing hexameter and *terza rima*, with echoes of Dante, Joyce, Montale, Hemingway, Conrad, Kipling, and the Bible, it recounts the war of jealousy for the wondrous Helen fought by a simple fisherman, the "quiet Achille, son of Afolabe," whose only slaughter is of fish, and "whose end, when it comes," will be the death by water of T. S. Eliot's Phlebas, and a Hector who has abandoned his canoe to turn taxi-driver. *Omeros* describes the wounds of Philoctetes, a tourist guide on the poet's native island, Saint Lucia, and narrates the story of Major Plunkett and his wife Maud, but its main concern is the Caribbean itself, which "goes on," and the magical landscape of the islands, which could almost redeem humanity from history: the dawns and sunsets and full moons of "our wide country." The protagonists of *Omeros* also include Seven Seas, a blind, wandering seer like Demodocus, and of course Homer himself: "O," he writes, "was the conch-shell's invocation, *mer* was / both mother and sea in our Antillean patois, / *os*, a grey bone, and the white surf as it crashes / and spreads its sibilant collar on a lace shore": *Omeros*, Homer as the whole world of nature, the voice of the sea, mother-tongue.

Walcott is soon on his trail, shadowing him across the meridian and finally reaching the "mud-caked settlement founded by Ulysses": Ulissibona, Lisbon.[67] Homer becomes Ulysses and *Odyssey*, Joyce and *Ulysses*. He appears in London, in a "bargeman's black greatcoat," his nose like a beacon in his sculpted face, his beard "like foam that exploded into the spray burst of eyebrows": in his "scrofulous claw his brown paper manuscript." He hunches, beggar-like, on a bench beside the Thames, his eyes closed, "frayed" lips chewing a beard "curled like the dog's-ears of his turned-down Odyssey," baptizing the various ships, contemplating the river, its shadows and fog which hide "the empires: London, Rome, Greece."[68] Cut to the Liffey in Dublin, and Anna Livia Plurabelle, the protagonist of Joyce's *Finnegans Wake*, "Muse of our age's Omeros, undimmed Master / and true tenor of the place!" Then "Mr. Joyce" himself appears, his voice "like sun-drizzled Howth" which closes Dublin's bay to the north (and where Joyce's *Ulysses* ends), "its violet lees / of moss at low tide," affably guiding his visitors, including the poem's narrator, and "the stone I rubbed in my pocket / from the Martello" (where Joyce's *Ulysses* begins). Joyce brings "one-eyed Ulysses to the copper-bright strand / watching the mail-packet pushing past the Head, its wake glittering like keys."[69] Lastly, we meet Ulysses himself, simultaneously in the Aegean and the Caribbean: a "tired shadow," his sail clinging "like a butterfly to the elbow / of an olive-tree," with his bride on her elderly father's arm, "scared of her future." This is a wandering Ulysses in full, mad flight, but brimming with desire and fearing his return.[70]

But these are all provisional shadows, like the poets Dante encounters: Omeros is the Virgil of the narrating voice, Joyce another guide, Ulysses a model. Just as Dante needs to shake off his mentor Virgil, and all the other poetic influences, from the two Guidos to Arnaut, so Walcott needs to find his own way, realize that everything that he has "read and rewritten till literature / was guilty as History" is not to be jettisoned, but transformed to meet his needs: "it was mine to make what I wanted of it, or / what I thought was wanted": "A cool wood off the road, a hut closed like a wound and the sound of a river / coming through the trees on a country Saturday, / with no-one in the dry front yard"; then "the track from which a man's shadow emerges, / then a girl carrying laundry, the road-smell like loaves, / the yellow-dressed butterflies" along the grassy banks. In short, "Why not see Helen / as the sun saw her, with no Homer shadow, / swinging her plastic sandals on that beach alone, / as fresh as the sea-wind?"[71]

Omeros traces with its metrical feet the bloodied, resentful tracks down which Europe and the West force-marched their own troops: Africa, the Caribbean, and Northern America. Nothing is omitted, but its glance is compassionate toward men, women, and the natural world: Achilles, Hector, Helen, and Philoctetes. In the end *Omeros* discovers what it is that distinguishes "mad flight" from the "right" journey, the Odyssey as undertaken by Homer and all poets: poetic composition, the poet crouched, immobile, silent, and sending Ulysses, his narrator, to face the tides, peoples and foreign tongues. Seven Seas, the bard of *Omeros*, describes the journey as follows:

"You ain't been nowhere," Seven Seas said, "you have seen
nothing no matter how far you may have travelled,
cities with shadowy spires stitched on a screen

which the beak of a swift has ravelled and unravelled;
you have learnt no more than if you stood on that beach
watching the unthreading foam you watched as a youth,

except your skill with one oar; you heard the salt speech
that your father once heard; one island, and one truth.
Your wanderer is a phantom from the boy's shore.

Mark you, he does not go; *he* sends his narrator
He plays tricks with time because there are two journeys
In every odyssey, one on worried water,

the other crouched and motionless, without noise.
For both, the 'I' is a mast; a desk is a raft
for one, foaming with paper, and dipping the beak

of a pen in its foam, while an actual craft
carries the other to cities where people speak
a different language, or look at him differently

while the sun rises from the other direction
with its unsettling shadows, but the right journey
is motionless; as the sea moves round an island

that appears to be moving, love moves round the heart —
with encircling salt, and the slowly travelling hand
knows it returns to the port from which it must start.

Therefore, this is what this island has meant to you,
why my bust spoke, why the sea-swift was sent to you:
to circle yourself and your island with this art."[72]

Love moves round the heart—with encircling salt: or, in a more Dantean vein,
love moves the heart in a circle, and the "high salt," the deep sea revolving in
a circle, as though they were wheels uniformly moved.[73] This is the poem's
message-in-a-bottle: this is why the sea-swift—not the halcyon nor swan nor

eagle—has been sent to the poet: to "encircle" him with the art whereby the line travels slowly toward the *nostos*: the hand which knowingly returns to the port it "must" depart from.

⸙

Even before *Omeros*, Walcott had already jettisoned the *Iliad* and found in Ulysses the more appropriate shadow for his Caribbean Everyman, going back to it some time later, in a stage version of the *Odyssey*.[74] "That sail which leans on light, / tired of islands, / a schooner beating up the Caribbean // for home," he writes in 1976 in *Sea Grapes*, "could be Odysseus, / homebound on the Aegean." Here, however, it is not just a question of finding a model, and tracing a tradition. Anyone connected with Western culture, directly or indirectly, who sees a sail and a lone man outlined against the sea, Walcott maintains, would think of Ulysses, Ulysses representing for us a sign, a conditioned image, a reflection of our own eyes.[75] But this won't do. That sail *could* be Odysseus: that fatherly, husbandly homesickness, "under gnarled, sour grapes" is "*like* the adulterer hearing Nausicaa's name in every gull's cry." But "this brings nobody peace":

> The ancient war
> between obsession and responsibility
> will never finish and has been the same
>
> for the sea-wanderer or the one on shore
> now wriggling on his sandals to walk home,
> since Troy sighed its last flame,
>
> and the blind giant's boulder heaved the trough
> from whose groundswell the great hexameters come
> to the conclusions of exhausted surf.
>
> The classics can console. But not enough.[76]

The classics can console. But not enough. The painful, stumbling steps of history are not to be forgotten. Before the *Odyssey* came the Trojan War; the hero returning to Ithaca is the person who reduced Ilium to ashes, the first European to destroy the "others" and haul them to slavery in the West. But poetry, Aristotle insists, is "more serious and more philosophical" than history. Poetry, Francis Bacon and Robert Lowth maintain, "seems to endow human nature with that which lies beyond the power of history, and to gratify the mind with at least the shadow of things where the substance cannot be had."[77] Poetry can therefore catch the primeval moment, its own beginnings and those of the world. Biblically, this is, of course, the moment of Creation. In the culture which, in a million metamorphoses, has come down to us from the Greeks, it is embodied in another moment of creation: a *poetic* one. Perhaps we can unwrite Walcott's *Sea Grapes* statement that the classics cannot console, by setting against it the *rewriting* of the classics in a mixed culture—in the *métissage* of the twenty-first century—as in Walcott's own "Map of the New World," where poetry goes back to its enchanted beginnings and a new Homer picks up the rain:

> At the end of this sentence, rain will begin.
> At the rain's end, a sail.
>
> Slowly the sail will loose sight of islands;
> into the mist will go the belief in harbours
> of an entire race.
>
> The ten-years' war is finished.
> Helen's hair, a grey cloud.
> Troy, a white ashpit
> by the drizzling sea.
>
> The drizzle tightens like the strings of a harp.
> A man with clouded eyes picks up the rain
> and plucks the first line of the *Odyssey*.[78]

⌘

This could be my conclusion. Instead of shoring fragments against our ruins, as T. S. Eliot preached at the end of *The Waste Land*, we should again marvel with the wonder possessed by children, first philosophers, and founding poets, recapture myth within history, "among peoples, amid events," and recreate poetry within ourselves, using the *poietike* each of us is endowed with. But my post-modern conscience obliges me to leave readers with an alternative, because history may in the end have its own revenge. In Battery Park, New York City, there stands a statue by the contemporary Italian artist, Ugo Attardi, a gift from Italy to the United States, as the Statue of Liberty was

. . .

Figure 3. Ugo Attardi. *Ulisse*. New York, Battery Park;
in the background the twin towers of the World Trade Center.
Photograph by Angelo Dicuonzo, 2000.

a gift from France. It represents Ulysses in mid-, mad, Dantean flight toward
knowledge of the unknown. He is clearly dancing, and pointing his staff
toward the newly discovered world of America: rejecting Leopold Bloom's
advice, he turns his back firmly on Wall Street. The ferocious helmet is
mask-like: multifaceted, "polytropic," and alien, but also a non-face, the face
of No one. As to the "real" face beneath, we could imagine it to be that of

a dead white European—Greek perhaps, that of Ulysses the Conquistador, rocking in war dance, spear and sword at the ready against the Cyclops—the "savages" of all new continents to be settled. Alternately, we might opt for a darker skin: a native American about to exact revenge on the paleface Suitors occupying his house and land. Or—the most unsettling hypothesis— the helmet might be concealing a Latino, African, Asian, or Middle Eastern grimace of hate, resentment, and incomprehension: a Ulysses threatening the Twin Towers, America, and the West through terrorism or immigration.

I ended a series of lectures held in New York and at Yale in the spring of 2000 with precisely that question. The answer came from two planes in mad, suicidal-homicidal flight on September 11, 2001, when the towers of the World Trade Centre were struck, and imploded into a Ground Zero unprecedented in America. The statue of Ulysses threatening the two towers from the middle of his own mad flight stands *behind the Towers*, a photograph highlighting their dangerous proximity.[79] The statue is still there, intact.

Epilogue: Winged Words

Readers will decide for themselves whether this book makes any sense. My view, of course, is that it does: that it is necessary for us to recount stories within history, reflect upon their connections, and experience poetry, trying to understand the beauty, the sublime, the good, and the just within it. Homer often speaks of *epea pteroenta*, "winged words": in traditional interpretations, this metaphor stood for the swift and lofty birdlike flight of language, particularly poetic language. This meaning has certainly sustained me throughout: as in a *psykhagogia*, the journey in which Hermes accompanied the dead to Hades, but also Icarus's anxiety for flight. I hope I have communicated these to readers. More recent interpretations, however, link the wings of words to the feathers that guide an arrow in flight, helping it fly straight, to reach its target. This is clearly the way in which the image is used by Pindar, the tragedians, and Plato. With these flights, my wish was to get to the *point*: if I have succeeded in offering readers a glimpse of the moment at which taking off, flying, or landing is "just" in my view (and hopefully in other people's as well), I will have achieved my aim, homed in upon my target.

By way of conclusion, let me offer here an epilogue pointing in a couple of directions. During the last century, there have been three, equally stunning, extremes of flight. The first two are instrumental to each other and are both found in Mikhail Bulgakov's *The Master and Margarita*. The first has Margarita Nikolaevna, who has become a witch, take off on a broomstick. Finally free, invisible, naked and weightless, she flies through the streets of Moscow in midair, wrecks the apartments of privileged writers and critics in Dramlit House—

the House for Dramatists and Literary Workers—smashes the windows, floods the building, and then flies off, away from the city and toward the forests, lakes, and rivers of Russia's vast territory. In flight she meets Natasha Prokofievna (whose mount is the writer Nikolai Ivanovich, who has been turned into a hog). In the moonlit night Margarita leaps into the silvery water. The witches and a goat-legged creature are gathered around a bonfire to pay homage to her: there is a feast in her honor. Immediately afterward, a flying convertible driven by a black sea-crow takes her back to Moscow, apartment number 302 B, Sadovaia Street. This is where Woland—Satan— has ensconced himself with his small demonic coterie, and where the devils' Grand Ball is soon to be held, crowning Margarita as "queen." Margarita's flight demolishes official literary criticism, and above all heads toward the infernal Sabbath, itself part of that Universal Judgment that commences with Woland's appearance in Moscow and that extends to the whole reality and horror of the Soviet Union under Stalinism. It leads to nothingness and damnation. Nonetheless, according to the epigraph from Goethe's *Faust* in Bulgakov's *The Master and Margarita*, the Devil is "That Power . . . which wills forever evil yet does forever good."[1]

Later in the novel there is another fantastic flight. Woland has just received word from Yeshua Ha-Notsri (Jesus of Nazareth), via tax collector Matthew Levi (coprotagonist, along with Pilate and Jesus himself, of the novel-within-the-novel in which the Master-author tells the story of the Passion and the Crucifixion), of a request to allow the Master and his beloved Margarita some "rest." Azazello, from Woland's coterie, poisons them with the Falernian wine drunk by Pontius Pilate. At this point the demon, Margarita, and the Master mount flying steeds in order to reach Satan. With Satan at their side, they continue on their celestial night flight until they reach a plain where boulders sparkle from dark depths untouched by moonlight. Pontius Pilate, procurator of Judea, has been sitting here for almost two thousand years, tormented prisoner of his own remorse. Upon the Master's request, he is freed. Soon after, while Woland and his coterie leap into the abyss, the Master and Margarita enter the small "eternal home" of refuge and silence. Flight leads to evil, but also to good: what changes its direction is Margarita's love and the Master's forgiveness of Pontius Pilate: transforming, within literature, the destiny that history and religion assigned to one man— a Roman, a foreigner, and a Gentile—at the outset of the entire Christian era. Stalin's Soviet Union and the Empire of Rome. How does one cope with such monstrous entities? With scorching irony and satire, on the one hand; with love, on the other. This is something that must be borne in mind.

There is also the third extreme of flight. In his *Sonnets to Orpheus*, Rilke dedicates a poem to the future of flight.[2] Only when flight is no longer a merely self-satisfied end unto itself—he says—will it rise into the celestial calm, soaring and hovering in luminous profiles. Only when it has become successful as an instrument, agile, and confident in playing the winds' darling; only when a pure destination takes over from the youthful pride of simply developing, growing machinery and gadgetry; only then, inebriated with triumph and quickened by victory, will one who has narrowed distances and ventured far, become what he pursues, the target of his solitary flight—

> will one, hellbent to win,
> closing on the distances
> *be* his lonely flight's own end.
> [wird, überstürzt von Gewinn,
> jener den Fernen Genahte
> *sein*, was er einsam erfliegt.][3]

We should meditate upon these lines. They invite us to free ourselves of airy exaltation, of self-complacency (that "complaisance dans le Même" of Western thought that Levinas criticizes in Ulysses), of art for art's sake, of the twentieth century's proud and conquering technology: of Icarian poetry and "mad flight." We need to move beyond, to rise into the *Himmelstillen*, into the silences and calm of the sky, towards *ein reines Wohin*, a pure *whereto*: straightforward and true. It is necessary to rise *in lichten Profile*, in the luminous profiles that are perfect "tools" and also favored by the wind: in tune and in *play* with it, *sicher, schlenkend und schlank*, confident, circling, and agile. In chapter 5, we have seen how Yeats's swans, "mysterious" and "beautiful" as they are, yet "build" their nests.[4] Rilke writes in the first of the *Duino Elegies* that "maybe birds will feel the air thinning as they fly *deeper into themselves*":[5] because they have a nest to return to, like the womb that is All. This is why, as if they knew that they are linked to the world "by a profound mystery"—so Rilke explains in a letter to Lou Andreas Salomé[6]—they sing in the world as though singing to themselves. Human beings and their winged words need to have a nest to which to return and at the same time to make of themselves luminous profiles: human tools and natural elements, but above all *instruments*, means—not ends. Perhaps then, in pursuing a target, flight and being will be one and the same.

Notes

CHAPTER 1

1. L. de Bosis, *The Story of My Death*, trans. Ruth Draper (Cambridge, Mass., 1971), p. 9. See also *La storia della mia morte*, ed. A. Cortese de Bosis (Rome, 1995), p. 67; L. de Bosis, *Storia della mia morte e ultimi scritti*, ed. G. Salvemini (Turin, 1948), p. 171.

2. F. Fucci, *Ali contro Mussolini. I raid aerei antifascisti degli anni trenta* (Milan, 1978).

3. M. Della Terza, "Lauro de Bosis (1901–1931)," *Harvard Library Bulletin* 30, no. 3 (July 1982): 253–81; I. Origo, *A Need to Testify. Portraits of Lauro de Bosis, Ruth Draper, Gaetano Salvemini, Ignazio Silone* (New York and London, 1984); J. M. Mudge, *The Poet and the Dictator: Lauro de Bosis Resists Fascism in Italy and America* (Westport, Conn. and London, 2002).

4. *Prometeo incatenato* (Rome, 1930); *Edipo re* (Rome, 1924); *Antigone* (Rome, 1927); *Il Ramo d'Oro* (Rome, 1925; and Turin, 1965, 1990); L. de Bosis, ed., *The Golden Book of Italian Poetry* (Oxford and New York, 1933). De Bosis also translated *The Private Life of Helen of Troy* by John Erskine (as *La vita privata di Elena di Troia* [Milan, 1928]) and *The Bridge of San Luis Rey* by Thornton Wilder (as *Il ponte di San Luis Rey* [Rome, 1929]).

5. *Story of My Death*, p. 9.

6. Hesiod, *Theogony*, 276–86, 325; Pindar, *Olympian* XIII, 60–92 and *Isthmian* VII, 44; Strabo, *Geography* 8.6.21; Apollodorus, *Library*, 2.3.2 and 4.2 ff.; Hyginus, *Fabulae* 151.

7. *Fasti* III, 450–58; see *Metamorphoses* IV, 785–89; V, 256–63.

8. G. Chaucer, *The Squire's Tale*, in *The Riverside Chaucer*, ed. L. D. Benson (Boston, 1987), *Canterbury Tales* V, 207.

9. See J. D. Reid, ed., *The Oxford Guide to Classical Mythology in the Arts, 1300–1990s* (New York and Oxford, 1993), s.v. "Pegasus"; P. Boitani, *Chaucer and the Imaginary World of Fame* (Cambridge, 1984), pp. 6, 42–45, 54, 57, 86, 131–34, 146.

10. Fulgentius, *Mitologiarum Liber*, ed. R. Helm (Stuttgart, 1970), I, xxi; III, i.

11. *Paradiso* XVIII, 82–87.

12. G. Bruno, *Spaccio de la bestia trionfante*, in *Dialoghi filosofici italiani*, ed. M. Ciliberto (Milan, 2000), p. 474; see also "Cabala del cavallo pegaseo," passim.

13. P. Valéry, "Au Platane," in *Charmes*, *Œuvres* (Paris, 1957), vol. 1, p. 115.

14. W. B. Yeats, "The Fascination of What's Difficult," in *Collected Poems* (London, 1965), p. 104.

15. R. Darío, "Pegaso," in *Cantos de vida y esperanza, Poesías completas*, 2nd ed. (Buenos Aires, 1987), vol. 2, pp. 540–41.

16. In *Storia della mia morte e ultimi scritti*, pp. 155–59.

17. Shakespeare, *Hamlet* II, ii, 553–54.

18. I have used the bilingual edition of *Icaro* with Ruth Draper's English translation and Gilbert Murray's preface (London, 1933).

19. Ibid., p. 200.

20. *Paradiso* I, 67–72; *Metamorphoses* XIII, 898–965.

21. *Icaro*, pp. 150–52.

22. *Icaro*, p. 170.

23. *Gerusalemme liberata* XV, 30 ss.

24. *Icaro*, p. 196.

25. *Icaro*, pp. 40–42.

26. In *Ramo d'Oro* (Turin, 1990), p. 826.

27. *Opera Omnia di Benito Mussolini*, ed. E. and D. Susmel (Florence, 1951), p. 187; F. Valli and A. Foschini, *Il volo in Italia* (Rome, 1939), p. 175. See also *Opera Omnia* (Florence, 1957), vol. 22, pp. 2–3: on November 7, 1925, Mussolini held an official welcome for Francesco de Pinedo at the Arnaldo da Brescia riverport, celebrating him as the "Dantean Ulysses who had turned oars into 'wings for the mad flight.'" On Mussolini, Fascism, and aviation, see R. Wohl, *The Spectacle of Flight: Aviation and the Western Imagination, 1920–1950* (New Haven and London, 2005), pp. 49–108.

CHAPTER 2

1. *Storia della mia morte e altri scritti*, ed. G. Salvemini (Turin, 1948), p. xv.

2. Cited in R. Wohl, *A Passion for Wings: Aviation and the Western Imagination, 1908–1918* (New Haven and London, 1994), p. 287.

3. F. Fucci, *Ali contro Mussolini. I raid aerei antifascisti degli anni trenta* (Milan, 1978).

4. *Forse che sì, forse che no*, in G. D'Annunzio, *Romanzi e novelle, Prose di Romanzi* (Milan, 1950), vol. 2, p. 906.

5. "Un'ala sul Mare è solitaria . . . Chi la raccoglierà? Chi con più forte / lega saprà rigiugnere le penne / sparse per ritentare il folle volo?" Ibid., vol. 2, p. 905.

6. F. Roncoroni, ed., *Alcyone* (Milan, 1995), p. 581. See also comment in P. Gibellini, ed., *Alcione* (Turin, 1995).

7. Ibid., pp. 584–85.

8. *Il secondo amante di Lucrezia Buti*, in *Prose di ricerca*, vol. 2, *Le faville del maglio* (Milan, 1950), p. 172.

9. Dithyramb IV, in *Alcyone*, pp. 592–622; here see 647–50.

10. "Non avevo mai sentito nel petto un animo tanto tirannico, tanto predace, tanto vorace . . . Mi rinchiudevo, mi affocavo e soffocavo. Mi sbattevo come un'aquila ardente in una gabbia cieca, come doveva sbattersi Icaro nella caverna dove il padre gli foggiava l'ali con troppa tardità. La poesia mi faceva groppo in gola, come il pianto, come il sangue. La

mia volontà di dire rompeva il metro, superava il numero. Ogni grande strofa del Ditirambo m'incominciava "Icaro disse," mi ricominciava "Icaro disse," mi si rifaceva "Icaro disse." Era come un'ambascia implacabile; era come uno struggimento di bevere il soffio dell'altezza titanica; era come una brama di eguagliare nel respiro il petto di Pan," *Prose di ricerca*, vol. 2, p. 172.

11. Ibid.

12. *Laudi*, pp. 2–3.

13. J. Farrell, "The Age of Icarus—the Adventure of Flight in G. D'Annunzio and L. De Bosis," in *Literature and Travel*, ed. M. Hanne (Amsterdam, 1994), pp. 123–36; cf. F. P. Ingold, *Literatur und Aviatik: Europäische Flugdichtung, 1909–1927* (Basel, 1978).

14. Since these journeys have been discussed in detail and cataloged in M. Dancourt, *Dédale et Icare: Metamorphoses d'un mythe* (Paris, 2002), it is unnecessary for me to deal with them thoroughly and systematically here. See also the *Nachwort* to *Mythos Ikarus*, ed. A. Aurnhammer and D. Martin (Leipzig, 1998).

15. *Aeneid* VI, 14–33.

16. *Ars amandi* II, 21–98; *Tristia* I, 87–90.

17. *Ars amandi* II, 42.

18. *Metamorphoses* VIII, 152–235.

19. "Paralipomeni alla Batracomiomachia" VII, in *Poesie e Prose*, ed. M. A. Rigoni (Milan, 1987), vol. 1, p. 289.

20. Apollodorus, *Epitome* I, 12.

21. *Carmina* II, xx, 1–3 and 12.

22. Suetonius, *De vita Caesarum, Nero XII.*

23. Aulus Gellius, *Noctes Atticae* X, xii, 8–10.

24. Lucian, *De astrologia* 14–15, 366–7.

25. Diodorus Siculus, IV, 77.

26. Pausanias, IX, 11, 4–5.

27. Pliny the Elder, *Naturalis Historia* VII, 57, 209.

28. F. Frontisi-Ducroux, *Dédale. Mythologie de l'artisan en Grèce ancienne* (Paris, 1975), pp. 79–82, 151–70.

29. *Odyssey* XXIII, 200.

30. At 1 Kings 12:10. P. Bersuire, *Ovidius moralizatus, Reductorium morale Liber XV, cap ii–xv* (Utrecht, 1962), pp. 128–29. Towards the end of the fifteenth century, in his *Narrenschiff* (40, 21–8), Sebastian Brant still associated Icarus with Phaethon and Jeroboam in order to claim that the "advice of the fathers" must be followed, M. Lemmer, ed., 2nd ed. (Tübingen 1968); translated as *The Ship of Fools*, trans. E. H. Zeydel (New York, 1962).

31. C. De Boer, ed., *Ovide moralisé en prose* (Amsterdam, 1954), pp. 228–9; and see C. De Boer, M. G. De Boer, and J. Th. M. Van 'T Sant, eds., *Ovide moralisé* (Amsterdam, 1931), book 8, ll. 1767–1928.

32. See C. Hart, *Images of Flight* (Berkeley, 1988).

33. See 2 Corinthians 12:2–5.

34. See 2 Kings 2:11–13.

35. Koran 17:1, translated by N. J. Dawood (1956; London, 1990); see E. Cerulli, *Il Libro della Scala e la questione delle fonti arabo-spagnole della Divina Commedia* (Vatican City, 1949). See also M. A. Amir-Moezzi, ed., *Le voyage initiatique en terre d'Islam. Ascensions célestes et itinéraires spirituels* (Louvain and Paris, 1996).

36. See C. Hart, *The Prehistory of Flight* (Berkeley, 1985).

37. M. Liborio et al., eds., *Alessandro nel Medioevo occidentale* (Milan, 1997), pp. 368–69.

38. Summaries and references in C. Hart, *The Dream of Flight: Aeronautics from Classical Times to the Renaissance* (London, 1972), pp. 90–91.

39. Niceta Choniates, *Chronica* IV, 7, 7–8, in *Grandezza e catastrofe di Bisanzio*, ed. Riccardo Maisano (Milan, 1994), vol. 1, pp. 268–75.

40. Hart, *Dream of Flight*, pp. 91–92.

41. Ibid., pp. 94–96.

42. Ibid., pp. 106, 168.

43. Leonardo da Vinci, *Scritti letterari*, ed. A. Marinoni, 2nd ed. (Milan, 1974), p. 175: "Piglierà il primo volo il grande uccello sopra del dosso del suo magno Cecero, empiendo l'universo di stupore, empiendo di sua fama tutte le scritture, e groria eterna al nido dove nacque."

44. S. Freud, *Leonardo da Vinci. A Study in Psychosexuality*, trans. A. A. Brill (New York, 1947).

45. Dancourt, *Dédale et Icare*; Hart, *Dream of Flight*.

46. *Orlando furioso*, ed. C. Segre (Milan, 1998), IV, 18.

47. Ibid., XXXIII, 96–114.

48. Ibid., XXXIV, 48–58.

49. Ibid., XXXIV, 68–75.

50. These are all available in *Mythos Ikarus*.

51. *Mythos Ikarus*, p. 63.

52. A. Alciato, in *Mythos Ikarus*, p. 54; W. Shakespeare, *Henry VI*, act IV, scene vi, 54–7; *Henry VI*, act V, scene vi, 18–29; Calderón de la Barca, *La vida es sueño*, II, xvii, (Madrid, 1969), p. 176; G. B. Marino, "Icaro in cera," in M. Pieri, ed., *La Galeria* (Padua, 1979), vol. 1, p. 301; *Adone*, ed. G. Pozzi, 2nd ed. (Milan, 1988), IX, 4; XI, 193.

53. L. de Góngora, *Soledades*, ed. R. Jammes (Madrid, 1994), book 1, ll. 397–434, 999–1019 (pp. 279, 403). See J. H. Turner, *The Myth of Icarus in Spanish Renaissance Poetry* (London, 1976); N. Von Prellwitz, "Góngora: el vuelo audaz del poeta," *Bulletin of Hispanic Studies* 74 (1997): 19–35. The authors of the *Emblems* are particularly passionate about the Icarus image. *Mythos Ikarus*, p. 263, n. 30, cites a rather interesting case from around 1600 when a Prince named Pompeo Colonna had his *impresa*, "Leave nothing to dare," illustrated with the image of Icarus in flight; the commentator linked it with the daring of Amerigo Vespucci: Jacobus Typotius, *Symbola divina et humana* (Graz, 1972), vol. 3, pp. 102–5. Vespucci thought of himself as a fortunate Dantean Ulysses.

54. L. de Góngora, *Sonetos completos* (Madrid, 1969), 72 (p. 131). Góngora's sonnet 118 is a burlesque treatment of the Icarus myth.

55. F. Bacon, *De sapientia veterum* XXVII, in *The Works of Francis Bacon*, vol. 6, ed. J. Spedding, R. L. Ellis, and D. D. Heath (London, 1861).

56. G. Bruno, *De gli eroici furori* I, iii, in *Dialoghi filosofici italiani*, ed. M. Ciliberto (Milan, 2000), p. 815.

57. Ibid.

58. Ibid., *De l'infinito, universo e mondi, Proemiale epistola*, p. 322.

59. C. Marlowe, *Doctor Faustus*, prologue 21–3: the Chorus implicitly compares Faustus to Icarus and Lucifer.

60. Sor Juana Inés de la Cruz, "El Sueño," 454–75, in *Poesía lírica*, ed. J. C. González (Madrid, 2001), pp. 284–85.

61. *Dialoghi filosofici italiani*, p. xxxi.

62. J. W. Goethe, *Faust II*, iii, 574–54, in *Werke*, ed. E. Trunz (Munich, 1988), vol. 7, emphasis added.

63. See W. Emrich, *Die Symbolik von Faust II*, 2nd ed. (Bonn, 1957); P. Citati, *Goethe* (Milan, 1990), pp. 459–71.

64. F. Nietzsche, *Also Sprach Zarathustra* (Stuttgart, 1988), p. 257; translated as *Thus Spoke Zarathustra*, trans. R. J. Hollingdale (Harmondsworth, 1961), p. 247. Nietzsche also composed a *Euphorion*, for which see Dancourt, *Dédale et Icare*, pp. 98–99.

65. See F. T. Marinetti, for example, "Le prospettive aeree del paesaggio italiano" and "L'aeropoema del Golfo della Spezia," in *Teoria e invenzione futurista*, ed. L. De Maria (Milan, 1983), pp. 197–201, 629–31, 1095–1137. And see Wohl, *Passion for Wings*, pp. 138–44, 196–200.

66. C. Baudelaire, *Œuvres complètes*, ed. C. Pinchois (Paris, 1975), vol. 1, p. 143.

67. *Mythos Ikarus*, pp. 102–5.

68. S. Mallarmé, *Œuvres completes* (Paris, 1988), vol. 1, p. 9.

69. Wohl, *Passion for Wings*, p. 110. Wohl's work is essential for understanding the aviation imaginary. See also R. D. Launius and J. R. Daly Bedmark, eds., *Reconsidering a Century of Flight* (Chapel Hill, 2003), and especially R. P. Hallion, *Taking Flight: Inventing the Aerial Age from Antiquity through the First World War* (New York and Oxford, 2003).

70. A. de Saint-Exupéry, *Vol de nuit*, in *Oeuvres complètes* (Paris, 1994), vol. 1, p. 154. Translated from the French by Stuart Gilbert as *Night Flight* (San Diego, 1932), p. 70. A Peter Greenaway exhibition, entitled Flying over Water: The Icarus Adventure, was held in Barcelona and Malmö in 1997, recounting the ancient story with extraordinary modern means, right up to the final fall of Icarus.

71. F. Kafka, "Die Aeroplane in Brescia" and "Der Kübelreiter," in *Ein Landarzt und andere Drucke zu Lebzeiten* (Frankfurt am Main, 1994), pp. 312–20, 345–47, translated as *The Penal Colony*, trans. W. and E. Muir (New York, 1948).

72. F. Kafka, *Hochzeits-vorbereitungen auf dem Lande und andere Prosa aus dem Nachlass* (Frankfurt am Main, 1983), p. 51. Icarus, flight, and wings survive in the lovely poems in S. Stewart, *Columbarium* (Chicago, 2003), pp. 10, 100–1.

73. P. Boitani, *The Shadow of Ulysses. Figures of a Myth* (Oxford, 1994), pp. 44–68.

74. S. Deane, in J. Joyce, *A Portrait of the Artist as a Young Man* (Harmondsworth, 1992), p. 329.

CHAPTER 3

1. Classical scholars continue to debate the resemblance versus metamorphosis issue: see a summary in G. S. Kirk, ed., *The Illiad: A Commentary* (Cambridge, 1990), vol. 2, pp. 239–41; and the commentaries by S. West and J. B. Hainsworth on *Odyssey* passages cited in note 3 (vol. 1 [Milan, 2003], vol. 2 [Milan, 2002]); see also P. Nilsson, *Geschichte der griechischen Religion*, 3rd ed., vol. 1 (Munich, 1967); F. Dirlmeier, "Die Vogelgestalt homerischer Götter," *Sitzungberichte der Heidelberger Akademie der Wissenschaften* 2 (1967); H. Erbse, *Untersuchungen zur Funktion der Götter im Homerischen Epos* (Berlin, 1986), p. 71. Athena's appearance as a vulture after the conversation between Telemachus and Nestor is a clear-cut case, since Nestor recognizes her precisely because she is a vulture.

2. *Iliad* VII, 59; XIV, 289–91; XV, 236–8; XIX, 350–1. Translations of the *Iliad* and the *Odyssey* are by Robert Fagles (New York 1990, 1996).

3. *Odyssey* I, 320; III, 371–79; XXII, 239–40; V, 333–53.

4. *Iliad* V, 778–79.

5. *Iliad* V, 768–72.

6. *Libellvs de Svblimitate Dionysio Longino fere Adscriptus*, ed. D. A. Russell (Oxford, 1968), chapter 9, paragraph 8; my translations are based on T. S. Dorsch's in Aristotle / Horace / Longinus, *Classical Literary Criticism* (Harmondsworth, 1965).

7. *Iliad* XIII, 17–31.

8. For various points concerning Hermes, see the Homeric "Hymn to Hermes," in *Inni omerici*, ed. F. Cassola (Milan, 1975); see also L. Kahn, *Hermès passe, ou les ambiguïtés de la communication* (Paris, 1978); J.-P. Vernant, *Myth and Thought among the Greeks*, (Boston, 1983); W. Otto, *The Homeric Gods*, 2nd ed. (London 1979), chap. 3; P. Citati, *La mente colorata. Ulisse e l'Odissea* (Milan, 2002), pp. 24–40; G. Chiarini, *I cieli del mito. Letteratura e cosmo da Omero a Ovidio* (Reggio Emilia, 2005), pp. 112–31, 194–222.

9. *Iliad* XXIV, 339–48.

10. *Inni Omerici*, II, 334–41.

11. *Odyssey* V, 43–58.

12. *Odyssey* I, 50.

13. Longinus, *De svblimitate* 7, 2–4.

14. Aristotle, *Poetics* 4, 1, 1448b 17.

15. I. Calvino, *Six Memos for the Next Millennium* (Cambridge, Mass., 1988), pp. 51–52.

16. *Odyssey* VIII, 579–80, emphasis added.

17. *Aeneid* IV, 238–58.

18. *Aeneid* IV, 223–37; here 227–31.

19. E. Fairfax's classic translation was published in 1600 as *Godfrey of Bulloigne* and is available as *Jerusalem Delivered* (Oxford, 1981).

20. *Aeneid* VIII, 622–23; *Georgics* I, 365–67; *Paradiso* XV, 13–14.

21. Fairfax's translation is too free, and I provide here my own.

22. *Gerusalemme liberata* ed. L. Caretti (Milan, 1979), IX, 60–62.

23. Heraclitus, *I frammenti e le testimonianze*, ed. C. Diano and G. Serra (Milan, 1980), test. 40, fr. 53, test. 42 (Maximus of Tyre).

24. Darkness and horror are Tasso's additions to Dante's image in *Purgatorio* II, 35.

25. R. M. Rilke, *Duino Elegies*, II, 13–14, 18–19, in *The Selected Poetry of Rainer Maria Rilke*, ed. and trans. S. Mitchell (New York, 1980).

26. *Aeneid* VIII, 622–3: "qualis cum caerula nubes / solis inardescit radiis longeque refulgent" [as a livid cloud / burns with the rays of the sun and shines afar].

27. *Paradise Lost* V, 246–87.

28. Acts 12:10.

29. *Paradiso* XXIX, 79–80.

30. Milton alludes to this in *Paradise Lost* I, 286–91. In *Areopagitica* he claims he visited Galileo at Fiesole.

31. A. Fowler sums up several of these ideas in his commentary on *Paradise Lost*, 2nd ed. (London, 1998).

32. Isaiah 6:2.

33. Pliny, *Historia naturalis* X, ii.

34. Revelation 1:13.

35. Tasso, *Gerusalemme liberata* I, 14.

36. F. G. Klopstock, *Werke in einem Band* (Munich and Vienna, 1969), *Der Messias* I, 158–226.

37. *Biblia Hebraica Stuttgartensia*, ed. K. Elliger and W. Rudolph (Stuttgart, 1990). The traditional interpretations of this verse are examined by K. Smorónski in "Et Spiritus Dei ferebatur super aquas: inquisitio historico-exegetica in interpretationem textus Gen. 1.2c," *Biblica* 6 (1925): 140–56, 275–93, 361–95.

38. Ellen van Wolde, *Stories of the Beginning* (London, 1996), p. 22.

39. *Paradiso* XXIX, 19–21.

40. Exodus 19:3–4, trans. R. Alter in *The Five Books of Moses* (New York and London, 2004).

41. Deuteronomy 32.10–12 (trans. R. Alter).

42. Isaiah 40:31.

43. Matthew 3:16, but also in the other Gospels: *Novum Testamentum Graece et Latine*, ed. E. and E. Nestle and B. and K. Aland (Stuttgart, 1994).

44. Isaiah 42:1.

45. *Paradise Lost* I, 20–22.

46. *Septuaginta*, ed. A. Rahlfs (Stuttgart, 1935): Genesis 1:2.

47. *Inferno* XVII, 100–36.

48. Mark 16:5; *Inferno* IX, 64–90; *Purgatorio* II, 13–51; lines 13–15, translated from the Italian by J. Sinclair. For the angels in Dante, Rilke, etc., see M. Cacciari, *L'angelo necessario*, 2nd ed. (Milan, 1994).

CHAPTER 4

1. *Greek Lyric Poetry*, trans. D. A. Campbell (Cambridge, Mass. and London, 1988), vol. 2, pp. 416–17. The meaning of the first and last lines is disputed: in the first, *hiarophonoi* could mean "holy-voiced" rather than "strong-voiced"; in the last *hiaros* could mean both "sacred" and, with the other words of the line, "of the first life" (or "spring").

2. Aristophanes, *The Birds*, 250–51.

3. Plutarch, *De sollertia animalium, Moralia* XII, 974; Democritus in Diels-Kranz, *Fragmente der Vorsokratiker*, fr. 154; see G. Lanata, ed., *Poetica pre-platonica* (Florence, 1963), pp. 41–43; B. Gentili, in *Studi . . . in onore di Vittorio de Falco* (Naples, 1971), pp. 59–67; M. C. Bowra, *Greek Lyric Poetry from Alcman to Simonides* (Oxford, 1961), pp. 16–73; H. Fränkel, *Early Greek Poetry and Philosophy*, trans. M. Hadas and J. Willis (Oxford, 1975), pp. 159–70.

4. Lucretius, *De rerum natura* V, 1379.

5. See P. Pucci, *The Song of the Sirens: Essays on Homer* (Lanham, MD, 1998); L. Mancini, *Il rovinoso incanto. Storie di Sirene antiche* (Bologna, 2005).

6. Pliny, *Historia Naturalis* X, 47 ff.

7. R. Graves, *The White Goddess*, ed. G. Lindop (London, 1997), p. 182.

8. *Metamorphoses* XI, 497–501.

9. *Metamorphoses* XI, 658–68.

10. Ibid., XI, 684–89.

11. *Metamorphoses*, XI, 731–33: this passage translated by F. J. Miller, *Metamorphoses* (Cambridge, Mass. and London, 1976), pp. 171–73.

12. On this, see Aristotle, *Historia animalium* V, viii; and Pliny, *Naturalis Historia* X, 47. Aristotle quotes a passage from a poem by Simonides with reference to the "holy season" when "the many-hued halcyon nurtures her young."

13. See R. Mussapi, *Inferni, mari, isole. Storie di viaggi nella letteratura* (Milan, 2002), pp. 29–33; H. Fränkel, *Ovid, a Poet between Two Worlds* (Berkeley, 1945); C. Segal, *Ovidio e la poesia del mito* (Venice, 1991); R. Esposito, *La narrativa inverosimile: Aspetti dell'epica ovidiana* (Naples, 1994); J. Fabre-Serris, *Mythe et poésie dans les Métamorphoses d'Ovide* (Paris, 1995); P. R. Hardie, *Ovid's Poetics of Illusion* (Cambridge, 2002).

14. Petrus Berchorius, *Ovidius moralizatus* (*Reductorium morale, Liber XV, capp. ii–xv*) (Utrecht, 1962), p. 161.

15. G. Chaucer, *The Book of the Duchess*, 62–230, in *The Riverside Chaucer*, ed. L. D. Benson (Boston, 1987); J. Gower, *Confessio amantis* IV, 2927–3123, G. C. Macaulay, ed., *Works*, vol. 2 (Oxford, 1901); Christine de Pisan, *L'epistre d'Othéa à Hector*, in *Œuvres poétiques*, ed. M. Roy (Paris, 1886–96), ch. 79; J. Dryden in J. Kinsley, ed., *Fables*, in *Poems and Fables* (Oxford, 1970); M. Ravel, *Alcyone*, cantata for voice and orchestra, libretto by E. and E. Adénis (Paris, 1902); S. T. Coleridge, "Domestic Peace," in *The Fall of Robespierre* (London, 1795).

16. Milton, "On the Morning of Christ's Nativity," V, 61–68: "But peaceful was the night / Wherein the Prince of Light / His reign of peace upon the earth began: / The winds with wonder whist, / Smoothly the waters kissed, / Whispering new joys to the mild ocean, / Who now hath quite forgot to rave, / While birds of calm sit brooding on the charmed wave." *Complete Shorter Poems*, ed. J. Carey (London, 1968).

17. Keats, "To the Ladies Who Saw Me Crowned," 5–7; *Endymion* I, 453–55, in *The Complete Poems*, ed. M. Allott (London, 1970).

18. "Albàsia," in *Alcyone*, ed. F. Roncoroni (Milan, 1995), ll. 32–38.

19. C. Ransmayr, *Die letzte Welt* (Nördlingen, 1988), translated from the German by J. E. Woods as *The Last World* (New York, 1990); see B. Vollstedt, *Ovids Metamorphoses, Tristia und Epistulae ex Ponto in Christoph Ransmayrs Roman Die letzte Welt* (Paderborn, 1998); H. Friedman, *Erzählte Verwandlung: Eine Poetik epischer Metamorphosen (Ovid, Kafka, Ransmayr)* (Tübingen, 2000).

20. *Last World*, pp. 28–29.

21. See F. Calvo, *L'esperienza della poesia*, ed. P. Boitani (Bologna, 2004), pp. 25–101.

22. E. Montale, *L'opera in versi*, critical ed. by G. Contini and R. Bettarini (Turin, 1980), p. 37; E. Montale, *Collected Poems, 1920–1954*, trans. J. Galassi (New York, 1998), p. 53.

23. See B. dal Fabbro, "Ornitologia di Montale," *Il Tesoretto* (1939): 38–40.

24. The lines are dated spring–summer 1924: they seem to echo the opening of T. S. Eliot's *The Waste Land*, published in 1922.

25. Montale, *L'opera in versi* (*Ossi di seppia*), p. 86; trans. Galassi, p. 117. Galassi has "gull," which, faithful to the original "alcione," I have replaced with "kingfisher."

26. And see Galassi's essay, pp. 415–27, and his commentary on these poems on pp. 457, 472–74.

27. *The Waste Land. A Facsimile and Transcript of the Original Drafts including the Annotations of Ezra Pound*, ed. Valerie Eliot (New York, 1971), p. 55.

28. *Four Quartets*, III, ii.

CHAPTER 5

1. *The Odes of Horace*, bilingual edition, trans. D. Ferry (New York, 1997), IV, ii, 1–4.

2. F. Hölderlin, *Gedichte*, in *Hölderlin Werke und Briefe*, ed. F. Beissner and J. Schmidt (Frankfurt am Main, 1969), vol. 1, pp. 248–49.

3. *Nemean* V, 1–8, 17–22, in Pindar, *Nemean Odes, Isthmian Odes, Fragments*, ed. and trans.

W. H. Race (Cambridge, Mass. and London, 1997). I basically adopt Race's translations of Pindar, at times slightly changing them.

4. *Isthmian* V, 63. And see *Pythian* V, 114; *Pythian* VIII, 34; *Nemean* VII, 22.

5. *Nemean* III, 80–83.

6. *Olympian* II, 83–91, in Pindar, *Olympian Odes, Pythian Odes*, ed. and trans. W. H. Race (Cambridge, Mass., and London, 1997).

7. *Isthmian* VI, 50–51.

8. *Pythian* II, 49–56.

9. Aeschylus, *Prometheus* 351–72.

10. *Olympian* I, 1–2.

11. *Pythian* I, 19–26.

12. *Libellvs de Svblimitate Dionysio Longino fere Adscriptus*, ed. D. A. Russell (Oxford, 1968), 33, 5; Engl. trans. by T. S. Dorsch in Aristotle/Horace/Longinus, *Classical Literary Criticism* (Harmondsworth, 1965).

13. Ovid, *Metamorphoses* V, 346ff.; XV, 340ff.; Virgil, *Georgics* I, 471 ff.; Seneca, *Epistles* 79; *De Svblimitate* 35, 4.

14. Aulus Gellius, *Noctes Atticae* XVII, 10; Virgil, *Aeneid* III, 570–87.

15. Lucretius, *De rerum natura* VI, 639–702.

16. *Pythian* I, 42–45.

17. Pliny, *Naturalis Historia*, XXXIV, 59.

18. *Pythian* I, 52–55.

19. *Pythian* I, 81–84.

20. F. Hölderlin, *Ubersetzungen*, in *Werke und Briefe* (Frankfurt am Main, 1969), vol. 2, p. 663; literally, "When you speak the opportune, many attempts summing up in brief."

21. *Nemean* I, 18; see C. T. Onians, *The Origins of European Thought* (Cambridge, 1954), pp. 343–48.

22. *Nemean* IV, 34.

23. *Pythian* IX, 133–37; the last two lines have also been interpreted to mean "for due proportion is supreme in everything alike."

24. As in *Olympian* XIII, 48–49, and *Pythian* IV, 286–87.

25. *Pythian* I, 93–95.

26. *Nemean* VI, 27–30.

27. See S. Hornblower, *Thucydides and Pindar* (Oxford, 2004).

28. *Pythian* I, 96–98.

29. Eraclito, *I frammenti e le testimonianze*, ed. C. Diano and G. Serra (Milan, 1980), fr. 14 and 15.

30. *Pythian* I, 1–24.

31. Pindar, *Nemean Odes, Isthmian Odes, Fragments*, pp. 228–31; Aeschylus, *Agamemnon* 160–83; and see B. Snell, *The Discovery of the Mind in Greek Philosophy and Literature* (New York, 1982), pp. 71–89.

32. G. Leopardi, *Zibaldone* [1856], ed. R. Damiani (Milan, 1997), vol. 2, pp. 1268–69. In *Zibaldone* 2049–51, Leopardi speaks of Horace's "constant and lively movement and action," of his transporting the spirit "at each step, and often brusquely, from one thought or image or idea or thing to some other, sometimes very remote and quite different." In other words, he attributes "Pindaric flights" to Horace.

33. *Olympian* I, 1–6.

34. *Pythian* I, 25–28.

35. *Pythian* IV, 287–88. The bibliography on Pindar is vast. Included here are works consulted for this section: introductions and commentaries from editions of the *Pythian Odes* and *Isthmian Odes* edited by B. Gentili, P. A. Bernardini, E. Cingano, and P. Giannini, respectively (Milan, 1995); and G. A. Privitera (Milan 1982); J. Rumpel, *Lexicon Pindaricum* (Hildesheim, 1961), and W. J. Slater, *Lexicon to Pindar* (Berlin and New York, 1969); O. Schroeder, *Pindars Pythien* (Leipzig, 1922); L. R. Farnell, *Critical Commentary to the Works of Pindar* (Amsterdam, 1961); R. W. B. Burton, *Pindar's Pythian Odes. Essays in Interpretation* (Oxford, 1962); D. C. Young, *Three Odes of Pindar* (Leiden, 1968); D. C. Young, *Pindar, Isthmian 7* (Leiden, 1971); C. Carey, *A Commentary on Five Odes of Pindar: Pythian 2, Pythian 9, Nemean 1, Nemean 7, Isthmian 8* (New York, 1981); K. Crotty, *Song and Action: The Victory Odes of Pindar* (Baltimore, 1982); D. E. Gerber, *Pindar's Olympian One: A Commentary* (Toronto, 1982); P. Bernardini, *Mito e attualità nelle odi di Pindaro: la Nemea 4, l'Olimpica 9, l'Olimpica 7* (Rome, 1983); G. W. Most, *The Measures of Praise: Structure and Function in Pindar's Second Pythian and Seventh Nemean Odes* (Göttingen, 1985); C. Segal, *Pindar's Mythmaking. The Fourth Pythian Ode* (Princeton, 1986); W. J. Verdenius, *Commentaries on Pindar* (Leiden, 1987); B. K. Braswell, *A Commentary on the Fourth Pythian Ode of Pindar* (Berlin and New York, 1988); O. Kollmann, *Das Prooimion der ersten Pythischen Ode Pindars* (Vienna, 1989); B. K. Braswell, *A Commentary on Pindar, Nemean One* (Fribourg, 1992); U. von Wilamowitz-Moellendorf, *Pindaros* (Berlin, 1922); E. Des Places, *Pindare et Platon* (Paris, 1949); J. Duchemin, *Pindare, poéte et prophète* (Paris, 1955); C. M. Bowra, *Pindar* (Oxford, 1964); J. K. Newman, *Pindar's Art, Its Tradition and Aims* (Hildesheim, 1984); T. K. Hubbard, *The Pindaric Mind* (Leiden, 1985); D. S. Carne-Ross, *Pindar* (New Haven, 1985); D. Steiner, *Crown of Song: Metaphor in Pindar* (New York and Oxford, 1986); E. L. Bundy, *Studia Pindarica* (Berkeley, 1986); W. Fitzgerald, *Agonistic Poetry: The Pindaric Mode in Pindar, Horace, Hölderlin, and the English Ode* (Berkeley, 1987); G. Nagy, *Pindar's Homer* (Baltimore, 1990); M. Trédé, *Kairos. L'à-propos et l'occasion* (Paris, 1992); L. H. Pratt, *Lying and Poetry from Homer to Pindar* (Ann Arbor, 1993); M. Theunissen, *Pindar: Menschenlos und Wende der Zeit* (Munich, 2000); J. T. Hamilton, *Soliticting Darkness: Pindar, Obscurity, and the Classical Tradition* (Cambridge, Mass., and London, 2003); W. Janke, *Archaischer Gesang. Pindar—Hölderlin—Rilke. Werke und Warheit* (Würzburg, 2005).

36. Aristophanes, *The Peace; The Birds; The Frogs*, vol. 2, trans. B. B. Rogers (Cambridge, Mass. and London, 1968); *The Birds*, 1373–1401.

37. See E. R. Schwinge, "Horaz, Carmen 2, 20," *Hermes* 93 (1965): 438–59, in particular pp. 438–40 and notes.

38. Euripides, fr. 911 N; Plato, *Phaedo* 60c8–61b7; 84e3–85b7.

39. See Schwinge, "Horaz, Carmen 2, 20."

40. Milton, *Paradise Lost*, I, 12–16.

41. J. Keats, "Ode to a Nightingale," in *The Complete Poems*, ed. M. Allott (London and New York, 1970), pp. 523–32, lines 7–10.

42. P. B. Shelley, "To a Sky-Lark," in *Shelley's Poetry and Prose*, ed. D. H. Reiman and S. B. Powers (New York and London, 1977), pp. 226–29.

43. L'Albatros" and "Le Cygne," in C. Baudelaire, *Œuvres complètes*, ed. C. Pichois (Paris, 1975), vol. 1, pp. 9–10, 85–87.

44. S. Mallarmé, *Oeuvres complètes*, éd. B. Marchal (Paris, 1998), vol. 1, pp. 36–37.

45. W. B. Yeats, *Collected Poems* (London, 1965), pp. 147–48.

46. For the "moment of moments" in Yeats, see G. Melchiori, *The Whole Mystery of Art* (London, 1960), pp. 283–86.

47. For a reading of this poem and Yeats's later use of the swan, see D. Stauffer, *The Golden Nightingale* (New York, 1949), pp. 64–79; on the formation of the swan image, Melchiori, *The Whole Mystery of Art*, pp. 99–114.

48. G. Leopardi, "Canto notturno di un pastore errante dell'Asia," pp. 133–38, in *Poesie e Prose* (Milan, 1987), pp. 87–88. It should be noted that Leopardi's "Nocturnal Song of a Wandering Asian Shepherd" also posited a second alternative: "O forse erra dal vero, / Mirando all'altrui sorte, il mio pensiero: / Forse in qual forma, in quale / Stato che sia, dentro covile o cuna, / E' funesto a chi nasce il dì natale" (Or perhaps my thought, looking at others' fate / errs from the truth: / perhaps, in whatever shape, in whatever state he be, / be it in den or cot, / the day of birth is deadly to him who is born).

49. *Odes* IV, ii, 27–32.

50. *Pythian* X, 50–54. Note also that the bees given by Apollo to Hermes at the end of *Homeric Hymns* IV (to Hermes) have the gift of prophecy and perhaps also of poetry.

51. R. M. Rilke to W. Hulewicz, letter dated November 15, 1925, in *Briefe*, vol. 3, p. 898: "Wir sind die Bienen des Unsichtbaren. Nous butinons éperdument le miel du visible, pour l'accumuler dans la grande ruche d'or de l'Invisible." See F. Calvo, *L'esperienza della poesia*, ed. P. Boitani (Bologna, 2004), pp. 207–57, especially pp. 246–47.

52. *Purgatorio* XXII, 70–72.

53. *Odes* III, iv, 1–20.

54. Ibid., 61–64.

55. *Odes* II, xx, 1–12.

56. Ibid., II, xx, 13–24.

57. *Odes* III, xxx, 1–6.

58. *Odes* IV, iii, 1–4.

59. Hesiod, *Theogony* 81–85, trans. D. Wender (Harmondsworth, 1973); Callimachus, *Aetia* I, fr.2, 1–2; IV, fr. 112, 5–6; *Epigrams*, XXIX.

60. *Odes* IV, iii, 10–12.

61. Ibid., IV, iii, 17–24.

62. *Odes* IV, iv, 1–11. For this discussion on Horace I am indebted to the following works: E. Fränkel, *Horace* (Oxford, 1957); E. Fränkel, *Das Pindargedicht des Horaz*, (Heidelberg, 1933); A. Rostagni, *Orazio* (Venosa, 1994); N. E. Collinge, *The Structure of Horace's Odes* (London, 1961); S. Commager, *The Odes of Horace: A Critical Study* (New Haven, 1962); C. O. Brink, *Horace on Poetry* (Cambridge, 1963); I. Troxler-Keller, *Die Dichterlandschaft des Horaz* (Heidelberg, 1964); G. Pasquali, *Orazio lirico*, ed. A. La Penna (Florence, 1966); J. V. Cody, *Horace and Callimachean Aesthetics* (Brussels, 1976); R. G. M. Nisbet, *A Commentary on Horace, Odes, Book II* (Oxford, 1978); M. C. J. Putnam, *Artifices of Eternity: Horace's Fourth Book of Odes* (Ithaca, N.Y., 1986); D. H. Porter, *Horace's Poetic Journey: A Reading of Odes 1–3* (Princeton, 1987); L. P. Wilkinson, *Horace and His Lyric Poetry* (London, 1968); M. Gigante, *Orazio: l'effimero diventa eterno* (Venosa, 1994); R. O. A. M. Lyne, *Horace: Behind the Public Poetry* (New Haven, 1995); E. A. Schmidt, *Zeit und Form: Dichtungen des Horaz* (Heidelberg, 2002).

63. Jeremiah 49:22; Hosea 8:1; Jeremiah 4:13; Habakkuk 1:8.

64. At 2 Samuel 1:23.

65. Job 9:26.

66. Job 9:26: "pertransierunt quasi naves poma portantes," not in the original.

67. Job 39:27–30.

68. Proverbs 30:19.

69. Matthew 24:28; Luke 17:37: "Wheresoever the body is, thither will the eagles be gathered together."

70. Matthew 6:26 and 10:29–31; Shakespeare, *Hamlet* V, ii, 213–18.

71. Proverbs 23:5; Obadiah 4.

72. Ezekiel 1.

73. Exodus 15:1; *Exodus Rabba* 23:13: see M. Greenberg, *Ezekiel 1–20* (New York, 1983), pp. 39–59, here p. 56.

74. Ezekiel 10:14 and 10:17.

75. Daniel 7.

76. At 4 Ezra 11–12.

77. Revelation 4:6–8.

78. Revelation 8:13.

79. Revelation 12:13–12.14. For an interpretation of Revelation, see the introduction and commentary in *L'Apocalisse di Giovanni*, ed. E. Lupieri (Milan, 1999).

80. Aristotle, *Historia animalium* CX, 32.

81. *Enciclopedia dell'arte medievale* (Rome, 1991), s.v. "aquila."

82. See 1 Corinthians 15:13–15:14.

83. Jerome, *Comm. In Matheum, Praefatio* 54–56, Corpus Christianorum, Series Latina 77 (Turnhout, 1969), p. 3; *Comm. in Ezechielem* I, i., 10, *Patrologia Latina* 25, 21–22; Irenaeus, *Contre les heresies* (Paris, 1974), III, 11, 8, pp. 162–71; Augustine, *De consensu Evangelistarum* I, vi, 9, *Patrologia Latina* 34, 1046–47.

84. Augustine, *In Iohannis Evangelium* I, 1–6, Corpus Christianorum, Series Latina 36, (Turnhout, 1954), pp. 1–3.

85. Origene, *Commentaire sur Saint Jean* I, iv, 21–24 (Paris, 1966), pp. 68–73.

86. *Paradiso* XXVI, 53.

87. Jerome, *In Matheum, Praefatio* 50–55, p. 3.

88. Augustine, *In Iohannis Evangelium* I, 1, 20–25, p. 1.

89. Johannes Scotus Eriugena, *Il Prologo di Giovanni*, ed. M. Cristiani (Milan, 1987), 1 and 4, pp. 8–15.

90. J. W. Goethe, *Faust* I, 1210–37; and see N. Frye, *The Great Code. The Bible and Literature* (New York and London, 1982), pp. 18–19.

91. John 19:26–7.

92. Origene, *Commentaire sur Saint Jean*, I, 23, pp. 70–71: the voice of the verb used by Origen is *anapeson*.

93. Ezekiel 1:25; Gregory, *Homélies sur Ézéchiel*, (Paris, 1986), vol. 1, VIII, 11–12, pp. 290–93.

94. Gregory, ibid., VIII, 16, 17–19, pp. 296–97. Alcuin also urges us to transcend on the wings of contemplation everything that began and will end with time, and to fly in our minds to the land time turns us to but where we shall live timelessly. Alcuin, *De Psalmorum usu*, I, v, *Patrologia Latina* 101, 474. See J. Leclercq and J. P. Bonnes, *Un maitre de la vie spirituelle au XIe siècle: Jean de Fécamp* (Paris, 1946), p. 90, n. 4.

95. Gregory, ibid., VIII, 17–19, pp. 298–303.

96. Agostino, *Confessioni*, ed. M. Cristiani, M. Simonetti, and A. Solignac (Milan, 1996), vol. 2, II 2-VI 8, pp. 106–17.

97. *Paradiso* XXV, 112–39; XXVI, 13–45; Aristotle, *Metaphysics* XII 7, 1072b; Exodus 33:19. One should bear in mind that Dante's formulation of this, *Io ti farò vedere ogne valore*, also echoes the opening words of a sonnet that Guido Cavalcanti had addressed to him, "Vedeste, al mio parere, onne valore." See B. Nardi, "Il canto XXVI del *Paradiso*," *L'Alighieri* 23, no. 1 (1985): 24–32; E. Ferrario, "Il linguaggio nel XXVI canto del *Paradiso*," in *Miscellanea di studi in onore di Aurelio Roncaglia* (Modena, 1989), pp. 559–79; K. Brownlee, "Language and Desire in *Paradiso* XXVI," *Lectura Dantis Virginiana* 6 (1990): 46–59.

98. *Inferno* IV, 95–96.

99. *Purgatorio* XXII, 101–2.

100. As Dante indicates in *Vita Nuova* (II, 8), *Convivio* (IV, xx, 4), and *Monarchia* (II, iii, 9), Aristotle cites the *Iliad* and *Odyssey* as definitive authorities in *Nicomachean Ethics* VII, 1, 1145a ff.

101. J. Keats, "On First Looking into Chapman's Homer," in *The Complete Poems*, pp. 60–62.

102. *De vulgari eloquentia* II, iv, 11.

103. *Purgatorio* IX, 1–33; see E. Raimondi, *Metafora e storia. Studi su Dante e Petrarca*, (Turin, 1970), pp. 95–146.

104. *Purgatorio* IX, 70–72.

105. *Inferno* II, 32: *Io non Enea, non Paulo sono* ("I am not Aeneas; I am not Paul").

106. G. Chaucer, *The House of Fame*, II, 529–1090, in *The Riverside Chaucer*, ed. L. D. Benson (Boston, 1987); and see P. Boitani, *Chaucer and the Imaginary World of Fame* (Cambridge, 1984), pp. 7–17, 73–90.

107. *Purgatorio* XXIX, 97–105.

108. *Purgatorio* XXIX, 37–42. See P. Dronke, *Dante and Medieval Latin Traditions* (Cambridge, 1986), pp. 55–81; P. Armour, *Dante's Griffin and the History of the World*, (Oxford, 1989).

109. *Purgatorio* XXIX, 105: *Giovanni è meco* ("John is with me"), an extraordinary claim; see P. S. Hawkins, *Dante's Testaments* (Stanford, 1999), pp. 54–71, but the whole book is relevant for my interpretation.

110. *Purgatorio* XXXII, 109–17; see K. Foster, *God's Tree* (London, 1957), pp. 33–49.

111. In *Purgatorio* XXXIII, 37–38, Beatrice announces that the empire will not be without an heir for long: "not for all time shall the eagle be without heir that left its feathers on the car."

112. *Paradiso* VI, 1–96; see E. Paratore, "Il canto dell'Aquila Romana," *Studi danteschi* 49 (1972): 49–77; J. H. Whitfield, "*Paradiso* VI," in D. Nolan, ed., *Dante Commentaries*, (Dublin, 1977), pp. 143–58.

113. Cfr. B. Nardi, *Saggi di filosofia dantesca*, 2nd ed. (Florence, 1967), pp. 215–75; C. T. Davis, *Dante and the Idea of Rome* (Oxford, 1957); C. T. Davis, *Dante's Italy and Other Essays*, (Philadelphia, 1984), pp. 23–41.

114. Wisdom of Solomon 3:7: "[the righteous] will shine forth, and will run like sparks through the stubble." For my entire reading of *Paradiso* XVIII–XX, I am indebted to the commentary by A. M. Chiavacci Leonardi, *Paradiso* (Milan, 1997).

115. Proverbs 8:27–9; *Paradiso* XIX, 40–41: *Colui che volse il sesto / a lo stremo del mondo* ("He that turned His compass about the bounds of the world").

116. Job 38:2; Romans 9:20: *Paradiso* XIX, 79–81.

117. Matthew 11:12: *Paradiso* XX, 94.

118. *Paradiso* XIX, 10: Revelation 8:13; *Paradiso* XX, 19–21: Revelation 1:15 and Ezekiel 43:2.

119. *Paradiso* XVIII, 51; see L. Pertile, "*Paradiso* XVIII tra autobiografia e scrittura sacra," *Dante Studies* 109 (1991): 25–49.

120. *Paradiso* XVIII, 72; 73–81, 88–114 for the rest of this paragraph.

121. *Paradiso* XIX, 1–33. For canto XIX, see K. Foster, *The Two Dantes* (London, 1977), pp. 137–55; V. Russo, *Il Romanzo teologico* (Naples, 1984), pp. 145–70.

122. *Paradiso* XIX, 70–8.

123. *Paradiso* XIX, 40–114; here, 106–11.

124. *Paradiso* XIX, 115–48.

125. *Paradiso* XX, 1–117; for this canto, see G. Barberi Squarotti, *L'ombra d'Argo* (Turin, 1986), pp. 241–71; M. Picone, "La viva speranza di Dante e il problema della salvezza dei pagani virtuosi. Una lettura di *Paradiso* 20," *Quaderni di italianistica* 10 (1989): 251–68.

126. *Paradiso* XX, 67–72, 118–29; *Aeneid* II, 426–28; see A. Battistini, " 'Rifeo Troiano' e la riscrittura dantesca della storia," *Lettere Italiane* 42 (1990): 26–50. The theory of "implicit revelation" is common to Augustine, Albert the Great, Thomas Aquinas, and many others.

127. *Paradiso* XX, 130–48.

128. *Paradiso* XVIII, 45; XVIII, 73–75 (the simile bears the stamp of Lucretius in *De rerum natura* II, 344–46, and Lucan in *Pharsalia* V, 711–16); XIX, 34–36; XIX, 91–93; XX, 73–75 (inspired by the Provençal troubadour Bernart de Ventadorn, "Can vei la lauzeta").

129. *Paradiso* XVIII, 100–1; XIX, 19–21.

130. Psalm 36:6, "Thy judgements are a great deep"; Ezekiel 43:2, "like a noise of many waters"; Revelation 1:15, "as the sound of many waters."

131. *Paradiso* XIX, 58–63; see P. Boitani, *The Tragic and the Sublime in Medieval Literature* (Cambridge, 1989), pp. 250–78.

132. *Paradiso* XX, 19–21.

133. *Paradiso* XX, 118–21.

134. J. Joyce, *A Portrait of the Artist as a Young Man*, ed. S. Deane (Harmondsworth, 1992), pp. 230–31. The concept is medieval and Thomistic: see U. Eco, *Il problema estetico in Tommaso d'Aquino*, 2nd ed. (Milan, 1970), pp. 132–53.

135. *Paradiso* XIX, 1–6; v. XVIII, 72.

136. *Paradiso* XX, 1–12.

137. *Paradiso* XVIII, 109–11.

138. Here as in *Paradiso* VII, XIII and XXIX.

139. *Paradiso* XIX, 40–45. God replies to Job's questions on justice with the Creation: Job 38. *Paradiso* XIX, 79–80 refers to Job 38:2, via Romans 9:20 ("O man, who art thou that repliest against God?").

140. *Paradiso* XX, 38; XXV, 72; XXV, 68–73.

141. *Paradiso* XVIII, 82–87.

142. *Paradiso* XIX, 7–9.

143. *Paradiso* XXV, 1–2.

144. At 2 Corinthians 12:2–4.

145. *Paradiso* I, 4–6.

146. Gregory, *Moralia in Iob* XXXI, xlvii, 94–liii, 106, Corpus Christianorum, Series Latina, 143 B (Turnhout, 1985), pp. 1614–23, and in particular 106, p. 1621; Job 39:27; *Paradiso* XXVIII, 133–35, with reference to *Moralia* XXXII, xxiii.

147. As *Inferno* II indicates, Paul was known as *vas d'elezione* ("Chosen Vessel"): Acts 9:15.

148. *Paradiso* I, 10–12.

149. *Paradiso* I, 49–54.

150. Benvenuto da Imola, *Comentum super Dantis Aldigherij Comoediam* (Florence, 1887), vol. 4, pp. 312–14; quotation on 314.

151. *Paradiso* XXII, 105; XXXII, 142–47; XXXIII, 83–84.

152. *Paradiso* XX, 22–27.

153. *Paradiso* XX, 142–48.

154. In *Paradiso* I, 18, Dante appropriately uses the term *aringo* ("arena").

CHAPTER 6

1. For a history of the painting, its attribution, an excellent reading, and an exhaustive bibliography, see E. M. Kavaler, *Pieter Bruegel: Parables of Order and Enterprise* (Cambridge, 1999), chap. 2, "The *Fall of Icarus* and the Natural Order," pp. 60–78 and pp. 283–91.

2. But note the objection in Leopardi, *Paralipomeni della Batracomiomachia* VII, 23, already mentioned in chapter 2, according to which Icarus's feathers, "sia per incidenza detto," "venner men dal caldo io non so come, / poiché nell'alta region del cielo / non suole il caldo soverchiar ma il gelo!"

3. Wolf Biermann, "Der Sturz des Dädalus" in *Mythos Ikarus*, ed. A. Aurnhammer and D. Martin (Leipzig, 1998), pp. 186–87.

4. See R. L. Delevoy, *Bruegel* (Geneva, 1959); M. Gibson, *Bruegel* (Paris, 1980); M. Seidel and R. H. Marijnissen, *Bruegel* (Stuttgart, 1970); R. H. Marijnissen, *Bruegel: Tout l'oeuvre peint et dessiné* (Anvers, 1988); F. Grossmann, *Bruegel. The Paintings. Complete Edition*, 2nd ed. (London, 1996).

5. E.g., besides the examples quoted by Kavaler, Langland's *Piers Plowman*, from the late fourteenth century, and the fifteenth-century Johannes von Tepl's *Ackermann aus Böhmen*. For a general discussion on the word-image relationship in this period, see L. Bolzoni, *La rete delle immagini* (Turin, 2002).

6. Cf. Kavaler, *Pieter Bruegel*, p. 73; Biermann, "Der Sturz des Dädalus," p. 187. The explanation is by the great Bruegel scholar C. de Tolnay, in his "Studien zu den Gemälden P. Bruegels d.Ä.," *Jahrbuch des Kunsthistorischen Sammlungen in Wien*, n.s., 8 (1934): 105–35.

7. Quoted by Kavaler, *Pieter Bruegel*, p. 283, n. 21. On Icarus as a symbol of ambition in the search for knowledge, see C. Ginzburg, "High and Low: The Theme of Forbidden Knowledge in the Sixteenth and Seventeenth Centuries," *Past and Present* 73 (1976): 28–41.

8. On this parallel, like the Ulysses-Hermes comparison, see the fascinating chapter 7 in C.-H. Rocquet, *Bruegel, or The Workshop of Dreams*, (Chicago, 1991), pp. 118–29. See also the evocative interpretation by André Breton in *De la survivance de certains mythes et quelques autres mythe en croissance ou en formation* (1942; Paris, 1988).

9. L. de Bosis, *Icarus* (London, 1933), p. 186: Theseus's sailors, who see Icarus flying over the Aegean, take him for Hermes.

10. Matthew 24:36–40.

11. *Metamorphoses* VIII, 236–59.

12. Only fragments of Antigonus's work survive anyhow, and they were not known in the sixteenth century.

13. Luke 9:62.

14. Cf. Kavaler, *Pieter Bruegel*, pp. 75–76.

15. *Gli oggetti desueti nelle immagini della letteratura*, a memorable book by F. Orlando (Turin, 1993).

16. Cf. W. Benjamin, "The Work of Art in the Age of Mechanical Reproduction," in his *Illuminations*, ed. H. Arendt (New York, 1968), pp. 217–51.

17. *Mythos Ikarus*, ed. A. Aurnhammer and D. Martin (Leipzig, 1998), pp. 190–91.

18. W. H. Auden, *Collected Poems*, ed. E. Mendelson, 2nd ed. (London, 1991), p. 179. See also S. Crivelli, "La caduta d'Icaro: Bruegel e la poesia di W. H. Auden, W. C. Williams e Sylvia Plath," in his *Lo sguardo narrato. Letteratura e arti visive* (Rome, 2003), pp. 23–38.

19. Raïssa Maritain, *Mythos Ikarus*, pp. 191–92.

20. Allan Curnow, "The Fall of Icarus. The Painting by Brueghel the Elder," in *Mythos Ikarus*, p. 195.

21. Michael Hamburger, "Lines on Brueghel's 'Icarus,'" in *Mythos Ikarus*, pp. 202–3.

22. William Carlos Williams, "Landscape with the Fall of Icarus," in *Mythos Ikarus*, p. 204.

23. Erich Arendt, "Pieter Breughel," part 3, in *Mythos Ikarus*, pp. 192–93.

24. The poem, from 1966, is in *Mythos Ikarus*, pp. 208–9.

25. Stephan Hermlin, "Landschaft mit dem Sturz des Ikarus," in *Mythos Ikarus*, p. 202.

26. Marie Luise Kaschnitz, "Wohin denn ich. Aufzeichnungen," in *Mythos Ikarus*, p. 207.

27. Ulrich Berkes, "Sturz des Ikarus" and "Warum Ikarus," in *Mythos Ikarus*, p. 212.

28. Gisbert Kranz, *Mythos Ikarus*, p. 213: note the alliteration and assonance of *pflügen* (to plow) and *fliegen* (to fly).

29. Jaroslaw Iwaskiewicz, in *Mythos Ikarus*, pp. 196–201, here p. 201.

30. Stephan Hermlin, "Ballade vom Gefährten Ikarus," in *Mythos Ikarus*, pp. 142–43.

31. Stephan Hermlin, *Abendlicht* (Berlin, 1979); Engl. trans., *Evening Light* (San Francisco, 1983).

32. W. G. Sebald, *Luftkrieg und Literatur* Munich and Vienna, 1999); Engl. trans., "Airwar and Literature," in *On the Natural History of Destruction* (London, 2003).

33. Kirsch, "Mauer," in *Mythos Ikarus*, p. 180.

34. Biermann, "Ballade vom preussischen Ikarus," in *Mythos Ikarus*, pp. 167–68.

35. Biermann, in *Mythos Ikarus*, p. 188.

36. Biermann, in *Mythos Ikarus*, pp. 215–17.

37. The passage corresponds (Biermann quotes the original almost verbatim) to W. Benjamin's "Theses on the Philosophy of History,". in *Illuminations*, ed. H. Arendt (New York, 1968), pp. 257–58. It should be remembered that an application of Benjamin's theories to America is discussed in *Approaching the Millennium: Essays on Angels in America*, ed. D. R. Geis and S. F. Kruger (Ann Arbor, 1997).

38. E. Ionesco, *Le piéton de l'air*, in *Théâtre complet* (Paris, 1991), pp. 731–36.

39. As proof of this, I should mention a poem that has reached me from England as I was revising this book for publication. The mythopoetic imagination that shapes it interprets Bruegel's *Fall of Icarus* as the indifference and ignorance of cultures toward each other, while Icarus and Ulysses on the one side, and David and Abel on the other, play the traditional roles of (Greek) discoverers (punished for their sin of hubris) and (Jewish) shepherds and contemplators of divinity, the "Phoenix city" representing Phoenician trade. The poem, by Emma Tristram, is entitled "Icarus again": "Maybe the picture means something completely different. / How blind the Israelites were (for we might be in Israel) / To the soar and splash of the Greeks. To a Phoenix city / And its trade routes too. David leans on his staff / In his small green pastures and contemplates heaven — but soon / He will be killed like Abel. The sun is

setting. / The pillars of Hercules gleam and loom in the background / Like a way out. And the white legs remain / Never quite drowned to kick us from indifference."

40. See F. Calvo, *L'esperienza della poesia*, ed. P. Boitani (Bologna, 2004), pp. 160–67.

CHAPTER 7

1. For all this, see R. Niccoli, *La storia del volo* (Vercelli, 2002); R. P. Hallon, *Taking Flight* (Oxford and New York, 2003); R. Wohl, *A Passion for Wings: Aviation and the Western Imagination, 1908–1918* (New Haven and London, 1994); and R. Wohl, *The Spectacle of Flight: Aviation and the Western Imagination, 1920–1950* (New Haven and London, 2005).

2. Readers are referred to my *The Shadow of Ulysses: Figures of a Myth* (Oxford, 1994), and *Sulle orme di Ulisse*, 2nd ed. (Bologna, 2007), pp. 17–21.

3. Apollinaire, "Zone," in *Œuvres Poétiques* (Paris, 1956), p. 728–29: "Et changé en oiseau ce siècle comme Jésus monte dans l'air . . . / Les anges voltigent autour du joli voltigeur / Icare Enoch Elie Apollonius de Thyane / Flottent autour du premier aéroplane."

4. D. Del Giudice, *Staccando l'ombra da terra* (Turin, 1994), p. 118, translated from the Italian by Joseph Farrell as *Takeoff: The Pilot's Lore* (New York, 1996), p. 160.

5. See M. Dancourt, *Dédale et Icare. Métamorphoses d'un mythe* (Paris, 2002), pp. 74–83, 109–20, 151–81.

6. See R. Wohl's fundamental *A Passion for Wings.*

7. W. Baum, *Ludwig Wittgenstein* (Berlin, 1985), pp. 14–15, 17–18; *The Autobiography of Bertrand Russell*, 2 vols. (London, 1968).

8. Del Giudice, *Staccando l'ombra*, p. 118; *Takeoff*, p. 160.

9. "An Irish Airman Foresees His Death," in *The Wild Swans at Coole*, in *Collected Poems of W. B. Yeats* (London, 1965), p. 152.

10. E. Ní Chuilleanáin, "Death and Engines," in *The Second Voyage*, 2nd ed. (Winston-Salem, N.C., 1986), pp. 50–51.

11. W. Faulkner, "All the Dead Pilots," in *Collected Stories of William Faulkner* (New York, 1950), pp. 511–12.

12. The section of the *Collected Stories* containing "All the Dead Pilots" is entitled "The Waste Land."

13. First published in 1935, now in *Novels, 1930–1935* (New York, 1985).

14. D. Del Giudice, *Le savoir du pilote*, Lectures held at the École des Hautes Études in Paris in 1993, p. 43. I am grateful to the author for providing me with his Italian manuscript. A modified version of this manuscript appears in *Staccando l'ombra* (published the following year), pp. 114–15. The English translation here is from *Takeoff*, p. 155.

15. Post–9/11 fiction is rapidly being produced and goes beyond the scope of this book. I need only mention Jonathan Safar Foer's *Extremely Loud and Incredibly Close* (2005) and Ian McEwan's *Saturday* (2005). To my mind the most important artistic contribution to the 9/11 events is Art Spiegelman's graphic novel, *In the Shadow of No Towers* (2004). A "disaster movie," *United 93*, dreadful in more than one way—is being shown in cinemas as this book goes to press.

16. *Le savoir du pilote*, p. 11, n. 10; Le Corbusier, *Aircraft* (London, 1935).

17. A. de Saint-Exupéry, *Courrier Sud*. My own English translation here is based on *Œuvres complètes*, ed. M. Autrand and M. Quesnel (Paris, 1994), vol. 1, p. 37. On Saint-Exupéry, see the *Notices* in *Œuvres*, vol. 1 (1994) and vol. 2 (1999); *Cahiers Saint-Exupéry*, vols. 1–3 (Paris, 1980, 1981, 1989); the monographic issues of *Icare, Revue de l'aviation française*, 69, 71, 75, 84, 96; and Wohl, *The Spectacle of Flight*, pp. 167–79, 195–204, 317–18.

18. *Courrier Sud*, in *Œuvres*, vol. 1, p. 108.

19. Ibid., vol. 1, pp. 108–9.

20. Saint-Exupéry to Rinette, 24 October 1926, in *Œuvres*, vol. 1, p. 805.

21. Saint-Exupéry to Rinette, November 1926, in *Œuvres*, vol. 1, p. 808.

22. Saint-Exupéry to Rinette, December 1926, in *Œuvres*, vol. 1, p. 810.

23. Saint-Exupéry to Rinette, 1926, in *Œuvres*, vol. 1, p. 793.

24. Ibid., vol. 1, p. 793.

25. Ibid., vol. 1, p. 796.

26. Ibid., vol. 1, p. 797.

27. Saint-Exupéry to his mother, 1925, in *Œuvres*, vol. 1, p. 749.

28. Saint-Exupéry to Rinette, no date, in *Œuvres*, vol. 1, pp. 786–77.

29. See S. Bernadie, "Pour moi, voler ou écrire, c'est tout un," in *Cahiers Saint-Exupéry* 3, pp. 123–32, quotation on p. 128.

30. F. Calvo, *Cercare l'uomo. Socrate Platone Aristotele* (Genoa, 1989).

31. *Night Flight*, translated from the French by Stuart Gilbert (San Diego, 1932), p. 51, *Œuvres*, vol. 1, p. 141.

32. *Reportage*, in *Œuvres*, vol. 1, p. 372.

33. "Here was a musician's face," Saint-Exupéry muses, that night in the train, "here was Mozart as a child, here was one of life's wondrous promises. The *petits princes* of legend were no different from him": ibid., p. 371. Saint-Exupéry's text was published on the front page of *Paris-Soir*, May 14, 1935, with the title "La Nuit dans un train où, au milieu de mineurs polonais repatriés, Mozart enfant dormait"; above the headline was written: "Vers l'U.R.S.S.;" the sub-headline: "Les petits princes de légende n'etaient point différents de lui." *Œuvres*, vol. 1, p. 1080.

34. Saint-Exupéry to his mother, January 1930, in *Œuvres*, vol. 1, pp. 780–81.

35. *Night Flight*, pp. 10 and 12; *Œuvres*, vol. 1, pp. 113 and 115. This is very different from the oneiric beginning, redolent with childhood memories, cited in the letter to his mother (see note 33 above).

36. *Night Flight*, p. 64, emphasis added; *Œuvres*, vol. 1, p. 151.

37. *Night Flight*, p. 66; *Œuvres*, vol. 1, p. 152.

38. *Night Flight*, p. 4; *Œuvres*, vol. 1, p. 963.

39. Aristotle, *Nicomachean Ethics* 1176a 31 ff., 1169b 29 ff.; *Metaphysics* VII, 1029b 5–7.

40. *Night Flight*, p. 45; *Œuvres*, vol. 1, p. 137.

41. *Night Flight*, p. 45; *Œuvres*, vol. 1, p. 137.

42. *Nicomachean Ethics* 1177b 33–34.

43. *Night Flight*, p. 87; *Œuvres*, vol. 1, p. 166–67.

44. *Cahiers Saint-Exupéry*, 1, p. 106.

45. Libretto for *Volo di notte* in M. Ruffini, *L'opera di Luigi Dallapiccola* (Milan, 2002), pp. 343–53, quotation on p. 350. I would like to thank Marco Ruffini for providing me with a recording of the opera. Note that in Saint-Exupéry's text, the words "They had only been married six weeks" are spoken not by Mme Fabien but rather by Inspector Robineau at the end of the conversation between Rivière and Mme Fabien.

46. Ruffini, *L'opera*, p. 127.

47. Ibid., p. 126.

48. Ibid., p. 125.

49. The text of the *Tre Laudi*, from the *Laudario dei Battuti di Modena* (1266), states, halfway through the first: "Stella marina che non sta' mai ascosa, / Luce divina vertù graziosa / Bellezza formosa de Deo sembianza." This is the *Stella maris* of Mary and the light, which resembles God.

50. Ruffini, *L'opera*, p. 127.

51. *Night Flight*, p. 70. *Vol de nuit*, in *Œuvres*, vol. 1, p. 154.

52. *Night Flight*, pp. 72 and 74.

53. *Paradiso* I, 70.

54. *Paradiso* XXXIII, 57.

55. *Night Flight*, p. 74.

56. *Terre des homes*, translated from the French by Louis Galantière as *Wind, Sand and Stars* (New York, 1940), p. 61; *Œuvres*, vol. 1, p. 197.

57. *Wind, Sand and Stars*, pp. 66–67.

58. Ibid., pp. 72–73.

59. T. S. Eliot, *Collected Poems, 1909–1962* (London, 1963), *Little Gidding* V. "Sermo humilis" is Erich Auerbach's famous definition of the style of Scripture (following Saint Augustine): see his "Sermo humilis" in *Literary Language and Its Public in Late Latin Antiquity and in the Middle Ages*, trans. R. Mannheim (New York, 1965), pp. 27–66.

60. *Wind, Sand and Stars*, p. 291.

61. Ibid., p. 306.

62. John 3:5–8; I have introduced into the King James translation the expression "from above," present in the Greek original.

63. *Wind, Sand and Stars*, p. 87.

64. Ibid., p. 94.

65. "The Elements," in *Wind, Sand and Stars*, p. 86.

66. *Pilote de guerre*, in *Œuvres*, vol. 2, p. 220. Translated from the French by Lewis Galantière as *Flight to Arras* (New York, 1942), p. 241.

67. Ibid., pp. 226–27; *Flight to Arras*, pp. 251–22.

68. The first draft of *Citadelle* dates from 1936. The book was published posthumously in 1948, and translated from the French by Stuart Gilbert as *The Wisdom of the Sands* (New York, 1950).

69. *Œuvres*, vol. 2, p. 371; *The Wisdom of the Sands*, pp. 10–11.

70. Matthew 18:5 and 18:2–4.

71. 1 Corinthians 13:11: "When I was a child, I spake as a child, I understood as a child, I thought as a child: but when I became a man, I put away childish things."

72. At 1 Corinthians 3:1–2. See *The Little Prince*, trans. by Katherine Woods (New York, 1945), pp. 17–19; *Œuvres*, vol. 2, pp. 245–47.

73. W. B. Yeats, *The Rose* (1893), in *Collected Poems* (London, 1965), pp. 35–58, and especially pp. 35, 41–43.

74. Rainer Maria Rilke, *Duino Elegies and The Sonnets to Orpheus*, trans. by A. Poulin, Jr. (Boston, 1977), pp. 148–49 (I have slightly modified the translation). And see F. Calvo, "Una rosa, prima del suo nome," in his *Il solco della parola: origine della poesia* (Naples, 1994), pp. 75–97.

75. Traces of the wreck and objects identifying the pilot were found in 2004.

76. D. Del Giudice, *Atlante occidentale* (Turin, 1985), p. 29; translated from the Italian by

Norman MacAfee and Luigi Fontanella as *Lines of Light* (San Diego and New York, 1988), p. 27.

77. *Lines of Light*, p. 60.

78. Ibid., p. 46.

79. Ibid., p. 107.

80. Ibid., p. 107.

81. Ibid., pp. 134–37.

82. Ibid., p. 141.

83. See Aristotle, *Metaphysics* 982b 11–19; S. Greenblatt, *Marvelous Possessions: The Wonder of the New World* (Oxford, 1991).

84. I would like to thank the author for providing me with the Italian typescript of *Taccuino*, on which my English translation here is based.

85. *Taccuino*, pp. 11–12.

86. Ibid., p. 16.

87. Ibid., p. 37.

88. Literally, "where 'every where' and 'every when'" (that is, all space and all time) come together: for Dante, to whom (*Paradiso* XXIX, 12) this is of course God.

89. Ibid., p. 29.

90. Ibid., p. 37.

91. It is worth noting that in recent decades an interest in the poles has resurfaced in literature. Besides several books on Scott and Shackleton, there is an excellent anthology edited by F. Marx, *Wege ins Eis* (Frankfurt, 1995), containing material from Dante to Camões, Coleridge, Poe, Paul Celan, Sten Nadolny, and Christoph Ransmayr; more recently, Roberto Mussapi has published a poem entitled *Antartide* (Parma, 2000).

92. *Staccando l'ombra da terra* (Turin, 1994); translated into English by Joseph Farrell as *Takeoff* (New York and San Diego, 1996).

93. *Staccando l'ombra da terra*, pp. 81–82; *Takeoff*, pp. 109–10.

94. Ibid., p. 110.

95. *Le savoir du pilote*, pp. 33–34.

96. *Takeoff*, p. 111.

97. *Le savoir du pilote*, pp. 35–41. The tragic example of the failure of language is the air crash in the Azores of February 2, 1989, when a charter flight from Bergamo crashed into a mountain because in communications between the plane and traffic control the word "over" was not used.

98. *Staccando l'ombra*, p. 71; *Takeoff*, p. 95.

99. *Staccando l'ombra*, pp. 34–35; *Takeoff*, pp. 43–45.

100. *Staccando l'ombra*, p. 19; *Takeoff*, p. 24.

101. *Takeoff*, p. 130.

102. *Takeoff*, p. 134.

103. *Takeoff*, p. 135.

104. *Takeoff*, p. 141.

105. S. Heaney, "The Flight Path," in *The Spirit Level* (London and Boston, 1996), pp. 22–26.

106. *Canto per Ustica* is available on cassette, accompanied by the libretto, *Quaderno dei Tigi: I-TIGI Canto per Ustica* (Turin, 2001).

CHAPTER 8

1. *Inferno* XXVI, 85–142.

2. Throughout this chapter I refer to several earlier books of mine, for which I apologize; for this point, see *The Shadow of Ulysses. Figures of a Myth* (Oxford 1994).

3. Victor Klemperer, *Ich will Zeugnis ablegen bis zum Letzten—Tagebücher, 1933–1941* (Berlin, 1995), p. 154; translated from the German by Martin Chalmers as *I Will Bear Witness: A Diary of the Nazi Years, 1933–1941* (New York, 1999).

4. J. Joyce, *Ulysses*, Gabler Edition (New York, 1986). All references and quotes are from this edition.

5. *Ulysses*, pp. 597–98.

6. Ibid. Cp. Exodus 13:21.

7. *Ulysses*, p. 598.

8. *Ulysses*, p. 599.

9. Niagara, "over which no human being had passed with impunity"; "the forbidden country of Thibet," whence, as Hamlet says of death, "no traveller returns."

10. See P. Boitani, *Esodi e Odissee* (Naples, 2004), pp. 35–53.

11. *Ulysses*, p. 598.

12. The film was made in 1968, one year before the Americans landed on the Moon. See *The Making of Kubrick's 2001*, ed. Jerome Agel (New York, 1970); A. Clarke, *2001, a Space Odyssey* (London, 1990); P. Scarpi, *La fuga e il ritorno. Storia e mitologia del viaggio* (Venice, 1992).

13. G. Leopardi, "Ad Angelo Mai," in *Poesie e prose*, edited by M. A. Rigoni (Milan, 1987), vol. 1, p. 18.

14. F. Nietzsche, *Thus Spoke Zarathustra*, trans. by R. J. Hollingdale (Harmondsworth, 1961), p. 246, slightly modified for closer rendering of the original, *Also sprach Zarathustra* (Stuttgart, 1988), p. 256.

15. E. Bloch, *Das Prinzip Hoffnung* (Frankfurt am Main, 1959), vol. 3, pp. 1201–4; and "Odysseus Did Not Die in Ithaca," in *Homer*, ed. G. Steiner and R. Fagles (Englewood Cliffs, N.J., 1962), pp. 81–85.

16. M. Horkheimer and T. W. Adorno, "Odysseus oder Mythos und Aufklärung," in *Dialektik der Aufklärung* (Frankfurt am Main, 1969), pp. 50–87. For Bloch, Horkheimer, Adorno, and other German philosophers and writers, see *Lange Irrfahrt-grosse Heimkehr. Odysseus als Archetyp—zur Aktualität des Mythos*, ed. G. Fuchs (Frankfurt am Main, 1994).

17. See my *Shadow*, pp. 3 and 125.

18. W. Benjamin, "Franz Kafka," in *Illuminations: Essays and Reflections*, ed. Hannah Arendt, trans. by H. Zohn (New York, 1968), pp. 111–40, at pp. 117–18.

19. F. Kafka, "The Silence of the Sirens," in *Parables and Paradoxes* (New York, 1961), pp. 88–91.

20. P. Citati, *Kafka* (Milan, 2000), pp. 160–63.

21. In *The Shadow of Ulysses*, pp. 213–19.

22. B. Brecht, *Odysseus und die Syrenen*, in *Berichtigungen alter Mythen, Gesammelte Werke. Prosa* (Frankfurt am Main, 1967), vol. 1, p. 207. M. Blanchot, "Le chant des Sirènes," in *Le livre à venir* (Paris, 1959), pp. 9–37; see my *Sulle orme di Ulysses*, (Bologna, 1998), pp. 119–23.

23. E. Levinas, *Humanisme de l'autre homme* (Paris, 1972), p. 40.

24. E. Levinas, *En découvrant l'existence avec Husserl et Heidegger* (Paris, 1974), p. 191.

25. Levinas, *En découvrant l'existence*, p. 188.

26. H. Fisch, *A Remembered Future. A Study in Literary Mythology* (Bloomington, Ind., 1984).

27. Philo, *Questions and Answers on Genesis*, book IV, in *Philo. Supplement* (Cambridge, Mass., and London, 1979), vol. 1, p. 274; Clement, *Exhortation to the Greeks*, IX, 71 (Cambridge, Mass., and London, 1953), pp. 190–91. And see H. Blumenberg, *Der Prozess der theoretischen Neugierde* (Frankfurt am Main, 1973), pp. 138–43, 282–83. Naturally, there is also a long-standing Christian reading of Ulysses (for example, in Paul Claudel), for which see H. Rahner, *Greek Myths and Christian Mystery*, trans. by B. Bradshaw (New York, 1963); H. Rahner, *Symbole der Kirche* (Salzburg, 1964).

28. Now collected in B. Fondane, *Le Mal des fantômes* (Paris, 1996).

29. B. Fondane, *Baudelaire et l'expérience du gouffre* (Brussels, 1994), pp. 254–433. See my *Esodi e Odissee*, pp. 107–24.

30. P. Levi, *Se questo è un uomo, Opere*, ed. M. Belpoliti (Turin, 1997), vol. 1, p. 111.

31. V. Klemperer, diary entries for September 1, 1942; March 2, 1943; and February 13, 1945; in *Ich will Zeugnis . . . Tagebücher 1942–1945; I Will Bear Witness*.

32. P. Celan, *Selected Poems*, trans. by M. Hamburger (Harmondsworth, 1996), pp. 178–79. References in the preceding paragraph are to pp. 102–3, 110–11, and 252–53 of this volume.

33. Levi, *Se questo è un uomo*, p. 109.

34. J. Derrida, *L'écriture et la différence* (Paris, 1967), ch. 4, note 2; *Ulysses*, p. 411.

35. For this, see R. Alter, "Joyce's Ulysses as Comic Messiah," in *Ulisse: archeologia dell'uomo moderno*, ed. P. Boitani and R. Ambrosini (Rome, 1998), pp. 265–80.

36. A. Desai, *A Journey to Ithaca* (London, 1995).

37. C. Kavafy, "Ithaka," in *Collected Poems*, trans. by E. Keely and P. Sherrard (London, 1984), pp. 29–30.

38. See J. Pépin, "The Platonic and Christian Ulysses," in *Odysseus / Ulysses*, ed. H. Bloom (New York, 1991), pp, 228–48; and P. Boitani, "Introduzione," in *Ulisse: archeologia dell'uomo moderno*, pp. 25–26.

39. Adonis, *Mémoire du vent. Poèmes, 1957–1990* (Paris, 1991), p. 56.

40. Adonis, *Mémoire*, pp. 57, 60.

41. Adonis, "A Memory of Wings," in *The Pages of Day and Night*, trans. by S. Hazo (Evanston, Ill., 1994), p. 27.

42. See the essays on Arab culture collected in Adonis, *La prière et l'épée*, ed. J. Y. Masson, trans. by A. Wade Minkowski (Paris, 1993).

43. I am grateful to Pino Blasone for these references, and for providing me with his Italian translations of Khàlid Abu Khàlid and Nur ed-Din Sammùd.

44. I rely on the Italian translation of "Il marinaio e il derviscio" by P. Blasone in *Linea d'ombra* 79 (February, 1993): 66–67. Other poems by Hawi are to be found in *Naked in Exile*, ed. A. Haydar and M. Beard (Washington, D.C., 1984). And see *From the Vineyards of Lebanon. Poems by Khalil Hawi and Nadeem Naimy*, ed. F. S. Haddad (Beirut, 1991), pp. 40–51.

45. W. Soyinka, "Ulysses Britannicus in Africa," in *Ulisse: archeologia*, pp. 367–74; and " 'No!' He said," in *Mandela's Earth and other Poems*, London 1990ý, pp. 21–23.

46. W. Soyinka, *Isarà. A Voyage Around Essay* (London, 1990); *Season of Anomy* (London, 1973). Soyinka makes an important contribution to the discussion on myth in his *Myth, Literature and the African World* (Cambridge, 1976).

47. W. Soyinka, *Selected Poems* (London, 2001), p. 185.

48. W. Soyinka, "Ulysses," in *Selected Poems*, pp. 125–27, and in *Ulisse: archeologia*, pp. 377–79.

49. On *métissage*, see S. Gruzinsky, *La pensée métisse* (Paris, 1999); on conflict, see D. Quint, *Epic and Empire. Politics and Generic Form from Virgil to Milton* (Princeton, 1992).

50. G. Steiner, *Language and Silence* (Harmondsworth, 1979), p. 83.

51. P. De Man, "Walter Benjamin's 'The Task of the Translator,'" in *The Resistance to Theory* (Manchester: Manchester University Press, n.d.), p. 92.

52. Milan Kundera, *Ignorance*, trans. by L. Asher (London 2002), p. 8.

53. Ibid., pp. 33–35

54. Ibid., p. 54.

55. Ibid., pp. 16–17.

56. Kundera examines some of these questions, touching on the way various languages deal with the word "nostalgia," at pp. 5–9 of *Ignorance*.

57. Ibid., pp. 193–94.

58. Ibid., p. 195.

59. Haroldo de Campos, now *Sobre Finismundo: A Última Viagem* (Rio de Janeiro, 1996); and see P. Boitani, "A Última Viagem de Ulisses no Brasil," in *A Sombra de Ulisses* (São Paulo, 2005), pp. 157–67.

60. The original has "trans-passar o passo." This is derived from Boccaccio's "per voler veder trapassò il segno / dal qual nessun poté mai in qua reddire" (for wanting to see, he [Ulysses] trans-passed / trespassed the sign from which no one was ever able to return; *Amorosa Visione*, A XXVII, 86–87, De Campos's epigraph for the first section of *Finismundo*). Boccaccio's lines in turn are a wonderful concretion of *Inferno* XXVI, 108–9 and 132, and *Paradiso* XXVI, 117, where Adam explains to Dante that the cause for the "exile" from earthly Paradise imposed on him and Eve was not the "tasting of the wood" (eating the fruit of the tree), "ma solamente il trapassar del segno," only the trespass of the "sign," the boundary. The "alto passo" of *Inferno* XXVI, 132 (the deep passage Ulysses says he and his companions crossed upon entering the Atlantic) also corresponds to the "passo / che non lasciò già mai persona viva" (the pass which never yet let any go alive) to which Dante himself had turned at the beginning of his own journey.

61. "Tupy or not tupy: that is the question," wonders De Andrade in *Manifesto Antropofágico*, 1928, paraphrasing Hamlet's famous *quaestio* by the Brazilian tribal name.

62. Haroldo de Campos, *Crisantempo* (São Paulo, 1998). Prior to his death in 2003 the poet had published the "transcreation" of the first twelve books of the *Iliade* (São Paulo, 2001).

63. H. de Campos, *A Máquina do Mundo Repensada* (São Paulo, 2000). See also his *Galáxias* (São Paulo, 1984). The poet had also "transcreated" *Bere'Shith—A Cena da Origem* (São Paulo, 1993); the *Rime petrose* and several cantos from *Paradiso* in *Pedra e Luz na Poesia de Dante* (Rio de Janeiro, 1998).

64. W. Harris, *Eternity to Season* (London, 1978): in particular *Tiresias, Anticlea, The Stone of the Sea (Odysseus to Calypso), Canje*, pp. 31, 34, 51, 72–79, 84–85; E. Brathwaite, *The Arrivants. A New World Trilogy* (Oxford 1973); a second "bajana" trilogy, which includes "Mother Poem" (1977), "Sun Poem" (1982), and "X/Self" (1987; all published in Oxford), narrates the discovery of Africa and the Caribbean; D. Dabydeen, *A Coolie Odyssey* (London and Coventry, 1988).

65. D. Walcott, "The Sea Is History," in *Collected Poems, 1948–1984* (London, 1992), pp. 364–67. On Walcott's poetry and poetics, see at least D. Walcott, *What the Twilight Says. Essays* (London, 1998); J. Brodsky, introduction to D. Walcott, *Poems of the Caribbean* (New York, 1983); R. Hamner, *Derek Walcott* (Boston, 1981); *The Art of Derek Walcott*, ed. S. Brown (Bridgend 1991); R. Terada, *Derek Walcott's Poetry. American Mimicry* (Boston, 1992); *Critical*

Perspectives on Derek Walcott, ed. R. D. Hamner (Washington, D.C., 1993); *Conversations with Derek Walcott*, ed. W. Baer (Jackson, 1996); G. Davis, ed., "The Poetics of Derek Walcott: Intertextual Perspectives," *South Atlantic Quarterly* 96, no. 2 (1997).

66. D. Walcott, *Omeros* (New York, 1990).

67. *Omeros*, book V, chapter xxxvii, i–iii, pp. 189–93.

68. *Omeros* V, xxxviii, i–ii, pp. 193–96.

69. *Omeros* V, xxxix, i–iii, pp. 198–201.

70. *Omeros* V, xl, i–ii, pp. 201–4.

71. *Omeros* VI, liv, ii–iii, pp. 270–72.

72. *Omeros* VI, lviii, ii, pp. 290–92.

73. *Paradiso* XXXIII, 143–45, the last lines of the *Comedy*: "Ma già volgeva il mio disio e 'l velle, / sì come rota ch'igualmente è mossa, / l'amor che move il sole e l'altre stelle" (but my / desire and will were moved already—like / a wheel revolving uniformly—by / the Love that moves the sun and the other stars.

74. D. Walcott, *The Odyssey. A Stage Version* (London, 1993).

75. D. Walcott, "A Sail on the Horizon," in *Ulisse: archaeologia*, pp. 47–48.

76. D. Walcott, "Sea Grapes," from *Sea Grapes*, in *Collected Poems*, p. 297. Walcott's Ulyssean poems are numerous: see, for instance, the whole of "The Schooner *Flight*" and "The Divided Child," ch. 6, IV, in *Collected Poems*, pp. 345–61, quotation on p. 181. The theme is frequently superimposed on that of the castaway or Robinson Crusoe.

77. Aristotle, *Poetics* IX, 1451b1; Francis Bacon, *The Advancement of Learning* (London, 1974), II, IV.2, pp. 96–97; Robert Lowth, *De Sacra Poesi Hebraeorum*, 2nd ed. (Oxford, 1821), I, p. 8; quotations come from the edition translated by G. Gregory (London, 1839), I, p. 9. Lowth elaborates on Bacon's more simple formulation: e.g., the idea of the "shadow" is Bacon's, but Lowth gives it his own special, metaphysical turn.

78. D. Walcott, "Map of the New World," in *Collected Poems*, p. 413.

79. It may be worth remembering, with Salvatore Settis, *Futuro del "Classico,"* Turin 2004, p. 6, that immediately after 9/11 the first comment by Mullah Muhammad Omar, chief of the Afghan talebans, "compared America to Polyphemus, 'a giant blinded by an enemy to whom he cannot give a name,' a Nobody!"

EPILOGUE

1. Mikhail Bulgakov, *The Master and Margarita*, trans. by Michael Glenny (New York, 1967).

2. Rainer Maria Rilke, *Duino Elegies and The Sonnets to Orpheus*, trans. by A. Poulin, Jr. (Boston, 1977), book 1, no. 23 (p. 129).

3. Ibid.

4. W. B. Yeats, "The Wild Swans at Coole," l. 27, in *Collected Poems* (London, 1965), p. 148.

5. Rilke, *Duino Elegies*, pp. 5–7.

6. Rainer Maria Rilke, *Briefe* (February 20, 1914) (Frankfurt am Main, 1987), vol. 2, p. 449.

Index

255